I0006209

Microsoft Loop for Everyone

A Simple Guide to Smarter Collaboration

Kiet Huynh

Table of Contents

Introduction

1.1 What is Microsoft Loop?

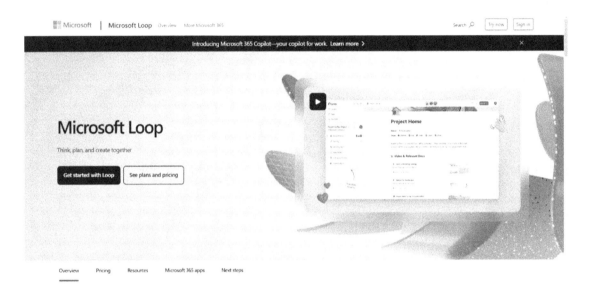

In today's digital workspace, collaboration tools are essential for teams to work efficiently, regardless of their physical location. Microsoft Loop is a groundbreaking productivity and collaboration tool designed to enhance teamwork through real-time, interactive components that can be shared across different Microsoft 365 apps. This chapter will explore what Microsoft Loop is, how it works, and why it is a game-changer for modern teams.

1. Introduction to Microsoft Loop

Microsoft Loop is a dynamic and flexible co-creation tool designed to help teams collaborate seamlessly. It integrates with Microsoft 365 apps like Teams, Outlook, Word, and OneNote, allowing users to create and share interactive components that remain synchronized across different platforms. Loop enables real-time collaboration, ensuring that everyone stays on the same page, no matter where they are working.

Loop consists of three core elements:

1. Loop Workspaces – A shared space where teams can collect and organize their work.

2. Loop Pages – Flexible, freeform pages where users can create and manage content.

3. Loop Components – Live, interactive elements (such as lists, tables, and task assignments) that can be embedded and edited in different Microsoft 365 applications.

2. The Evolution of Microsoft Loop

Microsoft Loop is part of Microsoft's vision for a more integrated and seamless digital workspace. The concept behind Loop originated from the increasing need for real-time collaboration tools that go beyond traditional document sharing.

How Loop Differs from Traditional Collaboration Tools

While traditional tools like Microsoft Word, Excel, and PowerPoint allow multiple users to edit documents collaboratively, Loop introduces a more modular and flexible approach. Unlike static documents, Loop components live independently, meaning they can be embedded in various applications while maintaining synchronization.

For example, a task list created in Loop can be embedded in a Teams chat and an Outlook email simultaneously. When someone updates the list in one location, the changes reflect everywhere in real time. This eliminates the need for copying and pasting content between different applications.

Microsoft Loop vs. Notion, Google Docs, and Other Tools

Microsoft Loop shares some similarities with tools like Notion, Google Docs, and Trello, but it stands out due to its deep integration with Microsoft 365 and its live, synchronized components.

Feature	Microsoft Loop	Notion	Google Docs	Trello
Real-time Collaboration	✓	✓	✓	✓
Modular Components	✓	✓	✗	✗
Microsoft 365 Integration	✓	✗	✗	✗
Task & Project Management	✓	✓	✗	✓
Live Synchronization Across Apps	✓	✗	✗	✗

As seen in the table, Microsoft Loop uniquely bridges document collaboration, modular workspaces, and live synchronization—something that traditional collaboration tools lack.

3. Core Features of Microsoft Loop

Microsoft Loop is built around three key components:

Loop Workspaces

Loop Workspaces are shared areas where teams can group related projects and content. Workspaces act as a central hub where members can contribute, track progress, and access essential documents.

- Users can create multiple workspaces for different projects.

- Workspaces allow real-time updates, ensuring that everyone has access to the latest information.

- Workspaces can be customized to suit different workflows.

Loop Pages

Loop Pages function like a hybrid of documents and project boards. They are freeform, allowing users to drag and drop content, add text, insert images, and embed interactive components.

- Loop Pages support multiple contributors, making it easy to collaborate.

- Pages are designed to be highly flexible, enabling different team members to structure them according to their needs.

- They serve as a living document, where teams can brainstorm, store meeting notes, or track project updates.

Loop Components

Loop Components are what set Microsoft Loop apart from traditional collaboration tools. These are live, interactive elements that can exist across different Microsoft 365 apps. Some examples include:

- Task Lists – Assign tasks to team members and track their progress.

- Tables – Organize and present data interactively.

- Lists – Create checklists or structured bullet points.

- Polls and Voting Tables – Gather feedback from your team in real time.

- Progress Trackers – Keep track of project milestones.

The magic of Loop Components lies in their synchronization—a table created in a Teams chat will be automatically updated if edited in Outlook or OneNote.

4. Benefits of Using Microsoft Loop

Increased Productivity

Microsoft Loop reduces context switching, allowing teams to work within their preferred tools without losing access to live, shared content. Instead of switching between different apps, users can interact with Loop Components embedded in their daily workflows.

Enhanced Team Collaboration

Loop makes collaboration seamless and interactive. Team members can co-edit documents, assign tasks, and share feedback instantly—without worrying about outdated versions of files.

Flexibility and Scalability

Loop is adaptable to various industries and team sizes, making it suitable for:

- Small teams working on creative projects.

- Enterprises managing large-scale projects with multiple departments.

- Remote teams needing real-time synchronization across different time zones.

Deep Integration with Microsoft 365

Since Loop is part of Microsoft 365, it integrates smoothly with:

- Microsoft Teams – Share and edit Loop components in chats and channels.

- Outlook – Embed interactive Loop elements in emails.

- OneNote – Use Loop to create interactive meeting notes.

- SharePoint and OneDrive – Store and manage Loop files efficiently.

5. Future of Microsoft Loop

Microsoft Loop is constantly evolving, with Microsoft adding AI-powered enhancements, better integrations, and new component types. Future developments could include:

- AI-powered suggestions for structuring workspaces.

- More automation features through Power Automate.

- Cross-platform enhancements, making Loop even more accessible on mobile and web.

6. Conclusion

Microsoft Loop is redefining the way teams collaborate by offering real-time, interactive, and synchronized content across Microsoft 365 apps. By combining the flexibility of modular workspaces with the power of Loop Components, it provides a unique solution for modern digital workplaces.

As businesses continue to shift towards hybrid and remote work models, Microsoft Loop will likely become an indispensable tool for enhancing productivity, reducing workflow friction, and improving team efficiency.

1.2 Why Use Microsoft Loop?

In today's digital work environment, collaboration is at the heart of productivity. As teams become more distributed and work becomes increasingly dynamic, traditional collaboration tools often fall short. Microsoft Loop is designed to address these challenges by providing a flexible, real-time, and component-based collaboration platform. But why should you use Microsoft Loop?

This chapter explores the key benefits of Microsoft Loop, how it enhances teamwork, and why it stands out from other collaboration tools. By the end of this section, you'll have a clear understanding of why Loop is an essential tool for modern professionals.

1. A New Era of Collaboration

The way we work has evolved significantly over the past decade. Traditional file-based collaboration, where documents are passed back and forth via email or stored in static locations, is no longer efficient. Microsoft Loop introduces a fluid, component-based approach that allows information to move dynamically across different applications and devices.

With Loop, collaboration is not limited to a single document or file; instead, content exists in flexible components that can be shared, edited, and updated in real time across multiple platforms. Whether you're in Microsoft Teams, Outlook, or another Microsoft 365 app, your content remains synchronized and accessible wherever you need it.

2. Key Benefits of Microsoft Loop

Real-Time Collaboration Across Teams

One of the most significant advantages of Microsoft Loop is its ability to facilitate real-time collaboration. Unlike traditional documents that require constant saving and refreshing, Loop allows multiple users to work on the same content simultaneously, ensuring that everyone sees the latest updates instantly.

How Real-Time Collaboration Works in Loop:

- Simultaneous Editing: Team members can edit a Loop component at the same time without conflicts.

- Automatic Updates: Changes appear instantly across all locations where the component is embedded.

- Seamless Communication: Users can add comments, tag teammates with @mentions, and receive feedback in real time.

This level of instant collaboration eliminates delays caused by version conflicts and ensures that teams are always working with the most up-to-date information.

Flexible and Reusable Components

Microsoft Loop introduces Loop Components, which are bite-sized pieces of content that can be inserted, edited, and synced across different applications. This is a major shift from the traditional way of working with static documents.

Examples of Loop Components:

- Task Lists: Assign tasks, set due dates, and track progress across different teams.

- Tables: Organize data dynamically with collaborative tables that update in real time.

- Notes and Brainstorming Boards: Capture ideas collaboratively without the constraints of traditional document formats.

- Voting Tables: Make decisions easier by gathering team input in a structured format.

Each component is independent yet connected, meaning that updating a component in one location automatically updates it everywhere it has been shared. This flexibility is particularly useful for cross-functional teams that need to share and update data across multiple platforms.

Deep Integration with Microsoft 365

Microsoft Loop is not a standalone tool—it's deeply integrated into the Microsoft 365 ecosystem, making it even more powerful. Whether you are using Microsoft Teams, Outlook, Word, OneNote, SharePoint, or Planner, Loop allows you to embed, edit, and synchronize content across different applications.

How Loop Works Within Microsoft 365:

- Teams: Share Loop components in chat and channels for real-time collaboration.

- Outlook: Embed Loop components directly in emails to keep discussions dynamic.

- OneNote & Word: Use Loop components for note-taking and document creation without duplicating content.

- SharePoint & OneDrive: Store and manage Loop content securely within Microsoft's cloud ecosystem.

This deep integration ensures that Loop fits **seamlessly into existing workflows**, reducing the need to switch between multiple tools.

Increased Productivity and Efficiency

Microsoft Loop enhances productivity by reducing time-consuming tasks such as manual document updates, email chains, and duplicated content. With Loop, teams can:

- Work from anywhere: Whether you're in the office, working remotely, or on the go, Loop keeps everyone connected.

- Reduce unnecessary meetings: Since updates happen in real time, there's less need for status meetings.

- Minimize context switching: By keeping everything within the Microsoft ecosystem, Loop reduces distractions caused by jumping between different apps.

Enhanced Team Communication

Effective communication is crucial for successful collaboration. Microsoft Loop encourages better communication by:

- Allowing instant feedback through comments and @mentions.

- Keeping everyone aligned with shared task lists and decision-making tools.

- Providing visual organization with customizable Loop pages for structured team collaboration.

Since communication happens directly within the workspace, there's less chance of misunderstandings or lost information.

Adaptability for Different Use Cases

Microsoft Loop is designed to be adaptable for a variety of use cases across different industries and professions. Whether you are a project manager, educator, software developer, content creator, or entrepreneur, Loop can be tailored to fit your needs.

Examples of Use Cases:

- Project Management: Track project progress, assign tasks, and manage deadlines.

- Marketing Teams: Collaborate on campaign planning, content creation, and brainstorming sessions.

- Human Resources: Organize hiring processes, onboarding materials, and employee training.

- Sales Teams: Share client updates, deal tracking, and sales reports.

- Education: Facilitate interactive learning with collaborative note-taking and discussion boards.

The ability to customize Loop pages and components makes it a **versatile tool** for both individuals and teams.

How Microsoft Loop Stands Out from Other Collaboration Tools

There are many collaboration tools available today, such as Google Docs, Notion, Trello, and Slack. While these tools offer great features, Microsoft Loop provides a unique combination of flexibility, real-time collaboration, and deep integration with Microsoft 365.

Feature	Microsoft Loop	Google Docs	Notion	Trello	Slack
Real-Time Collaboration	✓	✓	✓	✗	✓
Component-Based Editing	✓	✗	✓	✗	✗
Deep Integration with Microsoft 365	✓	✗	✗	✗	✗
Task Management	✓	✗	✓	✓	✗
Cross-Platform Accessibility	✓	✓	✓	✓	✓

The combination of dynamic components, real-time collaboration, and integration with Microsoft apps makes Loop a superior choice for Microsoft 365 users.

Conclusion: Why You Should Start Using Microsoft Loop Today

Microsoft Loop is a game-changer in the world of collaboration. By breaking down barriers between static documents and dynamic teamwork, Loop provides a flexible, real-time, and highly integrated workspace for individuals and teams.

Key Takeaways:

✓ Real-time collaboration keeps teams aligned.

✓ Loop components allow for reusable, dynamic content.

✓ Microsoft 365 integration enhances workflow efficiency.

✓ Better team communication through instant feedback and structured organization.

✓ Adaptable for different use cases, from project management to education.

If you're looking for a tool that helps you work smarter, collaborate seamlessly, and stay productive, Microsoft Loop is the solution.

1.3 Who This Book is For

More from Microsoft 365

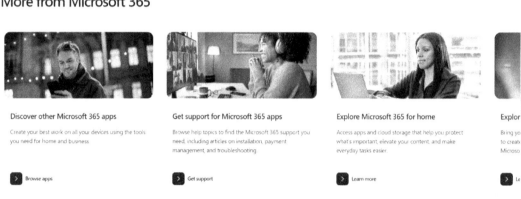

Microsoft Loop is an innovative tool designed to revolutionize collaboration, streamline workflows, and enhance productivity for individuals and teams. Whether you're an experienced professional looking to improve your workflow efficiency or a complete beginner exploring modern digital collaboration, this book is designed to help you master Microsoft Loop with ease.

This book is written for a diverse audience, including professionals, educators, students, freelancers, project managers, and teams across various industries. No matter your role, if you're looking to harness the full potential of Microsoft Loop, this guide will provide you with practical knowledge, step-by-step instructions, and best practices to optimize your workflow.

1. Business Professionals and Teams

In today's fast-paced business environment, effective collaboration is crucial. Microsoft Loop is built to help professionals streamline communication, manage tasks more efficiently, and reduce the need for endless email threads and scattered documents. This book is especially useful for:

Office Workers and Knowledge Workers

For professionals who deal with large amounts of information, documents, and teamwork, Microsoft Loop provides an intuitive workspace to organize ideas, collaborate in real time, and ensure that critical tasks don't get lost. If you work in an office environment, whether remotely or on-site, Loop can significantly enhance how you handle daily tasks, from taking meeting notes to managing reports.

Project Managers and Team Leaders

Project managers and team leaders can use Microsoft Loop to create a structured workflow for their teams. This book will show you how to:

- Set up Loop workspaces for different projects.

- Assign tasks and track progress using Loop components.

- Integrate Loop with Microsoft Teams and other Microsoft 365 apps for seamless collaboration.

- Foster real-time communication while reducing delays in decision-making.

Remote and Hybrid Workers

With the rise of remote and hybrid work models, it is essential to have a collaboration tool that ensures smooth communication. Microsoft Loop allows teams to work together in real time, regardless of location. This guide will teach you how to use Loop to:

- Share and edit documents simultaneously with colleagues.

- Keep project updates centralized and easily accessible.

- Ensure that workspaces remain organized, even with remote team members contributing from different time zones.

2. Educators and Students

Education is evolving, and digital collaboration is now a key component of effective learning. Microsoft Loop can help both teachers and students create interactive, engaging, and organized learning experiences.

Teachers and Educators

Educators can use Microsoft Loop to streamline lesson planning, facilitate classroom discussions, and encourage student engagement. This book will guide teachers on how to:

- Use Loop components to create interactive lesson plans.

- Organize course materials and resources in a structured way.

- Collaborate with students in real time for group projects and assignments.

- Track student progress and provide feedback efficiently.

Students and Academic Researchers

Students at all levels can benefit from Microsoft Loop's ability to organize notes, collaborate on group projects, and manage research efficiently. Whether you are a high school student working on a group assignment or a university researcher compiling data, this book will help you:

- Use Loop for structured note-taking.

- Manage group projects and ensure smooth communication.

- Integrate Loop with Microsoft Word, OneNote, and Teams for a comprehensive study experience.

3. Freelancers and Independent Professionals

For freelancers and independent professionals, managing multiple projects, clients, and tasks can be overwhelming. Microsoft Loop provides a centralized platform where freelancers can track their work, collaborate with clients, and ensure deadlines are met.

Writers and Content Creators

Freelance writers, bloggers, and content creators can use Microsoft Loop to draft, edit, and collaborate on content with clients or team members. This book will show you how to:

- Organize different writing projects within Loop workspaces.

- Collaborate with editors and clients in real time.

- Track revisions and ensure content remains structured and accessible.

Designers and Creative Professionals

For designers and other creatives, collaboration is an essential part of the workflow. Microsoft Loop allows teams to brainstorm ideas, gather feedback, and organize creative assets in one place. This guide will help you:

- Set up workspaces for different clients and projects.

- Collect feedback using comments and discussion threads.

- Integrate Loop with design tools like Microsoft Whiteboard and OneDrive.

Consultants and Business Coaches

If you work as a consultant or business coach, Microsoft Loop can be a powerful tool for organizing client information, creating business strategies, and maintaining detailed records of sessions and plans. This book will help you:

- Organize consulting notes and client records.

- Collaborate with clients on business plans and action steps.

- Use Loop components to create dynamic reports and presentations.

4. Entrepreneurs and Startup Teams

Entrepreneurs and startup teams need tools that allow them to move fast, stay organized, and collaborate effectively. Microsoft Loop is an excellent solution for managing business ideas, tracking progress, and ensuring alignment among team members.

Startup Founders and Business Owners

If you're running a startup or small business, Microsoft Loop can help you streamline operations. This book will teach you how to:

- Structure business plans and strategy documents.

- Collaborate with investors, partners, and employees in real time.

- Track progress on key business milestones.

Product Development Teams

For product development teams, staying organized and ensuring alignment is critical. Microsoft Loop helps teams manage brainstorming sessions, product roadmaps, and feedback cycles. In this book, you'll learn how to:

- Use Loop to create and update product roadmaps.

- Organize feature requests and bug reports.

- Collaborate with cross-functional teams efficiently.

5. Anyone Looking to Improve Productivity

Even if you don't fit into the specific categories above, Microsoft Loop can still benefit you. Whether you're managing personal projects, planning events, or simply looking for a better way to stay organized, this book will show you how to:

- Use Loop to create to-do lists and action plans.

- Manage household projects and personal organization.

- Enhance productivity through structured digital workspaces.

Conclusion: Is This Book Right for You?

If you:

- Struggle with scattered information and disorganized collaboration.

- Want to improve communication and teamwork in your professional or academic environment.

- Need a structured, user-friendly guide to learning Microsoft Loop.

Then **this book is for you**! Whether you're new to Microsoft Loop or looking to enhance your skills, this guide will provide the knowledge and strategies you need to become proficient in using Microsoft Loop for smarter collaboration.

1.4 How to Use This Book

Welcome to *Microsoft Loop for Everyone: A Simple Guide to Smarter Collaboration*! This book is designed to be a comprehensive yet easy-to-follow guide to Microsoft Loop, whether you're a beginner just getting started or a professional looking to optimize your workflow. In this section, you will learn how to get the most out of this book, how to navigate its chapters effectively, and how to apply what you learn in real-world collaboration scenarios.

1. A Practical Approach to Learning Microsoft Loop

Unlike traditional software manuals that simply list features and functions, this book takes a practical approach by guiding you through real-world use cases. Microsoft Loop is a dynamic tool designed for seamless collaboration, and learning how to use it effectively requires more than just knowing where to click. That's why this book emphasizes hands-on learning, step-by-step walkthroughs, and best practices.

Here's what you can expect from each chapter:

- **Clear Explanations** – Each chapter breaks down key concepts in an easy-to-understand way, ensuring that even users new to Microsoft Loop can follow along.

- **Step-by-Step Instructions** – You'll find detailed, guided steps on how to use various features, complete with screenshots and practical examples.

- **Best Practices & Tips** – Throughout the book, you'll find expert recommendations on how to use Microsoft Loop efficiently for maximum productivity.

- **Real-World Use Cases** – Instead of just explaining features, this book demonstrates how Microsoft Loop fits into different workflows—whether you're working on a personal project, managing a team, or collaborating with external partners.

- **Troubleshooting Advice** – Common issues and solutions are included so you can quickly resolve any problems you encounter.

2. How to Navigate This Book

This book is structured in a way that allows you to learn at your own pace. Whether you want to follow along chapter by chapter or jump directly to a specific topic, you'll find it easy to navigate.

A Breakdown of the Chapters

1. **Introduction** – Provides background on Microsoft Loop, its benefits, and why it is a valuable tool for collaboration.

2. **Chapter 1: Getting Started with Microsoft Loop** – Covers the basics of setting up Microsoft Loop, including understanding its core components (Workspaces, Pages, and Components).

3. **Chapter 2: Working with Loop Components** – Explains how to use the different Loop components effectively for various tasks.

4. **Chapter 3: Collaboration and Teamwork in Microsoft Loop** – Focuses on working with others, sharing content, and integrating Loop into team workflows.

5. **Chapter 4: Advanced Features and Customization** – Explores more advanced features such as automation, personalization, and integration with other Microsoft 365 tools.

6. **Chapter 5: Microsoft Loop for Different Use Cases** – Offers practical applications for individuals, teams, and businesses.

7. **Chapter 6: Troubleshooting and Best Practices** – Provides solutions to common issues and tips for optimizing your use of Microsoft Loop.

Each chapter is broken down into sections and subsections that allow you to quickly find the information you need. If you're a complete beginner, it's recommended to read the book sequentially. However, if you already have some experience, feel free to skip to the sections most relevant to your needs.

3. Who Can Benefit from This Book?

This book is designed for a wide range of users, including:

- **Beginners** – If you've never used Microsoft Loop before, this book will guide you step by step from setup to mastering key features.

- **Business Professionals** – If you work in a corporate environment, you'll learn how to enhance team collaboration, improve productivity, and streamline workflows.

- **Project Managers** – Learn how to use Microsoft Loop for managing projects, assigning tasks, and tracking progress.

- **Educators and Students** – Discover how to use Loop for classroom collaboration, organizing coursework, and working on group projects.

- **Freelancers and Entrepreneurs** – Use Microsoft Loop to manage your personal and business projects more efficiently.

No matter your background, this book will provide the insights and practical knowledge needed to integrate Microsoft Loop into your daily workflow.

4. Learning by Doing: How to Apply What You Learn

One of the best ways to master Microsoft Loop is by using it as you go through the book. Here are some suggestions on how to apply what you learn:

- **Follow Along with the Steps** – As you read through the book, open Microsoft Loop on your device and practice the steps in real time.

- **Experiment with Features** – Don't just read about features—test them out by creating a Loop workspace, adding pages, and experimenting with components.

- **Apply it to Real-World Scenarios** – Think about how Microsoft Loop can fit into your daily tasks and start incorporating it into your workflow.

- **Use Checklists and Exercises** – Many sections include best practices and recommended workflows—try implementing them to reinforce your understanding.

- **Revisit Chapters as Needed** – If you forget something or need a refresher, you can always jump back to the relevant chapter.

By actively engaging with the content and applying what you learn, you'll build confidence in using Microsoft Loop effectively.

5. Additional Resources and Support

To further enhance your learning experience, here are some additional resources you may find useful:

- **Microsoft Official Documentation** – Stay up to date with the latest features and updates from Microsoft.

- **Microsoft Loop Community** – Join online forums and discussion groups to share tips and ask questions.

- **Online Video Tutorials** – Supplement your learning with YouTube tutorials and Microsoft's official training videos.

- **Practice Workspaces** – Set up test workspaces to experiment with different features before implementing them in real-world projects.

By utilizing these resources along with this book, you'll maximize your ability to use Microsoft Loop efficiently.

Final Thoughts

This book is designed to be your ultimate guide to Microsoft Loop, whether you're just starting out or looking to refine your skills. By following the structured approach outlined here, you will develop a strong understanding of how to use Microsoft Loop to enhance collaboration, streamline workflows, and boost productivity.

Now that you know how to use this book effectively, let's dive in and explore **Microsoft Loop** in detail. Happy learning! 🚀

CHAPTER I
Getting Started with Microsoft Loop

1.1 Understanding Microsoft Loop Components

Before diving into the details of using Microsoft Loop, it is crucial to understand its fundamental components. Microsoft Loop is designed as a collaborative tool that enables teams to work seamlessly across applications, ensuring real-time synchronization and flexibility in managing tasks, documents, and ideas.

At its core, Microsoft Loop consists of three main components:

1. **Loop Workspaces** – The central hub where all your projects and collaborative efforts are organized.

2. **Loop Pages** – Sections within a workspace that allow for detailed organization of information.

3. **Loop Components** – The interactive and dynamic elements that can be embedded across different Microsoft 365 applications.

Each of these components plays a distinct role in fostering productivity and teamwork. This chapter will break down these components, starting with **Loop Workspaces**.

1.1.1 Loop Workspaces

What Are Loop Workspaces?

A Loop Workspace serves as the highest-level structure in Microsoft Loop. It acts as a centralized location where teams can organize projects, store information, and collaborate in real time. Workspaces are designed to be flexible, allowing users to bring together documents, notes, tasks, and interactive elements in a structured yet fluid environment.

Think of a Loop Workspace as a digital collaboration hub that enables seamless interaction between team members. Whether you are working on a marketing campaign, a software development project, or an event plan, a Loop Workspace provides a dedicated space to centralize all related information.

Key Features of Loop Workspaces

- **Centralized Collaboration** – All relevant documents, notes, and interactive components are stored within the workspace.

- **Real-Time Synchronization** – Updates are instantly reflected for all members, ensuring that everyone is on the same page.

- **Seamless Integration** – Workspaces connect with other Microsoft 365 apps, such as Teams, Outlook, and OneDrive.

- **Customizable Organization** – Users can structure their workspaces with pages and components based on their specific needs.

Creating a Loop Workspace

To get started with Microsoft Loop, the first step is to **create a workspace**. Follow these steps to set up your first Loop Workspace:

Step 1: Access Microsoft Loop

1. Open your web browser and navigate to Microsoft Loop.
   https://loop.cloud.microsoft/learn

2. Sign in using your Microsoft 365 account.

3. Once signed in, you will land on the **Loop homepage**, where you can manage existing workspaces or create a new one.

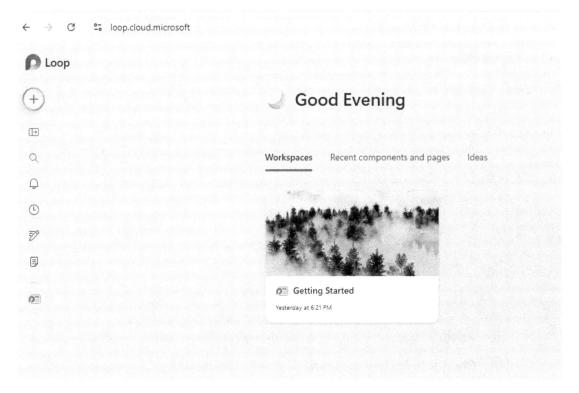

Step 2: Create a New Workspace

1. Click on **"New Workspace"** or the "+" icon.

2. Enter a **name** for your workspace. Choose a descriptive name that clearly identifies the project or purpose.

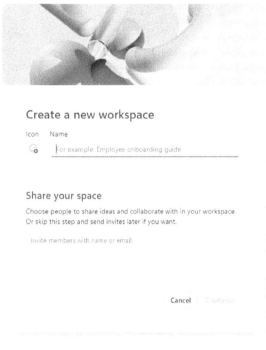

Create a new workspace

Icon   Name

For example: Employee onboarding guide

Share your space

Choose people to share ideas and collaborate with in your workspace.
Or skip this step and send invites later if you want.

Invite members with name or email

Cancel

3. Select a **color theme** or icon to personalize your workspace.

4. Click **"Create"** to finalize the setup.

Step 3: Invite Team Members

1. Once your workspace is created, click the **"Share"** button.

2. Enter the **email addresses** of the people you want to collaborate with.

3. Assign **permissions** (edit or view-only access).

4. Click **"Send Invite"** to notify your team members.

Now, your workspace is ready to use!

Organizing Your Workspace for Maximum Efficiency

Once a workspace is created, it's essential to structure it effectively to keep information organized and ensure smooth collaboration. Here are some best practices:

1. Categorize Your Workspaces

- Use different workspaces for **separate projects** (e.g., "Marketing Strategy 2024," "Product Launch Plan," "Team Meeting Notes").

- Avoid clutter by **archiving completed workspaces** that are no longer in use.

2. Use Clear Naming Conventions

- Name workspaces based on their **specific purpose** (e.g., "Website Redesign Project" instead of "Design Stuff").

- Keep names **concise and easy to recognize**.

3. Add Descriptions and Guidelines

- Use the **workspace description** field to provide an overview of the workspace's purpose.

- Include guidelines on **how team members should use the workspace** to maintain consistency.

4. Group Related Pages Together

- Within each workspace, create **Loop Pages** to organize specific aspects of a project.

- Example: A workspace for a marketing campaign might have pages for "Content Plan," "Social Media Strategy," and "Budget Overview."

Managing Loop Workspaces

Once your workspace is set up and organized, you will need to **manage** it effectively to ensure smooth collaboration. Microsoft Loop provides several tools to help users keep workspaces structured and up-to-date.

Adding Pages to a Workspace

- Click **"New Page"** within the workspace to create different sections.

- Pages can contain text, images, tables, checklists, and more.

- Drag and drop components to **rearrange content** as needed.

Customizing Workspace Settings

- Change the **color theme** for visual clarity.

- Set permissions to ensure only authorized members can edit critical information.

- Enable **notifications** to receive updates on changes within the workspace.

Archiving or Deleting a Workspace

- If a project is completed, consider **archiving** the workspace rather than deleting it. This allows you to **reference past work** without cluttering your active projects.

- To delete a workspace, navigate to **settings**, select **"Delete Workspace"**, and confirm the action.

Best Practices for Using Loop Workspaces

To make the most out of Microsoft Loop Workspaces, follow these best practices:

✓ **Keep Workspaces Focused** – Avoid adding unrelated content to a workspace. Stick to the **core topic** or project.

✓ **Encourage Team Collaboration** – Assign clear roles and responsibilities to ensure everyone contributes effectively.

✓ **Utilize Templates** – Save time by using pre-made templates for common workflows, such as meeting notes or project plans.

✓ **Leverage Microsoft 365 Integrations** – Use **Teams, Outlook, and OneDrive** alongside Loop for a fully connected workflow.

✓ **Maintain a Clean and Organized Structure** – Regularly review and update workspace content to prevent clutter.

Conclusion

Loop Workspaces are the foundation of Microsoft Loop, providing a structured yet flexible environment for collaboration. By understanding how to **create, organize, and manage workspaces effectively**, users can maximize productivity and streamline teamwork.

In the next section, we will explore **Loop Pages**, the second core component of Microsoft Loop, and how they help break down complex projects into manageable sections.

1.1.2 Loop Pages

Microsoft Loop is designed to revolutionize the way teams collaborate by providing a flexible and dynamic workspace. At the heart of Microsoft Loop's structure are Loop Workspaces, Loop Pages, and Loop Components—each playing a distinct role in fostering seamless teamwork.

In this section, we will explore Loop Pages, their functionality, structure, and best practices for using them effectively. Understanding Loop Pages will help you create organized, collaborative environments that enhance productivity.

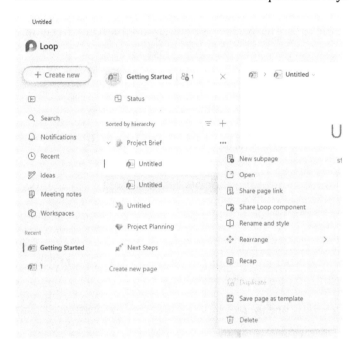

1. What Are Loop Pages?

Loop Pages are flexible, collaborative spaces where you can gather, organize, and work on content with your team in real time. Think of them as digital workspaces inside Loop Workspaces, where information is structured in an intuitive and interactive way.

Key Characteristics of Loop Pages:

- Real-time collaboration – Multiple team members can edit a Loop Page simultaneously.

- Modular design – Pages can contain different Loop Components like task lists, tables, and notes.

- Adaptive structure – Content within a Loop Page can be freely rearranged, formatted, and embedded.

- Integration with Microsoft 365 – You can embed documents, share data from OneDrive, and collaborate with Microsoft Teams users.

Loop Pages are not static like traditional documents. Instead, they are living documents that update dynamically, allowing teams to work together efficiently, no matter where they are.

2. How Loop Pages Fit into the Microsoft Loop Structure

To fully grasp the role of Loop Pages, let's see where they fit within Microsoft Loop's hierarchy:

- Loop Workspaces: The top-level structure that houses related projects or teams.

- Loop Pages: The main content area inside a workspace where users collect and collaborate on information.

- Loop Components: The smallest units inside a Loop Page, such as tables, task lists, and notes, which can also be shared outside the page.

This hierarchy ensures that content remains organized, making it easier to locate, edit, and manage.

3. Creating a Loop Page

Step-by-Step Guide to Creating a Loop Page

1. **Access Your Loop Workspace**

   o Open **Microsoft Loop** and navigate to the appropriate **workspace** where you want to create a new page.

2. **Create a New Page**

   o Click on the **"+" (plus) button** or select **"New Page"** in the left sidebar.

3. **Name Your Page**

   o Give your page a **clear, descriptive title** to reflect its purpose.

4. **Add Content and Components**

   o Start with **text, headings, and bullet points** to organize information.

   o Insert **Loop Components** such as task lists, tables, and voting polls.

   o Embed **documents, images, and links** from Microsoft 365 apps.

5. **Customize Formatting**

   o Use **bold, italics, and underlining** for emphasis.

   o Highlight key sections with **background colors**.

   o Insert **dividers** to separate content sections.

6. **Save and Share the Page**

   o Click **"Share"** to invite team members to view or edit.

   o Set appropriate **permissions** to control access levels.

---

4. Organizing Content in Loop Pages

Loop Pages allow for highly structured content organization. Here are some best practices:

4.1 Using Headings and Sections

- H1 for main topics, H2 for subtopics, and H3 for details.
- Keep headings concise and relevant to help readers quickly navigate.

4.2 Utilizing Tables for Data Organization

- Use tables to structure task lists, deadlines, and team responsibilities.
- Insert checklists to track project progress.

4.3 Embedding Links and Files

- Add links to related Loop Pages for better navigation.

- Embed OneDrive documents and Excel files to keep all project information in one place.

4.4 Pinning Important Information

- Pin key details at the top of the page to highlight critical tasks or updates.

- Use tags and labels to categorize information.

5. Collaboration Features in Loop Pages

5.1 Real-Time Editing and Syncing

- Changes made to a Loop Page update instantly for all collaborators.

- Microsoft Loop automatically saves progress, preventing data loss.

5.2 Commenting and Feedback

- Highlight text and use @mentions to direct feedback to team members.

- Add comments to specific sections for discussions.

5.3 Assigning Tasks and Responsibilities

- Create a task list inside a Loop Page and assign responsibilities.

- Use due dates and status updates to track progress.

6. Sharing and Permissions in Loop Pages

6.1 Sharing a Loop Page

- Click the "Share" button in the top-right corner.

- Choose to share with specific people or make it accessible to everyone in your workspace.

6.2 Setting Permissions

- Assign **"Can Edit"** or **"Can View"** permissions based on user roles.

- Restrict editing to prevent unintended modifications.

6.3 Embedding Loop Pages in Other Apps

- Paste a Loop Page link into **Microsoft Teams**, Outlook, or OneNote.

- The page remains **interactive and editable** across all platforms.

---

7. Best Practices for Using Loop Pages Effectively

To maximize productivity with Loop Pages, consider the following best practices:

1. **Keep Pages Concise and Well-Organized**
   - Avoid overcrowding a page with too much content.
   - Use separate **Loop Pages for different topics** rather than cluttering a single page.

2. **Use Templates for Standardized Workflows**
   - Create **template Loop Pages** for repeated processes (e.g., meeting notes, project planning).
   - Save time by reusing standardized formats.

3. **Regularly Review and Update Content**
   - Ensure that **Loop Pages remain relevant and up-to-date**.
   - Archive outdated information rather than deleting it.

4. **Encourage Team Participation**

   o   Motivate team members to contribute **by assigning sections** of a Loop Page.

   o   Use **feedback tools** to improve collaboration.

5. **Leverage Microsoft 365 Integrations**

   o   Embed files from **Word, Excel, and PowerPoint** for easy reference.

   o   Sync tasks with **Microsoft Planner** for better task management.

8. Conclusion

Loop Pages serve as **the core collaborative space within Microsoft Loop**, allowing teams to work efficiently with real-time updates and structured content. By understanding how to create, organize, and manage Loop Pages effectively, users can **enhance productivity, streamline teamwork, and integrate seamlessly with Microsoft 365**.

In the next section, we will explore **how to set up Microsoft Loop** and personalize your workspace to maximize efficiency. 🚀

1.1.3 Loop Components

Introduction to Loop Components

At the heart of Microsoft Loop lies its most powerful feature: **Loop Components**. These dynamic, modular elements allow users to create, edit, and share content seamlessly across different Microsoft 365 applications, such as Microsoft Teams, Outlook, Word, and Whiteboard. Unlike traditional documents or static notes, Loop Components are designed to be **collaborative, flexible, and always up-to-date**, ensuring that team members stay aligned no matter where they work.

In this section, we will explore:

- What Loop Components are and how they function.

- The different types of Loop Components.

- How to create, share, and edit Loop Components.

- Best practices for using Loop Components effectively.

By the end of this chapter, you will have a solid understanding of how to leverage Loop Components for improved productivity and collaboration.

What Are Loop Components?

Loop Components are **interactive content blocks** that can be embedded within different Microsoft 365 apps and updated in real-time. Instead of switching between multiple apps, users can work on a single component—whether it's a **task list, table, voting poll, or paragraph of text**—and see changes reflect instantly across all platforms.

These components are stored in **OneDrive**, allowing them to be accessed and edited from anywhere. They enable fluid collaboration, making them especially useful for teams working remotely or across different departments.

Key Features of Loop Components

1. **Real-Time Collaboration:** Multiple users can edit the same component simultaneously, with changes visible instantly.

2. **Cross-App Integration:** Components can be used within **Teams, Outlook, Word, and Whiteboard**, ensuring seamless collaboration.

3. **Version Control and History:** Changes are automatically saved, and users can track modifications over time.

4. **Adaptive Content:** Components can be used independently or as part of a **Loop Page or Workspace**, allowing for greater flexibility.

5. **Easy Sharing:** Loop Components can be shared via links, making it simple to collaborate with colleagues inside and outside an organization.

Types of Loop Components

Microsoft Loop offers a variety of **pre-built components** designed to facilitate team collaboration. Below are some of the most commonly used ones:

1. Text Component

The **Text Component** allows users to collaboratively write and edit text in real-time. It is ideal for drafting meeting notes, brainstorming ideas, or capturing key decisions.

◆ **Use Case Example:** A marketing team drafts a new product description inside a Loop Component in **Microsoft Teams Chat**. Each member can contribute, suggest edits, and finalize the content together.

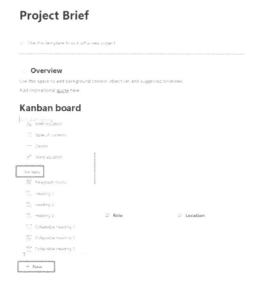

2. Table Component

A **Table Component** provides a structured way to organize and display data collaboratively. Users can add rows and columns, enter data, and format content within the table.

◆ **Use Case Example:** A project manager creates a task-tracking table in **Outlook** to monitor project milestones. Team members update their status in real-time.

3. Task List Component

The **Task List Component** helps teams assign, track, and complete tasks efficiently. Tasks can be marked as completed, and assignees receive updates automatically.

♦ **Use Case Example:** A software development team uses a Task List in **Microsoft Word** to manage bug fixes. Each developer updates their assigned tasks, ensuring smooth workflow management.

4. Voting Table Component

The **Voting Table Component** allows teams to make collective decisions by casting votes on different options.

◆ **Use Case Example:** A design team uses a Voting Table in **Microsoft Whiteboard** to decide on a final logo design. Each team member votes for their preferred choice, and the option with the most votes is selected.

5. Progress Tracker Component

The **Progress Tracker Component** helps teams keep track of work status, ensuring that everyone stays updated on the completion of key tasks.

◆ **Use Case Example:** An HR team uses a Progress Tracker in **Microsoft Teams** to monitor the onboarding process of new employees.

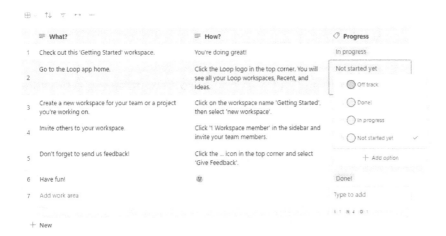

6. Number Component

The **Number Component** allows users to input and manipulate numerical data.

✦ **Use Case Example:** A finance team uses the Number Component inside **Microsoft Word** to track budget estimates for an upcoming project.

7. Date Component

The **Date Component** is useful for setting deadlines and scheduling meetings within a Loop Page or shared document.

✦ **Use Case Example:** A team leader adds a Date Component in **Outlook** to set deadlines for a report submission.

Creating and Using Loop Components

How to Create a Loop Component

To create a new Loop Component:

1. Open a Microsoft 365 application (e.g., Teams, Outlook, Word, or Whiteboard).

2. Click on the "Insert Loop Component" button (available in chat, email, or documents).

3. Select the type of component you want to create (e.g., Task List, Table, or Text Component).

4. Start editing the component and invite others to collaborate.

Sharing and Collaborating with Loop Components

Loop Components are designed for easy sharing:

- Copy the component's link and share it in a chat, email, or document.

- Control access permissions, allowing users to view or edit the component.

- Edit the component together in real time, with changes instantly reflected across all platforms.

Editing a Loop Component

- Click inside the component to edit text, add rows, or modify content.

- Changes are automatically saved, ensuring no updates are lost.

- @Mention colleagues to grab their attention and assign tasks within components.

Best Practices for Using Loop Components

To maximize the benefits of Loop Components, consider the following best practices:

✓ Use Loop Components for real-time collaboration. Avoid static documents when teamwork is required.

✓ Embed Loop Components in relevant applications. Use Teams for discussions, Outlook for decision-making, and Word for documentation.

✓ Keep components organized. Structure content clearly so team members can find information quickly.

✓ Regularly review and update components. Ensure data stays accurate and relevant.

✓ Use permissions wisely. Limit editing access when necessary to prevent accidental modifications.

Conclusion

Microsoft Loop Components redefine how teams collaborate by offering a fluid, real-time workspace that integrates seamlessly across Microsoft 365 apps. Whether you're managing tasks, collecting feedback, or brainstorming ideas, Loop Components ensure that your content stays up-to-date, accessible, and interactive.

By understanding how to create, edit, and share Loop Components, you can unlock a new level of efficiency and teamwork, making Microsoft Loop an essential tool for modern digital collaboration.

Now that you have a solid understanding of Loop Components, let's move on to how to set up Microsoft Loop and navigate its interface in the next section. 🚀

1.2 Setting Up Microsoft Loop

1.2.1 Accessing Microsoft Loop

Introduction to Accessing Microsoft Loop

Before you can start leveraging Microsoft Loop for collaboration and productivity, you need to understand how to access the platform. Microsoft Loop is a web-based and app-based service integrated into the Microsoft 365 ecosystem, designed to enhance teamwork and dynamic content creation.

This section will guide you through the different ways to access Microsoft Loop, including web access, mobile applications, and integration with other Microsoft tools. You'll also learn about system requirements, login procedures, and troubleshooting tips to ensure a smooth setup.

1. Accessing Microsoft Loop via the Web

The most common and straightforward way to use Microsoft Loop is through a web browser. Microsoft has designed Loop as a cloud-first application, meaning you don't need to install software to get started. Here's how you can access it:

Steps to Open Microsoft Loop on the Web

1. **Open Your Browser** – Microsoft Loop is optimized for modern browsers like Google Chrome, Microsoft Edge, and Safari. While other browsers may work, these three offer the best experience.

2. **Visit the Official Microsoft Loop Website** – Navigate to https://loop.microsoft.com.

3. **Sign in with Your Microsoft Account** – Use your Microsoft 365 account credentials. If your organization has Loop enabled, you will log in using your work email.

4. **Allow Permissions (if prompted)** – If this is your first time logging in, Microsoft may ask for permission to access certain features, such as OneDrive and Teams. Accept these permissions to use Loop's full functionality.

5. **Explore the Loop Dashboard** – After signing in, you will be directed to the Loop homepage, where you can create and manage your workspaces, pages, and components.

System Requirements for Web Access

To ensure the best performance, your system should meet these minimum requirements:

- **Operating System**: Windows 10 or later, macOS 10.14 or later

- **Browser**: Latest versions of Microsoft Edge, Google Chrome, or Safari

- **Internet Connection**: A stable broadband connection for real-time collaboration

- **Microsoft 365 Subscription**: Some features require an enterprise or business plan

If you experience issues accessing Loop via the web, ensure that your browser is updated, clear cache and cookies, and check if Loop is enabled in your Microsoft 365 admin settings.

2. Accessing Microsoft Loop on Mobile Devices

Microsoft Loop also provides a seamless experience on mobile devices, allowing you to collaborate on the go. The mobile app is available for both **iOS** and **Android**, offering essential features like workspace navigation, editing Loop components, and real-time updates.

Installing the Microsoft Loop Mobile App

1. **Go to the App Store (iOS) or Google Play Store (Android)** – Search for "Microsoft Loop."

2. **Download and Install** – Tap the install button and wait for the app to be installed on your device.

3. **Open the App and Sign In** – Use your Microsoft 365 account credentials to log in.

4. **Grant Necessary Permissions** – The app may request access to notifications, storage, and collaboration features. Approve them for a smooth experience.

5. **Start Using Loop** – You can now access your Loop workspaces, create pages, and edit components directly from your phone.

Features Available on the Mobile App

- **Real-time Editing** – Update your Loop pages and components just like on the web.

- **Push Notifications** – Get alerts for mentions, updates, and shared content.

- **Offline Mode** – Work on Loop content even without an internet connection, with automatic syncing when reconnected.

- **Dark Mode Support** – Customize the appearance for better visibility and reduced eye strain.

3. Troubleshooting Common Access Issues

While accessing Microsoft Loop is generally seamless, you may encounter some issues. Here are solutions to common problems:

Login Issues

- **Problem**: Unable to sign in

- **Solution**: Verify that your Microsoft 365 account has Loop access and that your subscription supports it.

Browser Compatibility Issues

- **Problem**: Loop is not loading properly

- **Solution**: Ensure you are using a supported browser (Chrome, Edge, Safari) and that it's up to date.

Mobile App Issues

- **Problem**: Syncing problems or app crashes

- **Solution**: Restart the app, check your internet connection, and ensure you're using the latest version.

Access Restrictions in Organizations

- **Problem**: Loop is disabled by your IT admin

- **Solution**: Contact your IT department to check if Microsoft Loop is enabled for your organization.

Conclusion

Now that you know how to access Microsoft Loop across different platforms, you're ready to dive deeper into its features. Whether you're using the web version, mobile app, or integrating with Microsoft Teams, Loop offers a dynamic way to collaborate efficiently.

In the next section, "1.2.2 Navigating the Loop Interface," you'll explore how to move around Loop, create workspaces, and use its key tools effectively. 🚀

1.2.2 Navigating the Loop Interface

Microsoft Loop provides an intuitive and collaborative environment designed to enhance productivity through dynamic workspaces, pages, and components. To make the most of Microsoft Loop, it's crucial to understand its interface, including how to navigate different sections efficiently. This chapter will guide you through the key elements of the Microsoft Loop interface, helping you get comfortable with its structure and functionalities.

1. Overview of the Microsoft Loop Interface

When you first open Microsoft Loop, you are presented with a clean and minimalist interface that focuses on simplicity and ease of collaboration. The interface is designed to help users quickly find their workspaces, pages, and components without unnecessary distractions.

The Microsoft Loop interface consists of the following key areas:

1. **Sidebar (Navigation Panel)** – Allows access to workspaces and recent pages.

2. **Main Workspace Area** – Displays the selected workspace, pages, and components.

3. **Top Navigation Bar** – Provides access to settings, search, and user profile.

4. **Page and Component Area** – The main content area where you work with Loop pages and components.

Now, let's explore each of these areas in detail.

2. Sidebar (Navigation Panel)

The **sidebar** in Microsoft Loop is a fundamental part of the interface, allowing users to navigate between workspaces, access recent pages, and find important documents. You can expand or collapse the sidebar depending on your preference.

Accessing Workspaces

At the top of the sidebar, you will find a section labeled **Workspaces**. This section contains a list of all your available workspaces, whether they are personal or shared with a team.

- Clicking on a workspace will open its contents in the main area.

- You can create a new workspace by clicking the **"+" button** next to the workspaces section.

- If you have many workspaces, a search bar within the sidebar allows you to find a specific workspace quickly.

Recent and Pinned Pages

Below the Workspaces section, you will see the **Recent** and **Pinned** pages sections:

- **Recent Pages:** Displays the pages you have accessed recently, making it easier to jump back into your work.

- **Pinned Pages:** If you frequently access a particular page, you can pin it for quick access. To pin a page, simply click on the pin icon next to its name.

Search Bar

At the top of the sidebar, you will find a **search bar** that helps locate specific workspaces, pages, or components. You can enter keywords to filter results quickly and jump directly to the relevant content.

3. Main Workspace Area

The **main workspace area** is where most of your work takes place. It serves as the primary interface where you interact with Loop pages, components, and collaborative content.

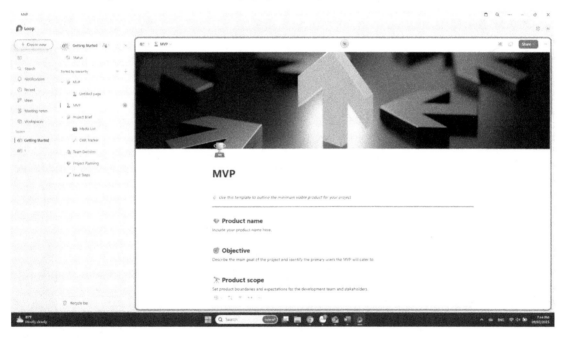

Workspace Layout

When you select a workspace, the main workspace area will display:

- **Workspace Title:** The name of the workspace is shown at the top.

- **List of Pages:** Displays all pages within the selected workspace.

- **Content Editor:** Where you can create and edit Loop pages and components.

Creating and Managing Pages

Each workspace contains **Loop pages**, which serve as digital canvases for collaboration.

- To create a new page, click the **"New Page"** button.

- You can rename pages by clicking on their titles and entering a new name.

- Drag and drop pages to reorder them within the workspace.

- Pages can be nested inside each other for better organization.

Adding Loop Components

Within each page, you can insert **Loop components**, which are dynamic, collaborative elements such as:

- Task lists

- Tables

- Polls

- Notes

- Embeddable content from Microsoft 365 apps

To add a component, type **"/" (forward slash)** to bring up the component menu and select the one you need.

4. Top Navigation Bar

The **top navigation bar** provides additional options for managing your workspace and settings.

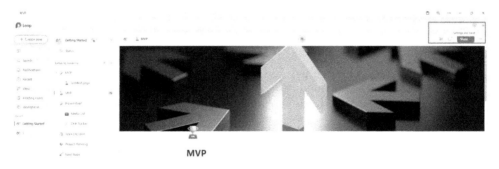

MVP

Profile and Settings

On the top-right corner of the interface, you will find your **profile picture**. Clicking on it allows you to:

- Change your account settings

- Manage workspace preferences

- Log out of Microsoft Loop

Collaboration and Sharing Options

Next to the profile section, you will find collaboration options, including:

- **Share Button:** Allows you to invite others to the workspace or specific pages.

- **Permissions Settings:** Lets you set edit or view permissions for different users.

Search and Notifications

- **Search Bar:** Helps you find pages, components, or workspaces quickly.

- **Notification Bell:** Displays recent activity, including updates from collaborators.

5. Page and Component Area

The **Page and Component Area** is where users interact with content directly. This area includes:

The Content Editor

The content editor is a flexible space where you can:

- Write and format text

- Insert media and interactive components

- Drag and rearrange elements

Formatting and Styling Options

Loop provides essential formatting tools, such as:

- Bold, Italic, Underline

- Bullet points and numbered lists

- Headings and subheadings

Using the formatting toolbar at the top of the content editor, you can enhance readability and structure your content effectively.

6. Customizing the Loop Interface

Microsoft Loop offers some customization options to enhance usability:

- Dark Mode and Light Mode: Change the appearance based on preference.

- Workspace Colors and Themes: Customize workspace visuals.

- Component Resizing: Adjust the size of embedded components for better readability.

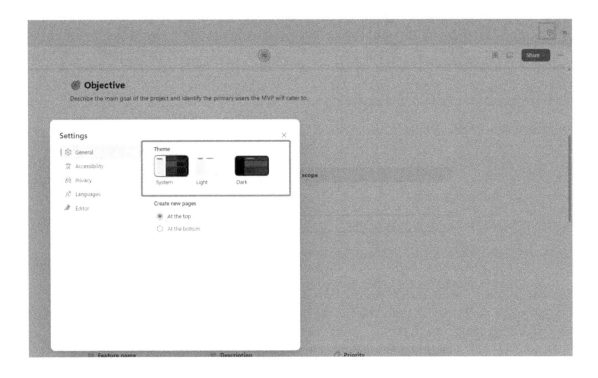

7. Conclusion

Navigating the Microsoft Loop interface effectively is crucial for maximizing productivity and collaboration. By understanding the sidebar, main workspace area, top navigation bar, and page editor, users can efficiently manage their workspaces and streamline teamwork.

Now that you're familiar with the interface, the next step is learning how to create and structure workspaces for collaboration, which we will cover in the next section.

1.2.3 Personalizing Your Loop Experience

Microsoft Loop offers a highly customizable experience, allowing users to tailor their workspaces, pages, and components to best suit their workflow. Personalizing Microsoft Loop can enhance productivity, improve collaboration, and create a more organized and visually appealing work environment. In this section, we will explore various ways to personalize Microsoft Loop, from adjusting workspace settings to customizing pages and components.

Customizing Your Loop Workspace

Setting a Workspace Name and Icon

When creating a workspace in Microsoft Loop, giving it a meaningful name and selecting an appropriate icon can help team members quickly identify its purpose. To customize the workspace name and icon:

1. Open your **Loop workspace**.

2. Click on the workspace name at the top of the screen.

3. Enter a new name that clearly represents the project or team using the workspace.

4. Click on the **Edit Icon** button and select an icon that visually represents your workspace.

5. Save the changes.

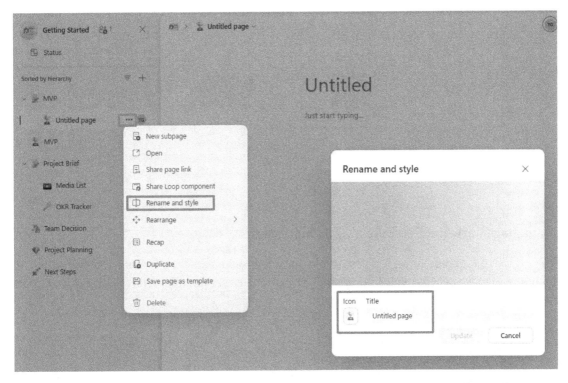

By naming workspaces descriptively and using icons, you ensure that all members can quickly navigate between multiple workspaces without confusion.

Choosing a Color Theme for Your Workspace

Loop allows users to apply different color themes to workspaces to visually differentiate between various projects. To change the color theme:

1. Click on the workspace settings menu.

2. Navigate to **Appearance or Theme Settings**.

3. Choose from the available color themes or customize your own.

4. Save the settings to apply the new color scheme.

Using distinct colors for different workspaces can help users quickly recognize and switch between them, reducing cognitive load.

Managing Workspace Members and Permissions

For effective collaboration, it's essential to manage who can access and modify content in a Loop workspace. Microsoft Loop provides options to set permissions for individual users or groups. To customize permissions:

1. Open the workspace settings.

2. Click on **Members & Permissions**.

3. Add or remove users by entering their email addresses.

4. Assign roles:

    o **Viewer** (read-only access)

    o **Editor** (can edit and collaborate)

    o **Owner** (can manage workspace settings)

5. Save changes.

By carefully managing permissions, teams can ensure that the right people have the appropriate level of access.

Personalizing Loop Pages

Organizing Pages for Better Navigation

A well-structured workspace makes it easier to find information and improves overall efficiency. To organize pages within a workspace:

1. Use **nested pages** to group related content.

2. Drag and drop pages to rearrange their order.

3. Use page titles and subtitles to clearly define sections.

4. Add page descriptions to provide context.

Using a logical structure for pages ensures that team members can quickly locate relevant information without unnecessary searching.

Customizing Page Layouts

Loop allows users to format pages according to their needs. To customize a page layout:

1. Click on **Page Settings**.

2. Choose a layout style (e.g., single-column, multi-column, grid view).

3. Adjust **text formatting** (bold, italic, underline) to highlight important content.

4. Use bullet points, checklists, and tables for better organization.

5. Insert **images, links, and files** to enrich the content.

By customizing layouts, users can create visually appealing and easy-to-read pages that enhance collaboration.

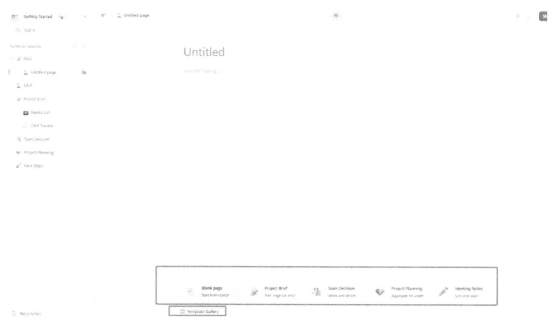

Using Templates for Consistency

For recurring tasks, using **templates** can save time and maintain consistency across multiple pages. To create and apply a template:

1. Open an existing page with a well-structured layout.

2. Click on **Save as Template**.

3. Name the template and choose whether it should be available to all workspace members.

4. When creating a new page, select the saved template to apply the same structure.

Templates are especially useful for project management, meeting notes, and brainstorming sessions.

Customizing Loop Components

Modifying Component Styles

Loop components are at the core of Microsoft Loop's collaboration features, allowing users to share interactive content across Microsoft 365 apps. To personalize components:

1. Change text colors and fonts to highlight key information.

2. Adjust the **size and width** of tables and lists.

3. Use **background highlights** to differentiate sections.

4. Embed interactive elements like **task lists, voting tables, and progress trackers**.

Personalizing component styles makes content more engaging and easier to digest.

Reusing and Sharing Components

Loop allows users to **reuse** and **share** components across multiple locations. To do this:

1. Select a Loop component.

2. Click on **Copy Component Link**.

3. Paste the link into Microsoft Teams, Outlook, or OneNote.

Since Loop components update in real time, any changes made in one location will automatically reflect everywhere else, ensuring information remains consistent.

Enhancing Collaboration with Custom Settings

Integrating Loop with Other Microsoft Apps

To enhance productivity, users can integrate Loop with other Microsoft 365 applications, such as:

- **Microsoft Teams** – Share Loop pages and components in chat.

- **Outlook** – Embed Loop components in emails for real-time updates.

- **OneNote** – Use Loop for interactive note-taking.

- **Planner** – Convert Loop tasks into structured project plans.

These integrations streamline workflows by reducing the need to switch between apps.

Setting Up Notifications and Alerts

To stay updated on changes within a workspace, users can enable notifications:

1. Click on **Workspace Settings**.

2. Navigate to **Notifications**.

3. Enable alerts for:

   o Page edits

   o New comments or mentions

   o Assigned tasks

4. Customize how notifications are delivered (email, Teams, or in-app alerts).

By fine-tuning notifications, users can stay informed without being overwhelmed by unnecessary updates.

Best Practices for Personalizing Microsoft Loop

To maximize efficiency while using Microsoft Loop, follow these best practices:

- **Keep workspaces organized** – Use clear naming conventions and categorize pages logically.

- **Use consistent formatting** – Standardize fonts, colors, and layouts across pages.

- **Minimize clutter** – Regularly archive old pages and remove outdated content.

- **Encourage team adoption** – Train team members on personalization features to ensure a consistent experience.

By implementing these strategies, users can create a highly customized Microsoft Loop experience that enhances both personal productivity and team collaboration.

Conclusion

Personalizing Microsoft Loop is key to making collaboration seamless and efficient. From customizing workspaces and pages to modifying Loop components and integrating with Microsoft 365, there are numerous ways to tailor Loop to your specific needs. By leveraging these customization options, users can create a workspace that is visually appealing, well-organized, and optimized for productivity.

1.3 Creating Your First Loop Workspace

1.3.1 Structuring a Workspace for Collaboration

Introduction

Microsoft Loop is designed to revolutionize collaboration by providing a flexible and dynamic workspace for individuals and teams. Before diving into creating your first workspace, it's essential to understand how to structure it for maximum efficiency. A well-organized workspace enhances productivity, streamlines communication, and ensures that all team members can easily access and contribute to shared content.

In this section, we will explore the key principles of structuring a Microsoft Loop workspace, best practices for organizing content, and strategies to maintain clarity and efficiency within your workspace.

Understanding the Role of a Workspace in Microsoft Loop

A Loop workspace serves as the central hub where all project-related content is stored and managed. Within this workspace, users can create Loop pages and Loop components to facilitate collaboration.

A structured workspace offers several benefits:

- Improved Organization: Helps teams keep documents, notes, and tasks neatly arranged.

- Efficient Collaboration: Enables team members to contribute and track progress in real-time.

- Easier Navigation: Ensures that all necessary information is accessible without excessive searching.

- Enhanced Productivity: Reduces clutter and duplication, allowing teams to focus on their goals.

To achieve these benefits, a workspace should be carefully planned and structured from the beginning.

Step 1: Defining the Purpose of Your Workspace

Before setting up your workspace, clarify its purpose. Ask yourself the following questions:

- **Who will be using this workspace?** Is it for a specific team, department, or cross-functional project?

- **What type of work will be done in this workspace?** Is it for brainstorming, project management, documentation, or general collaboration?

- **What information needs to be stored and shared?** Will it include meeting notes, project updates, reports, or task lists?

- **How frequently will team members access this workspace?** Is it a daily collaboration space or an archive for reference?

Having a clear purpose ensures that your workspace is designed to support the needs of your team.

Step 2: Naming and Structuring Your Workspace

2.1 Choosing a Meaningful Name

A well-named workspace makes it easy for team members to identify and access relevant content. Use descriptive names that reflect the purpose of the workspace.

Examples of Effective Workspace Names:
✅ "Marketing Team Hub" – for a marketing department's central collaboration space.
✅ "Product Development Sprint Q2" – for tracking a product development cycle.
✅ "Client Onboarding Resources" – for managing client onboarding documentation.

Avoid vague or overly generic names like:
🚫 "Work"
🚫 "Miscellaneous"
🚫 "Stuff to Do"

2.2 Organizing Your Workspace with Loop Pages

Once your workspace is created, it should be structured using **Loop pages**, which serve as folders or sections for organizing information.

Best Practices for Loop Page Organization:

- **Create a Homepage** – This should act as the central dashboard summarizing key information.

- **Use a Logical Hierarchy** – Group related pages together (e.g., a "Project Management" page can contain sub-pages for different project phases).

- **Number or Label Pages for Clarity** – Use consistent naming conventions like "1.0 Project Overview" or "📌 Key Resources."

- **Archive Old Content** – Keep the workspace clean by moving outdated information to an archive section.

Example of a Well-Structured Workspace:

💼 **Marketing Team Hub**
📌 Homepage (Quick links & workspace overview)
📰 Meeting Notes
—— Weekly Team Meetings
—— Client Strategy Sessions
📊 Campaign Planning
—— Social Media Strategies
—— Email Marketing Plans
✓ Task Management
—— Sprint Backlog
—— Assignments & Deadlines

Step 3: Utilizing Loop Components for Flexibility

Microsoft Loop's **dynamic components** allow content to be easily shared and updated across Microsoft 365 apps. These components can be embedded within a workspace to enhance collaboration.

3.1 Types of Loop Components

1. **Text Components** – For shared notes, brainstorming, and documentation.

2. **Tables** – For organizing data, tracking tasks, and creating simple databases.

3. **Task Lists** – For assigning and tracking work progress.

4. **Voting Tables** – For decision-making through quick feedback collection.

5. **Progress Trackers** – For visualizing team progress on projects.

3.2 How to Use Components Effectively

- **Keep Components Small & Modular** – Each component should serve a specific function.

- **Embed Components in Multiple Locations** – For example, a task list can appear both in Microsoft Teams and within Loop.

- **Use Tags & Mentions (@username)** – To assign tasks and notify team members.

Step 4: Establishing Collaboration Guidelines

A well-structured workspace is only effective if team members know how to use it properly. Setting **collaboration guidelines** ensures consistency and productivity.

4.1 Defining User Roles and Permissions

- **Editors** – Can create, modify, and delete content.

- **Contributors** – Can add and edit content but cannot delete critical documents.

- **Viewers** – Can access and read content but cannot make changes.

4.2 Setting Expectations for Communication

- **Use Comments for Discussions** – Instead of editing content directly, use comments to discuss changes.

- **Update Task Status Regularly** – Ensure that everyone marks their assigned tasks as "In Progress" or "Completed."

- **Avoid Duplicate Content** – Check for existing documents before creating new ones.

Step 5: Maintaining and Optimizing Your Workspace

Once your workspace is set up, it requires ongoing maintenance to remain effective.

5.1 Conducting Regular Reviews

- **Weekly Clean-Up** – Remove or archive outdated information.

- **Monthly Review Meetings** – Evaluate how well the workspace is functioning.

- **Gathering Feedback** – Ask team members for suggestions on improvements.

5.2 Leveraging Microsoft Loop Updates

Microsoft frequently updates Loop with new features. Stay informed by:

- Checking Microsoft's official blog and release notes.

- Participating in Microsoft Loop user communities.

- Exploring integration with emerging AI and automation tools.

Conclusion

Structuring a Microsoft Loop workspace effectively is essential for ensuring seamless collaboration and efficiency. By carefully planning the purpose, naming conventions, page organization, Loop components, and collaboration rules, teams can maximize their productivity and make the most out of Microsoft Loop's features.

With a well-structured workspace, your team will benefit from better organization, streamlined workflows, and enhanced teamwork, making Microsoft Loop an indispensable tool for modern digital collaboration.

Now that you understand how to structure a workspace, the next section will guide you through adding and organizing Loop **pages** to enhance your collaborative experience further. 🚀

Example: Structuring a Microsoft Loop Workspace for a Marketing Team

To illustrate how to properly structure a Microsoft Loop workspace, let's walk through an example: a **Marketing Team Hub** for a digital marketing department.

Step 1: Define the Purpose of the Workspace

The **Marketing Team Hub** is designed to:
✓ Centralize all marketing documents, meeting notes, and project plans.

✅ Enable collaboration between team members working on campaigns.

✅ Provide easy access to key resources and performance metrics.

Step 2: Name and Organize the Workspace

A clear and descriptive name is chosen:

📌 **Marketing Team Hub**

Inside this workspace, Loop **Pages** are created to organize information:

💼 **Marketing Team Hub**
```
├── 📌 Homepage (Overview & Quick Links)
├── 📷 Meeting Notes
│   ├── Weekly Team Meetings
│   ├── Client Strategy Sessions
├── 📊 Campaign Planning
│   ├── Social Media Strategies
│   ├── Email Marketing Plans
├── ✅ Task Management
│   ├── Sprint Backlog
│   ├── Assignments & Deadlines
```

Each **Loop Page** acts as a section containing relevant **Loop Components** for easy collaboration.

Step 3: Utilize Loop Components for Collaboration

Within the **"Social Media Strategies"** page, the team uses **Loop Components** for dynamic updates:

📄 **Social Media Strategies**

◆ **Campaign Goals:** Improve engagement by 20%, grow followers by 10%

◆ **Target Audience:** Young professionals (ages 25-34)

◆ **Key Platforms:** Instagram, LinkedIn, TikTok

📌 **Task List (Loop Component)**

Task	Assigned To	Due Date	Status
Research trending hashtags	@Emma	Feb 15	☐ In Progress
Create Instagram post drafts	@Jake	Feb 18	⬤ Not Started
Schedule TikTok videos	@Lena	Feb 20	☐ Pending Review

📊 Engagement Metrics Table (Loop Component)

Platform	Likes	Shares	Comments
Instagram	1,200	300	150
LinkedIn	800	250	100
TikTok	3,500	1,000	500

✅ Since **Loop Components are live**, updates made here are instantly reflected across Microsoft Teams and Outlook, ensuring real-time collaboration.

Step 4: Establish Collaboration Guidelines

To maintain an efficient workspace, the team follows these rules:
📌 **Naming Conventions**: All campaign pages start with "📊 [Campaign Name] - [Date]"
📌 **Comments Over Direct Edits**: Feedback is given using @mentions instead of modifying content directly.
📌 **Weekly Review Sessions**: Every Monday, team members update the workspace.

Step 5: Maintain and Optimize the Workspace

☐ Monthly Check-in:

- Archive old campaign pages into a "Past Campaigns" section.
- Review and improve collaboration guidelines.
- Add new Loop Components for improved tracking.

By structuring the Marketing Team Hub in this way, team members can quickly find relevant information, collaborate effectively, and streamline marketing efforts. 🚀

This example showcases how **Microsoft Loop** can transform a workspace into an interactive and organized collaboration hub! ⊙⃗

1.3.2 Adding and Organizing Loop Pages

Once you've set up your first **Loop workspace**, the next step is to build **Loop pages** to structure your content and collaboration. Loop pages act as dynamic canvases where you can organize text, images, tasks, and interactive components. Whether you're managing a project, brainstorming ideas, or collaborating on documents, organizing your pages effectively will help you and your team work more efficiently.

This section will guide you through **adding, customizing, and organizing Loop pages** within your workspace to ensure clarity, productivity, and smooth collaboration.

---

1. Understanding Loop Pages

1.1 What Are Loop Pages?

Loop pages are flexible digital documents within a Loop workspace that support real-time collaboration. Unlike static documents, Loop pages allow users to add Loop components, including lists, tables, task trackers, and even embedded content from Microsoft 365 apps. These pages are highly interactive, enabling seamless updates and modifications by multiple users at the same time.

Each Loop page serves as a centralized hub for specific topics or projects. For example, within a marketing workspace, you can have separate Loop pages for:

- Campaign Planning – Tracking key milestones and brainstorming strategies.
- Content Calendar – Scheduling and managing content releases.
- Meeting Notes – Keeping a shared record of discussions and decisions.

1.2 Key Features of Loop Pages

- Real-time Collaboration: Multiple users can edit and contribute at the same time.
- Dynamic Content: Embed task lists, polls, checklists, and more.

- Integration with Microsoft 365: Insert files, tables, and data from Word, Excel, and Teams.

- Customizable Structure: Arrange content using sections, bullet points, headers, and interactive elements.

2. Adding a New Loop Page

2.1 Creating a Loop Page

Adding a new page to your workspace is straightforward:

1. Open your Loop Workspace: Navigate to the workspace where you want to create a new page.

2. Click on "New Page": You'll see this option in the sidebar or workspace menu.

3. Name Your Page: Give your page a clear and descriptive title (e.g., "Marketing Strategy 2024" or "Weekly Sprint Review").

4. Start Adding Content: Begin by typing or inserting Loop components to structure your page.

2.2 Adding Content to a Loop Page

Once your page is created, you can start building its content. Loop pages support various elements, including:

- Text Sections: Use rich text formatting to highlight key points.

- Tables and Lists: Organize data into structured formats.

- Task Lists: Assign action items with due dates and responsible team members.

- Embedded Media: Insert images, videos, and links for reference.

Best Practices for Adding Content

- Use Headers and Sections: Break content into logical sections using H1, H2, and bullet points.

- Keep It Concise: Avoid long paragraphs—use lists, tables, and highlights for clarity.

- Leverage Loop Components: Utilize checklists, voting tables, and progress trackers for interactive collaboration.

3. Organizing Loop Pages for Maximum Efficiency

As your workspace grows, keeping your pages well-organized becomes essential. Here are some methods to **categorize and structure your Loop pages** effectively.

3.1 Structuring Pages with Categories and Sections

Grouping related pages into logical categories improves navigability and team efficiency. Some effective ways to organize Loop pages include:

- **By Project:** Create a separate Loop page for each project phase (e.g., "Project Kickoff," "Execution Plan," "Final Review").

- **By Department:** Maintain individual pages for Marketing, Sales, HR, and Operations.

- **By Task Type:** Keep dedicated pages for reports, task lists, and meeting notes.

Example: Marketing Team Loop Structure

📁 **Marketing Strategy 2024**
- 📄 Campaign Planning
- 📄 Social Media Calendar
- 📄 Ad Budget Allocation

📁 **Weekly Meetings**
- 📄 Monday Standup Notes
- 📄 Client Feedback Tracker

📁 **Content Creation**
- 📄 Blog Post Ideas
- 📄 Video Script Planning

This method allows teams to quickly locate pages and maintain clarity in complex projects.

3.2 Using Tags and Labels

Microsoft Loop allows users to apply tags and labels to pages, making it easier to find relevant information. Consider these best practices for tagging your pages:

- **Project-Based Tags:** #Marketing, #Finance, #Operations
- **Priority Labels:** 🔥 Urgent, ☐ In Progress, ✅ Completed
- **Team-Specific Identifiers:** @DesignTeam, @HR, @ITSupport

When searching for content, simply use the Loop search bar and filter results by tags to locate relevant pages instantly.

3.3 Linking Between Pages

For seamless navigation, Microsoft Loop enables internal linking between pages. You can create hyperlinks to reference related content within your workspace.

How to Link Between Pages:

1. Highlight the text you want to hyperlink.
2. Click on the Link icon or use the shortcut Ctrl + K (Windows) / Cmd + K (Mac).
3. Select the target Loop page from the list.

🔗 **Example:** On your "Marketing Strategy 2024" page, you can add a link to "Social Media Calendar" for easy access.

---

4. Managing Access and Permissions for Loop Pages

Controlling who can view or edit your Loop pages ensures smooth collaboration while protecting sensitive information.

4.1 Setting Page Permissions

Microsoft Loop allows users to adjust permissions at the workspace, page, or component level.

Permission Levels:

🔹 **Full Access:** Users can edit and share the page.
🔹 **Comment Only:** Users can add comments but not edit content.
🔹 **View Only:** Users can read but not modify content.

4.2 Sharing Loop Pages with External Users

You can share Loop pages with people outside your organization while maintaining security:

1. Click the **Share** button in the top-right corner.

2. Choose **"Anyone with the link"** or **"Only people in your organization"**.

3. Select the desired **permission level** (Edit, Comment, View).

4. Copy and share the generated link.

Conclusion

Effectively adding and organizing Loop pages is key to streamlining collaboration, maintaining clarity, and improving productivity. By structuring pages logically, using labels, and implementing best practices for organization, teams can maximize the benefits of Microsoft Loop and stay on top of their tasks effortlessly.

Examples of Loop Workspaces

To help you understand how Microsoft Loop Workspaces can be structured and utilized in real-world scenarios, let's explore several practical examples across different industries and team functions. Each example demonstrates how teams can organize Loop pages and components to optimize collaboration and productivity.

Example 1: Marketing Team Workspace

Use Case: A marketing team managing campaigns, content planning, and performance tracking.

📁 **Marketing Strategy 2024**
  - 📄 Campaign Planning
  - 📄 Social Media Calendar
  - 📄 Budget Allocation

📁 Content Creation
- 📄 Blog Post Ideas
- 📄 Video Script Planning
- 📄 Graphic Design Requests

📁 Analytics and Performance
- 📄 Monthly Report (Linked with Power BI)
- 📄 Website Traffic Overview
- 📄 SEO Analysis

📁 Meeting Notes & Collaboration
- 📄 Weekly Team Standups
- 📄 Client Feedback Summary

Key Loop Components Used:

✅ **Task Lists** – Assign marketing tasks to team members.

📊 **Data Tables** – Embed Google Analytics or Power BI reports.

🎥 **Embedded Media** – Insert videos and social media content drafts.

✍️ **Real-time Notes** – Shared notes during brainstorming sessions.

💡 **Benefit:** Helps **centralize all marketing activities** in one workspace, ensuring seamless communication between content creators, designers, and analysts.

Example 2: Software Development Team Workspace

Use Case: A development team tracking project progress, sprints, and documentation.

📁 Project: Mobile App Development
- 📄 Feature Roadmap
- 📄 Sprint Backlog
- 📄 Bug Tracking

📁 Documentation
- 📄 API Reference
- 📄 User Guide Draft
- 📄 Troubleshooting FAQ

📁 **Team Collaboration**
- ▪ Daily Standup Notes
- ▪ Code Review Comments

Key Loop Components Used:

⚙️▢ **Task Trackers** – Assign development tasks to engineers.

👓 **Embedded GitHub Issues** – Link directly to code repositories.

▦ **Timeline View** – Visualize sprint cycles and release dates.

💬 **Live Commenting** – Collaborate on documentation edits in real time.

💡 **Benefit:** Helps engineers, designers, and product managers **stay aligned** with project milestones and efficiently track development progress.

Example 3: Human Resources (HR) Workspace

Use Case: An HR team managing recruitment, onboarding, and employee engagement.

📁 **Recruitment & Hiring**
- ▪ Job Postings & Descriptions
- ▪ Interview Schedule (Linked with Outlook Calendar)
- ▪ Candidate Evaluation Tracker

📁 **Onboarding Process**
- ▪ New Employee Checklist
- ▪ Training Materials
- ▪ HR Policies & Documents

📁 **Employee Engagement & Benefits**
- ▪ Performance Review Guidelines
- ▪ Wellness & Employee Perks
- ▪ Monthly HR Newsletter

Key Loop Components Used:

📌 **Checklists** – Ensure smooth onboarding with step-by-step guides.

▢▢ **Embedded Forms** – Gather employee feedback with Microsoft Forms.

Policy Documents – Maintain HR guidelines in one accessible place.
Survey Results – Track employee engagement statistics.

Benefit: Provides **a single platform for HR teams** to manage hiring, onboarding, and employee engagement initiatives.

Example 4: Sales Team Workspace

Use Case: A sales team managing leads, tracking deals, and analyzing performance.

Lead Management
- Lead Tracking Sheet
- Contact List & Follow-ups
- Outreach Email Templates

Sales Performance
- Monthly Sales Reports
- Key Account Reviews
- Sales Forecasting

Team Collaboration
- Weekly Sales Calls Notes
- Competitive Analysis

Key Loop Components Used:

Live Excel Charts – Embed sales metrics from Excel.
CRM Integration – Connect Microsoft Dynamics or Salesforce data.
Deal Progress Trackers – Monitor ongoing negotiations.
Meeting Summaries – Log insights from client calls.

Benefit: Enables sales teams to **track leads efficiently**, analyze performance, and optimize outreach strategies.

Example 5: Event Planning Workspace

Use Case: A team organizing an annual conference, managing logistics, and coordinating speakers.

📁 Event Planning
- 📄 Event Timeline & Deadlines
- 📄 Venue & Catering Arrangements
- 📄 Speaker Coordination

📁 Marketing & Registration
- 📄 Event Website Content
- 📄 Social Media Promotions
- 📄 Attendee Registration List

📁 Day-of-Event Logistics
- 📄 Session Schedule
- 📄 Volunteer Assignments
- 📄 Emergency Contacts

Key Loop Components Used:

🗓 **Event Calendar** – Schedule sessions and deadlines.

✏ **Speaker Profiles** – Keep bios and talk details handy.

✅ **Task Assignments** – Allocate responsibilities to team members.

📌 **Quick Links** – Provide easy access to documents and vendor details.

💡 **Benefit:** Ensures **efficient coordination** between event planners, speakers, and vendors for a smooth event execution.

Conclusion

These examples demonstrate how Microsoft Loop Workspaces can be customized for different teams and workflows. By structuring Loop pages strategically and using interactive Loop components, businesses can enhance team collaboration, transparency, and efficiency.

Whether you're leading a project, managing a team, or organizing information, Loop provides the flexibility needed to create a dynamic and connected workspace.

🚀 Next Steps: Now that you understand how Loop Workspaces function, the next chapter will cover how to work with Loop Components to make collaboration even more powerful!

1.3.3 Customizing Workspace Settings

Once you have created your first Microsoft Loop workspace, customizing its settings can significantly enhance your workflow, organization, and collaboration experience. Proper customization ensures that your workspace aligns with your needs and makes it easier for you and your team to navigate and use Loop effectively.

This section will guide you through the various customization options available in Microsoft Loop, including workspace naming, privacy settings, user permissions, layout customization, and notification preferences.

1. Customizing the Workspace Name and Description

1.1 Choosing a Clear and Descriptive Name

When creating a workspace in Microsoft Loop, giving it a meaningful and recognizable name is crucial. A well-named workspace helps users quickly identify its purpose and content.

Best Practices for Naming Your Workspace:

- **Be Specific**: Instead of naming a workspace "Project 1," consider "Q1 Marketing Campaign – 2025."

- **Keep It Concise**: Avoid overly long names that make navigation difficult.

- **Use Consistent Naming Conventions**: If your organization uses a structured naming system, follow it (e.g., "Department - Project - Year").

- **Avoid Special Characters**: Some special characters may not be supported in naming and can create issues in file management.

1.2 Adding a Workspace Description

A brief description can help clarify the workspace's purpose, especially when multiple users are involved. When adding a description:

- Explain the workspace's primary objective.

- Mention key users or stakeholders if applicable.

- Provide a quick overview of what kind of content will be stored or collaborated on.

For example:

- **Workspace Name:** "Product Launch – Spring 2025"

- **Description:** "This workspace is dedicated to planning, executing, and tracking all activities related to the Spring 2025 product launch. Team members from marketing, sales, and product development will collaborate here."

2. Managing Privacy and Access Settings

2.1 Understanding Privacy Levels

Microsoft Loop allows users to set privacy levels depending on how accessible the workspace should be:

- **Private Workspace:** Only invited members can access it. Ideal for confidential projects or internal team discussions.

- **Organization-Wide Access:** Anyone within your organization can view or edit, depending on permissions. Useful for company-wide initiatives.

- **Public Workspace (if available):** In some enterprise settings, a workspace can be made publicly accessible within a broader network.

To set privacy settings:

1. Click on the workspace settings icon (⚙☐).

2. Navigate to **Privacy Settings**.

3. Choose between **Private** or **Organization-wide** access.

2.2 Managing User Permissions

Microsoft Loop provides granular control over who can access and edit workspace content. When inviting users, you can assign them different roles:

- **Owner:** Full control over the workspace, including settings and user management.

- **Editor:** Can modify, add, and delete content but cannot change settings.
- **Viewer:** Can only view content but cannot edit or comment.

Steps to Manage Permissions:

1. Open the **Workspace Settings** panel.
2. Navigate to **Manage Members**.
3. Click **Invite Users** and select their permission level.
4. Adjust existing members' roles as needed.

3. Organizing the Workspace Layout

3.1 Customizing Sections and Pages

A well-structured workspace improves collaboration and makes it easier to find relevant content. Microsoft Loop provides a flexible approach to organizing pages and sections.

Best Practices for Structuring Your Workspace:

- Use Clear Page Titles: Instead of "Notes," name it "Weekly Team Meeting Notes."
- Create Sections for Major Topics: Organize content into separate pages for tasks, brainstorming, and meeting notes.
- Pin Important Pages: Keep frequently accessed pages at the top of the workspace for quick reference.

3.2 Using Templates for Efficiency

Microsoft Loop offers templates that streamline workspace setup and maintain consistency across teams. You can create custom templates for:

- Meeting agendas
- Project planning
- Brainstorming sessions

Steps to Use a Template:

1. Click **New Page** in the workspace.

2. Select **Use a Template** instead of a blank page.

3. Choose a pre-built template or customize one for future use.

4. Customizing Notifications and Alerts

Managing Notifications for Workspace Activity

Microsoft Loop provides notification settings to keep you updated without overwhelming you with alerts. You can customize notifications for:

- Comments and mentions

- New content added

- Task updates and deadlines

Setting Up Reminders and Alerts

For time-sensitive tasks, Loop allows users to set reminders:

- **Task Reminders:** Automatically notify you when a deadline approaches.

- **Comment Mentions:** Alert you when someone responds to your input.

- **Workspace Updates:** Notify you of significant changes made by other members.

5. Integrating with Other Microsoft 365 Apps

Embedding Loop Components in Other Applications

Microsoft Loop is designed to work seamlessly with Microsoft 365 apps like Teams, Outlook, and OneDrive.

How to Embed Loop Components in Teams:

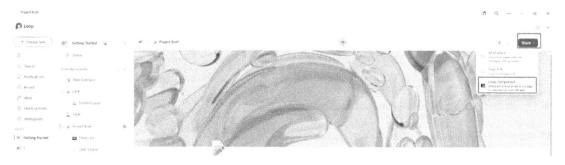

1. Open Microsoft Teams.

2. Select a chat or channel where you want to add Loop content.

3. Click **Insert Loop Component** and choose a relevant document or note.

Using Loop with Outlook:

1. Compose a new email in Outlook.

2. Click **Insert > Loop Component**.

3. Select an existing workspace page or create a new one.

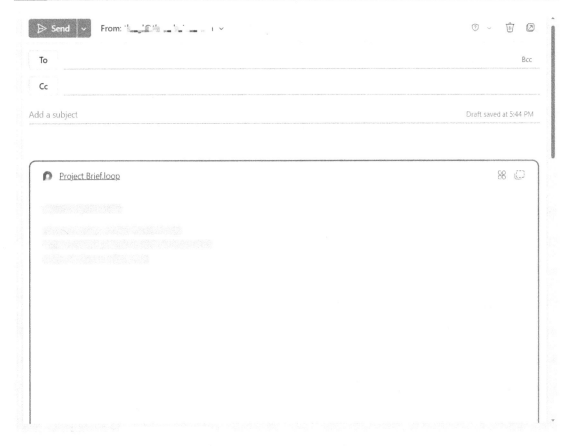

Syncing Loop Workspaces with OneDrive

Loop workspaces can be automatically backed up to OneDrive, ensuring data security and easy recovery.

To enable auto-sync:

1. Open **Settings** in Microsoft Loop.

2. Navigate to **Storage & Backup**.

3. Enable **Sync with OneDrive** for automatic updates.

6. Ensuring Security and Compliance

Data Protection Measures

Microsoft Loop follows enterprise-grade security protocols, but users should still take precautions:

- Enable multi-factor authentication (MFA) for added security.

- Set expiration dates for shared links to prevent unauthorized access.

- Regularly review workspace member access to remove inactive users.

Compliance with Organizational Policies

If you work in a regulated industry, ensure that your Loop workspaces follow company policies regarding:

- Data retention

- Information classification

- GDPR or HIPAA compliance (if applicable)

Conclusion

Customizing your Microsoft Loop workspace ensures a more structured, efficient, and productive environment for collaboration. By tailoring settings such as naming conventions, user permissions, page organization, notifications, and integrations with other Microsoft 365 tools, you can create a workspace that aligns with your specific needs.

As you continue using Microsoft Loop, revisit these settings periodically to optimize your workflow and ensure that your workspace remains well-organized and secure.

CHAPTER II
Working with Loop Components

2.1 Introduction to Loop Components

2.1.1 What Are Loop Components?

Microsoft Loop is a revolutionary tool designed to enhance collaboration by allowing teams to work seamlessly on shared content. At the core of Microsoft Loop are Loop Components, which are modular, flexible, and highly interactive content blocks that can be used across different Microsoft 365 applications. These components provide a dynamic way for users to create, share, and edit content in real time, making teamwork more efficient and connected.

Loop Components are not just static documents or simple text boxes; they are live, constantly updating elements that can be embedded in emails, chats, documents, and even other applications within the Microsoft ecosystem. They allow users to collaborate without switching between multiple apps, keeping work synchronized and accessible to all team members, no matter where they are.

1. The Purpose of Loop Components

The primary goal of Loop Components is to streamline collaboration and enhance productivity by providing teams with interactive, shareable content that can be updated in real time. Unlike traditional documents or notes that require manual updates and version control, Loop Components stay in sync across all locations where they are embedded.

For example:

- If a team member updates a task list inside a Loop Component within a Teams chat, that update will instantly reflect wherever the component is also being used, such as in an Outlook email or a Word document.

- If another user modifies a table within a Loop Component on a shared page, everyone else will see the changes in real time, eliminating the need to send multiple versions of a document.

This fluid approach to content management allows teams to stay aligned, reduce miscommunication, and eliminate redundant work caused by outdated information.

2. Key Features of Loop Components

Loop Components bring several unique capabilities that set them apart from traditional document collaboration tools:

a. Real-Time Synchronization

Loop Components **update instantly** across all platforms where they are shared. If a user edits a component inside Microsoft Teams, that same component updates inside an Outlook email, a Word document, or anywhere else it has been shared. This eliminates the need for version tracking and manual syncing.

b. Cross-Application Usability

One of the biggest strengths of Loop Components is that they can be used across multiple Microsoft 365 applications, including:

- Microsoft Teams – Embedded in chat conversations for live collaboration.

- Outlook – Used inside emails to share and edit content directly within the message.

- Word and OneNote – Integrated into documents and notes for enhanced content creation.

- SharePoint and OneDrive – Stored and accessed easily from cloud-based platforms.

This versatility ensures that users can collaborate in their preferred workspace without being confined to a single app.

c. Modular and Flexible

Loop Components are modular, meaning they can be broken down into different elements, moved around, or even used independently. A component that starts as a simple task list can be expanded into a detailed project plan, with assigned owners and due dates, all within the same shared space.

d. Interactive and Engaging

Unlike static text, Loop Components allow for real-time engagement. Users can:

- Edit content collaboratively, seeing changes as they happen.

- React with emojis or comments to provide quick feedback.

- Mention team members using @mentions to draw attention to specific updates.

This interactive approach makes Loop Components highly effective for brainstorming sessions, project planning, and information sharing.

e. Seamless Integration with Microsoft 365 AI Features

Loop Components leverage Microsoft AI capabilities to enhance productivity. For instance:

- Smart suggestions help users organize and format content automatically.

- AI-driven insights can summarize information or provide recommendations based on the component's content.

- Microsoft Copilot (if enabled) can assist users in creating or refining Loop Components efficiently.

This integration ensures that teams can work faster and smarter, reducing manual effort while maintaining high accuracy and consistency.

3. Types of Loop Components

While Chapter 2.1.2 (Types of Loop Components) will cover each component in detail, here is a high-level overview of the key types of Loop Components:

- Text Components – Simple, shareable text blocks for notes, lists, and discussions.

- Tables – Interactive tables for organizing structured data.

- Task Lists – To-do lists that allow for assignments, due dates, and progress tracking.

- Checklists – Actionable lists for task management and workflow tracking.

- Voting Tables – A polling tool to gather team feedback and make decisions collectively.

- Progress Trackers – Visual tools for monitoring tasks, goals, or project milestones.

- Embedded Files – Components that integrate files, images, and links within workspaces.

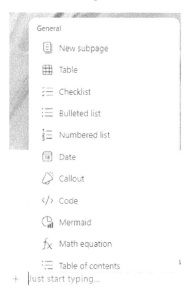

Each of these components serves a unique purpose, allowing teams to tailor their collaboration experience based on their needs.

4. Benefits of Using Loop Components

a. Increased Efficiency

Because Loop Components eliminate the need for duplicate documents and manual updates, they significantly reduce wasted time spent tracking changes, searching for the latest version, or consolidating feedback.

b. Enhanced Collaboration

With real-time updates and cross-application functionality, Loop Components make it easier for teams to stay aligned, whether working remotely or in an office environment.

c. Simplified Workflows

Instead of switching between multiple apps and files, users can work directly inside shared components, making workflows smoother and more intuitive.

d. Better Organization

Since Loop Components stay synchronized across platforms, they help maintain a single source of truth, reducing miscommunication and document clutter.

e. Improved Transparency

By allowing all team members to see updates instantly, Loop Components create a culture of transparency, ensuring that everyone is on the same page without the need for excessive meetings or email chains.

5. The Future of Loop Components

Microsoft is continuously expanding the capabilities of Loop Components, integrating them deeper into Microsoft 365 and AI-driven automation. Future updates may include:

- More component types, such as interactive dashboards or data-driven charts.

- Expanded integration with third-party tools like Trello, Slack, or Jira.

- AI-powered automation for smarter workflows and content suggestions.

As these features evolve, Loop Components will continue to redefine how teams collaborate and manage work in the modern digital workplace.

Conclusion

Loop Components represent a fundamental shift in digital collaboration, offering a flexible, real-time, and cross-platform approach to teamwork. Whether you're working on project plans, brainstorming ideas, or managing tasks, these components help keep everything connected and up to date, eliminating inefficiencies caused by outdated information or scattered documents.

In the next section, "2.1.2 Types of Loop Components," we will explore each component type in detail, explaining how to use them effectively to **boost productivity and streamline workflows** in Microsoft Loop.

2.1.2 Types of Loop Components

Microsoft Loop is a powerful collaboration tool designed to streamline teamwork and enhance productivity. One of its core features is **Loop Components**, which are modular, interactive content blocks that can be used across various Microsoft 365 applications such as Outlook, Teams, and OneNote. These components allow users to create, edit, and share content in real-time, making collaboration more dynamic and efficient.

In this section, we will explore the different types of Loop Components, their functionalities, and how they can be effectively used in various workflows.

Overview of Loop Components

Loop Components are designed to be **lightweight, flexible, and adaptable**. Unlike traditional documents that remain static, these components can be edited by multiple users in real-time, ensuring that content is always up to date. They can be embedded in emails, chats, and shared documents, making them accessible across multiple platforms.

Each component serves a unique purpose, whether it's for text-based collaboration, task management, brainstorming, or data tracking. Understanding these different types will help you leverage Microsoft Loop effectively.

Types of Loop Components

Microsoft Loop offers a variety of components tailored to different collaboration needs. The main types of Loop Components include:

General

☰ New subpage

⊞ Table

☷ Checklist

☰ Bulleted list

☷ Numbered list

⊡ Date

◊ Callout

</> Code

⌸ Mermaid

ƒx Math equation

☰ Table of contents

1. **Text Components**

2. **Table Components**

3. **Task List Components**

4. **Voting Table Components**

5. **Checklist Components**

6. **Numbered List Components**

7. **Bullet List Components**

8. **Progress Tracker Components**

9. **Q&A Components**

Let's explore each type in detail.

Text Components

The **Text Component** is one of the most fundamental elements in Microsoft Loop. It allows users to create and edit rich text collaboratively. This component is useful for:

- Taking shared notes during meetings

- Brainstorming ideas in a free-form text area

- Drafting content for documents, emails, or reports

Users can apply formatting options such as bold, italics, underlining, and bullet points to enhance readability. Additionally, @mentions can be used to tag team members, ensuring they are notified of important updates.

📌 **Example Use Case**: A marketing team drafts key messaging for an upcoming campaign in a Loop Text Component shared within a Microsoft Teams chat.

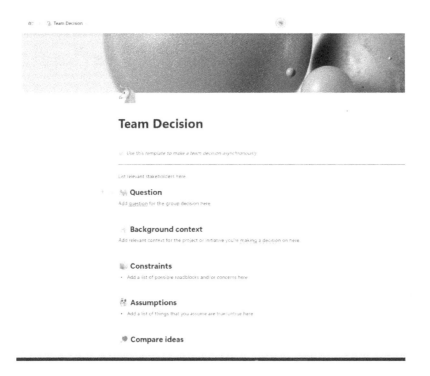

Table Components

The **Table Component** allows users to structure information in a grid format, making it easier to organize and analyze data. Tables can be customized with column headers and cell formatting to suit different needs.

Key features include:
✓☐ Customizable rows and columns
✓☐ Live updates from multiple users
✓☐ Sorting and filtering capabilities

★ **Example Use Case**: A project team tracks deliverables and deadlines using a Loop Table embedded in an Outlook email.

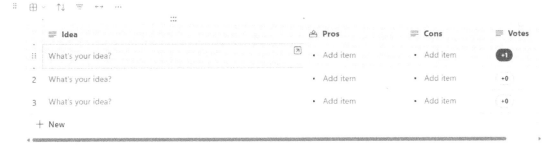

Task List Components

The **Task List Component** is an interactive to-do list that enables teams to assign tasks, set due dates, and track progress. It is ideal for project management and ensures that everyone is aligned on their responsibilities.

◆ **Key Features:**

- Assign tasks to specific users

- Set priorities and deadlines

- Check off completed tasks in real-time

★ **Example Use Case**: A software development team uses a Loop Task List to track bug fixes, ensuring that each task is assigned and completed efficiently.

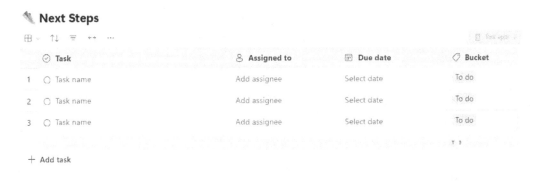

Voting Table Components

The **Voting Table Component** is a powerful decision-making tool that allows team members to vote on different options within a structured table.

◆ **Key Features:**

- Add multiple options for voting

- Team members can vote by adding checkmarks or rating items

- Real-time updates to reflect consensus

✦ **Example Use Case**: A product development team uses a Voting Table to prioritize new feature ideas based on team feedback.

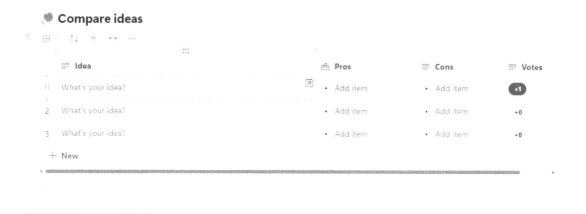

Checklist Components

The **Checklist Component** is a variation of the Task List Component that focuses on **step-by-step completion tracking**. It is particularly useful for process-driven tasks or quality control workflows.

◆ **Key Features:**

- Create a sequential list of tasks

- Check off items as they are completed

- Keep track of incomplete tasks

★ **Example Use Case**: A retail store manager uses a Loop Checklist to ensure all daily operational tasks are completed by the team.

🔗 **Relevant links**

Add relevant links here.

○ Check list 1

○ Check list 2

Numbered List Components

The **Numbered List Component** is used for creating ordered lists. This is useful for:

- Outlining step-by-step instructions

- Listing ranked priorities

- Structuring hierarchical information

★ **Example Use Case**: A training manager uses a Numbered List in Microsoft Loop to outline the onboarding steps for new employees.

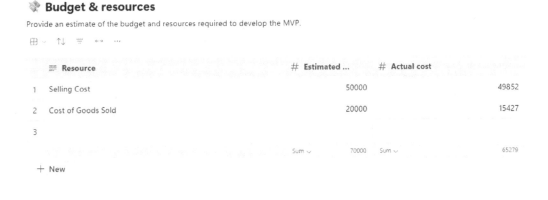

🏵 **Budget & resources**

Provide an estimate of the budget and resources required to develop the MVP.

⊞ ⌄   ↑↓   ☰   ↤   ⋯

	Resource	# Estimated ...	# Actual cost
1	Selling Cost	50000	49852
2	Cost of Goods Sold	20000	15427
3			
		Sum ⌄ 70000	Sum ⌄ 65279

+ New

Bullet List Components

The **Bullet List Component** is similar to the Numbered List but without numerical ranking. It is useful for:

- Brainstorming ideas

- Creating quick reference lists

- Structuring informal meeting notes

✦ **Example Use Case**: A content team creates a Bullet List in Loop to outline blog post ideas.

- - - - - - - -

🪨 Constraints

- Add a list of possible roadblocks and/or concerns here
- Add item

Progress Tracker Components

The Progress Tracker Component helps teams visualize the status of ongoing projects. It includes color-coded progress indicators and allows users to update project status dynamically.

◆ **Key Features:**

- Color-coded progress bars

- Customizable project milestones

- Real-time updates from team members

✦ **Example Use Case**: A marketing team tracks the progress of an advertising campaign with a Loop Progress Tracker embedded in a Teams chat.

⊞ ⌄   ↑↓   ☰   ↔   ⋯

	☰ What?	☰ How?	◇ Progress
1	Check out this 'Getting Started' workspace.	You're doing great!	In progress
2	Go to the Loop app home.	Click the Loop logo in the top corner. You will see all your Loop workspaces, Recent, and Ideas.	Not started yet
3	Create a new workspace for your team or a project you're working on.	Click on the workspace name 'Getting Started', then select 'new workspace'.	Not started yet
4	Invite others to your workspace.	Click '1 Workspace member' in the sidebar and invite your team members.	Not started yet
5	Don't forget to send us feedback!	Click the ... icon in the top corner and select 'Give Feedback'.	Not started yet
6	Have fun!	☺	Done!
7	Add work area		Type to add

I I N 4 D I

+ New

Q&A Components

The Q&A Component provides a structured format for team members to ask and answer questions. It is ideal for knowledge-sharing and troubleshooting sessions.

⬥ **Key Features:**

- Users can submit questions
- Team members can provide responses
- Responses can be upvoted for visibility

📌 **Example Use Case**: A company's IT support team uses a Loop Q&A Component to answer frequently asked questions about software troubleshooting.

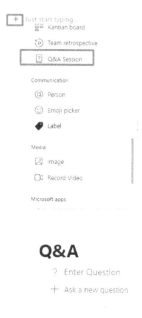

Q&A

? Enter Question

+ Ask a new question

Choosing the Right Loop Component for Your Needs

Selecting the appropriate Loop Component depends on your **specific collaboration and productivity goals**. Below is a quick reference guide to help you choose:

Need	Recommended Loop Component
Quick brainstorming	Text Component, Bullet List
Structured information	Table Component
Task tracking	Task List, Checklist
Decision-making	Voting Table
Project management	Progress Tracker
Information gathering	Q&A Component

Understanding these Loop Components and how they interact within the Microsoft 365 ecosystem will help you streamline your workflow, improve communication, and enhance collaboration.

Conclusion

Loop Components are at the heart of Microsoft Loop's collaborative experience. By leveraging Text, Tables, Task Lists, Voting Tables, Checklists, Numbered Lists, Progress Trackers, and Q&A Components, teams can work together more efficiently in real-time.

In the next section, we will dive deeper into Using Text and Table Components, where we will explore how to create, format, and customize these components for better readability and usability.

2.2 Using Text and Table Components

2.2.1 Creating and Editing Text Components

Introduction to Text Components in Microsoft Loop

Text components are one of the fundamental elements in Microsoft Loop, allowing users to create, edit, and collaborate on text-based content in a flexible and dynamic manner. Unlike traditional word processors, Loop's text components are designed for real-time collaboration, meaning multiple users can edit and format text simultaneously while changes are updated instantly for everyone.

This section will guide you through the process of creating, editing, and managing text components efficiently. You will learn how to add text, format it for readability, and optimize it for team collaboration.

Creating a New Text Component

Step 1: Accessing Microsoft Loop

Before you start working with text components, ensure that you are logged into Microsoft Loop via the Microsoft 365 portal or a dedicated Loop app (if available). Once inside, navigate to an existing Loop workspace or create a new workspace to begin.

Step 2: Adding a Text Component to a Page

To create a new text component in **Microsoft Loop**, follow these steps:

1. Open a **Loop page** within your workspace.

2. Click anywhere on the page to activate the **editor**.

3. Start typing directly—Loop will automatically recognize and create a **text component**.

4. Alternatively, type **"/text"** and press **Enter** to insert a new **text component** explicitly.

Step 3: Organizing Text Components

Once your text component is created, you can organize it efficiently:

- **Drag and drop** text components to rearrange them on the page.

- Use **headings (H1, H2, H3)** to structure content logically.

- Create **bulleted or numbered lists** for better readability.

- Convert a text component into another format (e.g., a table, checklist, or task list) using the **context menu**.

Editing Text Components

Editing in **Microsoft Loop** is designed to be intuitive and collaborative. Since all changes are updated in real-time, multiple users can work together without the need for manual saving.

Basic Editing Functions

To edit a text component, simply click inside it and make changes as needed. The system automatically saves all modifications.

Common text editing actions:

- Typing and deleting text normally.

- Copying and pasting (Ctrl + C / Ctrl + V on Windows, Cmd + C / Cmd + V on Mac).

- Dragging and dropping text to reorganize paragraphs.

Text Formatting Options

Microsoft Loop offers basic formatting to enhance text readability and structure. These options can be accessed via the floating toolbar that appears when you select text.

Bold, Italics, and Underline

- **Bold**: Select text and press **Ctrl + B** (Windows) or **Cmd + B** (Mac).

- *Italics*: Select text and press **Ctrl + I** (Windows) or **Cmd + I** (Mac).

- **Underline**: Select text and press **Ctrl + U** (Windows) or **Cmd + U** (Mac).

Headings and Subheadings

To structure your text effectively, use the heading options:

- Heading 1 (H1): # Your Title then press Enter

- Heading 2 (H2): ## Your Subtitle then press Enter

- Heading 3 (H3): ### Your Section Title then press Enter

Using headings improves document organization and makes navigation easier for team members.

Lists (Bulleted and Numbered)

Lists are useful for organizing information concisely.

- Bulleted list: Type - or * followed by a space.

- Numbered list: Type 1. followed by a space.

Example:

- Task 1

- Task 2

1. Step 1

2. Step 2

Block Quotes

To format a block quote, type > followed by a space. This is useful for emphasizing important statements.

Example:

This is a block quote in Microsoft Loop.

Collaborative Editing in Text Components

One of Microsoft Loop's biggest strengths is its ability to facilitate real-time collaboration. When working in a shared workspace, multiple team members can edit the same text component simultaneously, with changes reflected instantly.

Features for Collaborative Editing

Live Cursors and User Presence

When multiple users are editing a text component, **Loop displays their cursors** in real-time, each identified by their name or initials. This feature prevents **overwriting issues** and improves coordination.

@Mentions for Team Collaboration

You can tag colleagues by using **@username** to notify them about important updates. Example:

@JohnDoe Please review this section.

Tagged users receive a **notification**, ensuring timely collaboration.

Commenting and Feedback System

Microsoft Loop allows users to **add comments** to text components. This is useful for discussions without modifying the original content.

To add a comment:

1. Highlight the text you want to discuss.

2. Click the **comment icon** in the floating toolbar.

3. Type your comment and press **Enter**.

Using Templates for Text Components

To save time, Microsoft Loop offers **pre-designed templates** for frequently used content structures, such as:

- **Meeting notes**

- **Brainstorming sessions**

- **Project outlines**

To use a template:

1. Type **"/template"** and select a relevant **pre-made format**.

2. Customize the template as needed.

Using templates ensures **consistency** across different projects.

Best Practices for Using Text Components in Loop

To maximize efficiency, follow these **best practices** when working with text components:

1. **Keep It Concise** – Avoid unnecessary text clutter.

2. **Use Headings and Lists** – Improve readability with structured formatting.

3. **Leverage @Mentions** – Ensure team members stay engaged.

4. **Utilize Comments for Discussions** – Keep feedback separate from content.

5. **Regularly Review and Update** – Maintain document accuracy over time.

Conclusion

Text components in Microsoft Loop are a powerful tool for collaborative writing and brainstorming. With real-time editing, formatting options, and team collaboration features, they help users create structured and efficient content. By following best practices and utilizing features like @mentions and comments, teams can maximize productivity and ensure effective communication.

The next section, 2.2.2 Formatting Text for Better Readability, will cover advanced formatting techniques to enhance document clarity and presentation.

2.2.2 Formatting Text for Better Readability

Effective text formatting is a crucial aspect of using Microsoft Loop efficiently. Well-structured text improves readability, enhances collaboration, and ensures that information is easily digestible by your team. In this section, we will explore best practices for formatting text in Microsoft Loop, covering everything from basic styling options to advanced techniques that optimize your workspace.

1. Why Formatting Matters in Microsoft Loop

Microsoft Loop is designed for dynamic, real-time collaboration, and formatting plays a key role in:

- **Enhancing Readability:** Well-structured text ensures clarity, making it easier for collaborators to process information quickly.

- **Improving Organization:** Consistent formatting helps structure information logically, preventing messy, cluttered workspaces.

- **Highlighting Key Points:** Using emphasis techniques (bold, italics, highlights) can draw attention to important content.

- **Maintaining Professionalism:** A well-formatted document creates a polished and organized impression.

Without proper formatting, Loop pages can become difficult to read, leading to miscommunication and inefficiencies in teamwork.

2. Basic Text Formatting Options

Microsoft Loop provides several formatting tools that allow users to refine text presentation. These tools are accessible from the formatting toolbar or using keyboard shortcuts.

2.1.1 Bold, Italics, and Underline

Emphasizing text using **bold**, *italics*, or *underline* can help highlight key points or differentiate sections.

Formatting Style Shortcut Purpose

Bold	Ctrl + B	Emphasize key points or headings
Italics	Ctrl + I	Highlight terms or subtle emphasis
Underline	Ctrl + U	Indicate important notes

💡 **Best Practice:** Use bold for important terms, italics for technical words, and underline sparingly to avoid clutter.

2.1.2 Font Size and Headers

Using different text sizes and headers improves content hierarchy, making it easier to navigate large documents.

- **Heading 1 (H1):** Used for main sections

- **Heading 2 (H2):** Subsections under main headings

- **Heading 3 (H3):** Further subdivisions

To apply a heading in Microsoft Loop, type **# (H1)**, **## (H2)**, or **### (H3)** before the text.

Example:

Main Topic (H1)

Subsection (H2)

Smaller Detail (H3)

💡 **Best Practice:** Use headers strategically to break down content into manageable sections.

2.1.3 Bullet Points and Numbered Lists

Organizing information with bullet points or numbered lists enhances clarity.

- **Bullet Points (Unordered Lists):**
    - Used for general lists
    - Good for brainstorming ideas
    - Helps separate key concepts

- **Numbered Lists (Ordered Lists):**

0. Ideal for step-by-step instructions

1. Helps track progress

2. Ensures sequence clarity

💡 **Best Practice:** Use bullets for general information and numbers for steps or processes.

3. Advanced Formatting Techniques

3.1 Highlighting and Color Coding

Microsoft Loop allows you to highlight text with colors to improve visibility.

- **Yellow highlight:** Draws attention to urgent details
- **Green highlight:** Can indicate approved information
- **Red text:** Used for warnings or critical points

To highlight text:

1. Select the text
2. Click the formatting toolbar
3. Choose "Highlight" and select a color

💡 **Best Practice:** Use color coding consistently to avoid confusion.

3.2 Indentation and Block Quotes

Indentation can help structure responses, while block quotes are useful for referencing key information.

- **Indent Text:** Press Tab to indent a paragraph.
- **Block Quotes:** Start a line with > to format a quote.

Example:

> "Microsoft Loop enhances team collaboration by keeping content synchronized in real-time."

💡 **Best Practice:** Use block quotes for important references or external citations.

3.3 Hyperlinks and Embedded Links

Embedding links keeps documents clean while providing easy access to external resources.

- To insert a hyperlink: Press **Ctrl + K** and enter the URL.

- To link existing text: Select text, then add a hyperlink.

Example:

☞ <u>**Visit Microsoft Loop**</u>

💡 **Best Practice:** Use descriptive link text rather than raw URLs for better readability.

4. Structuring Content for Readability

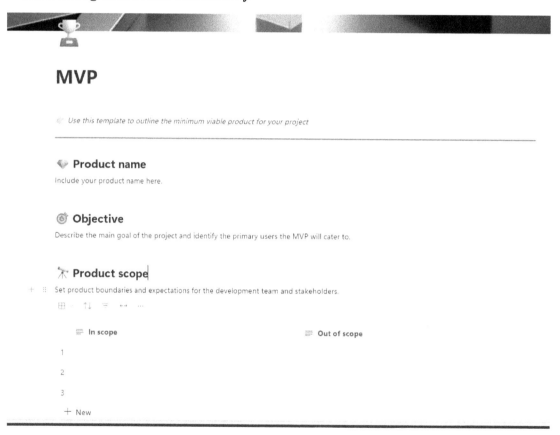

4.1 Grouping Related Information

Grouping related text together improves comprehension.

Example (Good Structure):

✓ "In this section, we cover three formatting techniques: bold text, headers, and bullet points."

Example (Poor Structure):

✗ "Bold text helps emphasize. Headers structure content. Bullet points improve clarity."

💡 **Best Practice:** Organize content in logical order with smooth transitions.

4.2 Using White Space Effectively

Avoid long paragraphs—use white space to improve readability.

✗ **Bad Example:**

This is an example of a paragraph that is too long. It contains too much information without proper spacing, making it difficult to read. Readers may struggle to find the key points, which can lead to information overload.

✓ **Good Example:**

- Use short paragraphs (2-3 sentences)

- Insert line breaks between sections

- Avoid large text blocks

💡 **Best Practice:** Break up content with headings, lists, and spacing.

5. Formatting Best Practices in Microsoft Loop

Best Practice	Description
Use headers	Improves document structure
Keep text concise	Avoids overwhelming readers
Use bold for emphasis	Highlights key information
Organize lists properly	Enhances content flow
Avoid excessive formatting	Too many styles create clutter

💡 **Final Tip:** Keep formatting simple and consistent to ensure readability across all devices.

Project Planning

Use this template to define, scope and plan milestones for your next project

Status : Not Started

Roles

Roles	Assignees
1	
2	
3	

+ New

Background context

Explain the information that your team needs to know, such as the industry, why this need arises.

Add relevant quote here.

Opportunity statement

Here, explain what the problem is, why it's important and what value it has.

Consider using the Problem Framing template to formulate your team's statement.

Conclusion

Formatting text properly in Microsoft Loop enhances readability, improves collaboration, and makes information easier to digest. By using structured headers, bullet points, color coding, and whitespace effectively, you can create a well-organized workspace that keeps your team engaged and productive.

💬 **Next Section:** Now that we've mastered text formatting, let's move on to **2.2.3 Adding and Customizing Tables** to further enhance content organization in Microsoft Loop! 🚀

2.2.3 Adding and Customizing Tables

Tables are a fundamental tool for organizing and displaying structured information in Microsoft Loop. Whether you're tracking tasks, comparing data, or structuring project details, tables allow you to present information in an easy-to-read format. This section will guide you through adding, formatting, and customizing tables in Microsoft Loop to enhance collaboration and productivity.

Understanding Tables in Microsoft Loop

Tables in Microsoft Loop function similarly to tables in other Microsoft 365 applications like Word or Excel, but with a focus on real-time collaboration and flexibility. Unlike static tables in traditional documents, Loop tables are **dynamic and interactive**, meaning multiple users can edit them simultaneously.

Key Features of Tables in Microsoft Loop:

- **Real-Time Collaboration:** Any changes made to a table are instantly visible to all collaborators.

- **Customizable Columns and Rows:** Add, remove, and resize table components to fit your needs.

- **Interactive Components:** Insert checkboxes, dates, and mentions within table cells.

- **Integration with Microsoft 365:** Easily link and embed table data across other Microsoft applications.

Tables in Loop provide a structured way to manage content while maintaining the flexibility needed for effective teamwork.

How to Add a Table in Microsoft Loop

Creating a table in Microsoft Loop is straightforward and can be done in just a few clicks. Here's how:

Method 1: Using the Slash Command

1. **Open a Loop Page** where you want to insert a table.

2. **Type "/table"** in the editor. This will automatically create a basic 3x3 table.

3. Press **Enter** to insert the table, then begin customizing it.

Method 2: Using the Toolbar

1. **Click on the "+" icon** in the Loop editor.

2. Select **"Table"** from the list of available components.

3. A table will be inserted into your Loop page, where you can adjust its size and content.

Method 3: Copying from Another Microsoft 365 App

1. Open an existing **table in Excel, Word, or OneNote**.

2. Copy the table using **Ctrl + C** (Windows) or **Cmd + C** (Mac).

3. Paste it into your Loop page using **Ctrl + V** (Windows) or **Cmd + V** (Mac).

4. The table will be inserted, and you can edit it directly in Loop.

Customizing Tables in Microsoft Loop

Once a table is added, you can modify its structure, appearance, and functionality to better suit your needs.

1. Adding and Removing Rows and Columns

- **To add a row:** Click the **"+" icon** below the last row or right-click a row and select **"Insert Row Below"** or **"Insert Row Above"**.

- **To remove a row:** Right-click any cell in the row you want to delete and select **"Delete Row"**.

- **To add a column:** Click the **"+" icon** to the right of the last column or right-click a column and choose **"Insert Column Left"** or **"Insert Column Right"**.

- **To remove a column:** Right-click any cell in the column you want to delete and select **"Delete Column"**.

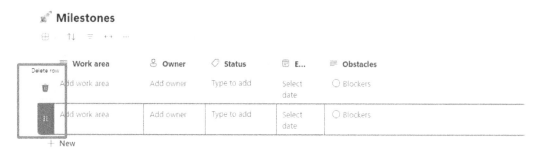

2. Resizing Columns and Rows

- **Drag column edges** to adjust width. This helps fit longer text without cluttering the table.

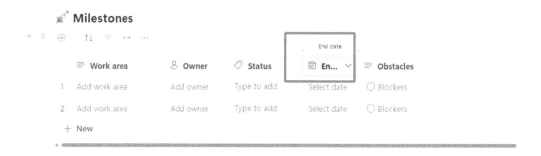

- **Adjust row height** by clicking inside a cell and adding extra space using the **Enter key**.

3. Formatting Text Inside Table Cells

- Bold, Italic, and Underline: Use Ctrl + B, Ctrl + I, or Ctrl + U to format text.
- Text Alignment: Align text to the left, center, or right using the toolbar.
- Highlighting Cells: Use color coding to differentiate sections.

4. Adding Interactive Elements

One of the most powerful features of Loop tables is the ability to add interactive elements:

- Checkboxes: Convert a table into a task tracker by adding checkboxes to a column.
- Mentions (@): Use @mentions to assign tasks to team members within table cells.

- Date Pickers: Add a date field to track deadlines.

- Links and Attachments: Embed external links and attach files for easy reference.

Using Tables for Specific Use Cases

1. Project Management

A well-structured table can serve as a project tracker:

Task Name	Assigned To	Due Date	Status
Design Website	@JohnDoe	2024-02-10	In Progress
Write Blog Post	@JaneSmith	2024-02-12	Not Started
Review Content	@AlexBrown	2024-02-15	Completed

Tips:

- Use color coding to indicate task priority.

- Add a progress column with % completion.

2. Meeting Notes and Action Items

Tables can help keep track of meeting notes and next steps:

Discussion Topic	Key Points	Action Item	Owner
Marketing Plan	Launch in Q2	Prepare campaign brief	@SarahLee
Budget Review	Reduce expenses	Identify cost-cutting areas	@MichaelScott

Tips:

- Use @mentions to assign responsibilities.

- Add checkmarks to track completed items.

3. Content Planning

A content calendar can be managed efficiently using tables in Loop:

Content Title	Author	Due Date	Status	Notes
Blog on AI Trends	@LisaK	2024-02-14	Drafting	Needs graphics
Social Media Post	@TomH	2024-02-16	Scheduled	Facebook & LinkedIn

Tips:

- Embed links to drafts for quick access.

- Add deadline reminders using the **date picker**.

Best Practices for Using Tables in Microsoft Loop

1. **Keep It Simple** – Avoid unnecessary columns; focus on essential information.

2. **Use Color Coding** – Highlight important rows and categories for quick scanning.

3. **Leverage Interactive Features** – Checkboxes, mentions, and date pickers improve usability.

4. **Regularly Update and Maintain Tables** – Keep information accurate and up to date.

5. **Integrate with Other Apps** – Connect Loop tables with Microsoft Teams and Outlook for enhanced productivity.

Conclusion

Tables in Microsoft Loop provide a powerful and flexible way to organize and manage information collaboratively. Whether you're using them for task tracking, meeting notes, or project management, Loop tables help teams stay aligned and efficient. By leveraging interactive elements, customization options, and seamless integration, users can maximize the potential of Microsoft Loop for smarter collaboration.

Ready to take your Loop experience to the next level? In the next section, we'll explore task management with Loop components, helping you streamline workflows even further!

2.3 Task Management with Loop Components

2.3.1 Creating To-Do Lists

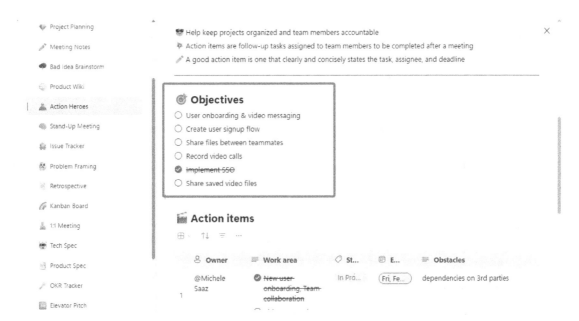

Microsoft Loop offers a dynamic and flexible way to manage tasks through interactive To-Do Lists, helping individuals and teams stay organized. Unlike traditional static lists, Loop To-Do Lists are collaborative, real-time, and seamlessly integrated with other Microsoft 365 applications. This section will guide you through everything you need to know about creating, managing, and optimizing To-Do Lists in Microsoft Loop.

Understanding To-Do Lists in Microsoft Loop

A To-Do List in Microsoft Loop is an interactive component that allows users to:
✓ Add and update tasks dynamically
✓ Assign tasks to team members
✓ Track completion status in real-time
✓ Collaborate across different Microsoft 365 platforms

Unlike traditional task lists in Word or Excel, Loop To-Do Lists are always synchronized, meaning updates are instantly visible to everyone who has access to the workspace.

Creating a Basic To-Do List

Step 1: Open Microsoft Loop

To begin, access Microsoft Loop through your web browser or desktop app:

1. Go to loop.microsoft.com (or open Loop from Microsoft 365).

2. Sign in with your Microsoft account.

3. Open an existing workspace or create a new one.

Step 2: Add a To-Do List Component

Once inside a Loop Page, you can insert a To-Do List component:

1. **Click on an empty space** in your Loop Page.

2. **Type "/"** to bring up the component menu.

3. **Select "Task List"** from the dropdown.

4. A new interactive task list will appear.

Step 3: Add Tasks

To add tasks to your **Task List**:

- Click on the **empty task field** and start typing.

- Press **Enter** to create a new task below.

- Use **Tab** to create **subtasks** under a main task.

- Use **Shift + Tab** to move a subtask back to the main level.

Tasks

	Task	Assigned to	Due date	Bucket
1	11	Add assignee	Select date	To do
2	Task name	Add assignee	Select date	To do
3	Task name	Add assignee	Select date	To do
4	Task name	Add assignee	Select date	To do

Step 4: Mark Tasks as Complete

- Click the **checkbox** next to a task to mark it as completed.

- Completed tasks will **fade out** or move to the bottom (depending on your settings).

Assigning Tasks to Team Members

Collaboration is one of Microsoft Loop's strongest features. You can assign tasks to specific people directly within the To-Do List.

Step 1: Mention a Team Member

- Type "@" followed by the team member's name to tag them.

- Select the name from the suggested list.

- The assigned person's profile picture will appear next to the task.

Step 2: Assign Multiple People

- You can assign a task to multiple team members by adding more "@mentions".

- Each assigned person can track and update progress.

Step 3: Set Due Dates

Currently, Microsoft Loop doesn't have built-in due dates for To-Do Lists, but you can manually include dates in the task description or use an Outlook or Planner integration.

Tracking and Managing Progress

A To-Do List is only useful if you can effectively track progress. Microsoft Loop provides real-time updates, allowing everyone to see changes instantly.

Step 1: Monitor Task Completion

- Completed tasks will show a checkmark.

- Updates appear instantly for all collaborators.

- Use @mentions in comments to request updates.

Step 2: Organizing Tasks Effectively

To keep your To-Do List structured, you can:

✦ Use sublists for detailed task breakdowns.

✦ Drag and drop tasks to rearrange priorities.

✦ Use color codes or labels to highlight critical tasks.

Advanced Features and Best Practices

1. Integrating Loop To-Do Lists with Microsoft 365

To-Do Lists in Loop are designed to work seamlessly with Microsoft 365 tools like Outlook, Teams, and Planner:

- Outlook: Copy the Loop To-Do List link and paste it into an email.

- Teams: Share a Loop To-Do List directly in a chat.

- Planner: Manually transfer Loop tasks into Planner for advanced tracking.

2. Using Comments for Collaboration

Team members can comment on individual tasks to provide updates, feedback, or clarification.

- Click on a task and type a comment.

- Use "@" mentions to notify a team member.

- Reply to comments for better communication.

3. Keeping To-Do Lists Organized

- Review tasks daily to keep progress on track.

- Clear completed tasks regularly to keep the list clean.

- Use a shared naming system for consistency across the team.

Common Mistakes and How to Avoid Them

⊘ Forgetting to Assign Tasks – Always use "@mentions" to ensure accountability.
⊘ Letting the List Become Cluttered – Regularly archive or delete old tasks.
⊘ Not Updating Task Status – Encourage team members to mark tasks as completed.
⊘ Ignoring Collaboration Features – Use comments and mentions to keep everyone aligned.

Final Thoughts

Microsoft Loop's To-Do List feature is a powerful tool for task management, collaboration, and real-time productivity. Whether you're managing personal projects or working with a team, Loop To-Do Lists keep everything organized, visible, and up to date.

◆ Next Up: Learn how to assign tasks and track progress effectively in Section 2.3.2: Assigning Tasks to Team Members.

2.3.2 Assigning Tasks to Team Members

Introduction

Assigning tasks effectively is a crucial aspect of any collaborative workflow, and Microsoft Loop makes this process seamless. With Loop, users can create interactive task lists, assign responsibilities, set due dates, and monitor progress in real-time. This functionality is particularly useful for teams working on shared projects, ensuring everyone is aligned and accountable for their respective roles.

This section will guide you through the process of assigning tasks to team members in Microsoft Loop, including how to create task lists, use mentions for task assignment, track task completion, and integrate with other Microsoft 365 tools for a more streamlined workflow.

1. Understanding Task Assignment in Microsoft Loop

Microsoft Loop provides a dynamic and flexible way to manage and assign tasks within workspaces and pages. Unlike static task lists, Loop components are interactive and can be updated in real-time by multiple users.

Key Benefits of Task Assignment in Loop:

- **Real-Time Collaboration:** Changes are instantly reflected across all shared spaces.

- **Task Ownership:** Each assigned task is linked to a specific team member, ensuring clear responsibility.

- **Cross-Platform Accessibility:** Loop components work seamlessly across Microsoft Teams, Outlook, and other Microsoft 365 apps.

- **Efficient Tracking:** Integrated progress updates help teams stay on top of deadlines and deliverables.

---

2. Creating a Task List for Assignment

Before assigning tasks, you need to create a structured task list. Microsoft Loop provides task list components that allow users to add tasks, assign them to team members, and track their status.

Step-by-Step Guide to Creating a Task List in Loop:

1. **Open Microsoft Loop** and navigate to your workspace or create a new page.

2. **Insert a Task List Component:**

    o Type **"/task list"** in a Loop page to quickly insert a new task list component.

    o Alternatively, use the "+" menu to select "Task List" from available components.

3. **Add Tasks to the List:**

    o Click on an empty row and type a task description.

    o Press **Enter** to add multiple tasks in a structured format.

4. **Format the Task List for Better Readability:**

o   Use bullet points or numbering to organize complex task lists.

o   Add **subtasks** by pressing **Tab** under a main task item.

5. **Enable Completion Tracking:**

o   Each task includes a **checkbox** for marking completion.

o   Click the checkbox to track progress in real-time.

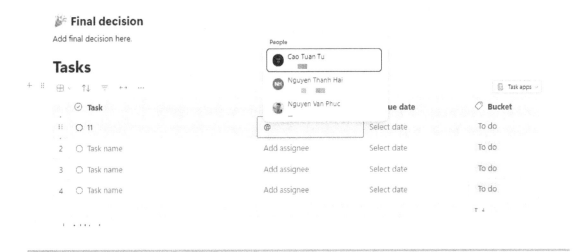

3. Assigning Tasks to Team Members

Once you have created a task list, the next step is to assign specific tasks to team members. Microsoft Loop allows for easy task assignment using @mentions and integrated collaboration features.

Method 1: Using @Mentions for Task Assignment

@Mentions allow you to quickly tag a team member within a task list, notifying them instantly.

How to Assign a Task Using @Mentions:

1. Click on the task that needs to be assigned.

2. Type "@" followed by the team member's name (e.g., **@JohnDoe**).

3. Select the correct person from the dropdown suggestion list.

4. The task now appears with the assigned person's name next to it.

5. The assignee receives a **notification** in Microsoft Teams or Outlook, depending on their Loop settings.

Method 2: Assigning Tasks with Due Dates

Setting due dates helps in managing priorities and ensuring timely task completion.

How to Add a Due Date to a Task:

1. Click on the task description.

2. Select the **calendar icon** (if available) or type the due date manually.

3. Choose a deadline from the date picker.

4. The assigned person will see the due date next to their task.

Method 3: Integrating Task Lists with Microsoft Planner

For teams managing multiple projects, syncing Loop task lists with **Microsoft Planner** can enhance task tracking and accountability.

How to Sync Loop Task Assignments with Planner:

1. Open **Microsoft Planner** in your Microsoft 365 account.

2. Select "New Plan" or use an existing project board.

3. Copy and paste task details from Loop into a Planner bucket.

4. Assign tasks within Planner, and the updates will reflect in both platforms.

---

4. Tracking Task Progress and Updates

Once tasks have been assigned, it's important to monitor progress to ensure deadlines are met. Microsoft Loop provides multiple ways to track task completion and collaborate efficiently.

Tracking Task Status in Loop:

1. **Marking Tasks as Complete:**

    o   Each task has a **checkbox** that can be ticked when completed.

o   Completed tasks appear with a strikethrough effect.

2. **Using Status Updates:**

o   Team members can add notes under tasks to provide progress updates.

o   Comments can be added using @mentions for team-wide visibility.

3. **Reviewing the Task History:**

o   Use **version history** to see who made changes and when.

o   Restore previous versions if needed.

Using Notifications and Reminders:

- Automated Reminders: Assigned users receive notifications for upcoming deadlines.

- Email and Teams Alerts: Loop integrates with Outlook and Teams to send reminders.

- Follow-Up Actions: Managers can add priority tags to overdue tasks.

5. Best Practices for Assigning Tasks in Loop

To ensure effective task management, follow these best practices:

1. Clearly Define Responsibilities

- Assign tasks to specific individuals rather than entire groups.

- Provide detailed task descriptions to avoid confusion.

2. Use Deadlines Effectively

- Set **realistic due dates** to maintain a balanced workload.

- Use priority labels for critical tasks.

3. Encourage Team Collaboration

- Encourage assignees to update task progress regularly.

- Use comments to discuss obstacles and propose solutions.

4. Integrate with Other Microsoft 365 Tools

- Use **Microsoft To Do** for personal task tracking.

- Sync tasks with **Planner** for advanced project management.

5. Regularly Review and Adjust Task Assignments

- Hold weekly check-ins to review progress.

- Reassign or redistribute tasks if workloads change.

Conclusion

Assigning tasks in Microsoft Loop is a powerful way to enhance team productivity and collaboration. By leveraging @mentions, due dates, real-time tracking, and integrations with Microsoft 365 tools, teams can ensure accountability and efficient project execution.

By following best practices, managers and team members can create a transparent and organized task workflow, making Microsoft Loop a central hub for dynamic teamwork.

2.3.3 Tracking Progress Effectively

Managing tasks efficiently is essential for productivity, whether you are working individually or as part of a team. Microsoft Loop provides robust features that allow you to track progress effectively, ensuring that projects stay on course and deadlines are met. This section will guide you through the best practices for tracking progress using Loop components, organizing workflows, and leveraging Loop's integration with Microsoft 365 tools.

Understanding Task Tracking in Microsoft Loop

Task tracking in Microsoft Loop revolves around Loop task components, which allow users to create, assign, update, and monitor tasks dynamically. Unlike static to-do lists, Loop components provide real-time collaboration, meaning updates are instantly reflected for all team members.

Key features that support task tracking include:

- Dynamic To-Do Lists: Changes to task lists update in real-time.

- Task Assignment and Status Updates: Easily assign tasks and track progress.

- Integration with Microsoft Planner and To Do: Sync Loop tasks with other Microsoft productivity apps.

- Real-Time Notifications: Stay informed about task updates and changes.

Setting Up an Effective Task Tracking System in Loop

1. Creating a Task List for Project Tracking

A well-structured task list is the foundation of effective progress tracking. Follow these steps to create one in Microsoft Loop:

1. **Add a To-Do List Component:**

   o Open a Loop page and type "/", then select **To-Do List** from the component options.

   o This will create a structured checklist where you can enter task details.

2. **Define Clear Tasks and Milestones:**

   o Break down larger projects into manageable tasks.

   o Assign deadlines for each milestone to keep the project on track.

3. **Categorize Tasks for Better Organization:**

   o Group tasks under relevant sections, such as "In Progress," "Pending Review," and "Completed."

   o Use tags or labels to differentiate task priority (e.g., **Urgent, High, Medium, Low**).

2. Assigning Tasks and Tracking Ownership

Task ownership is crucial for accountability and transparency. Microsoft Loop allows seamless task assignments through **@mentions**:

1. **Assign a Task to a Team Member:**

   o Click on a task within a To-Do List component.

- Type **"@"** followed by the team member's name to assign the task.

- The assignee will receive a notification and the task will be linked to their Microsoft To Do or Planner.

2. **Set Due Dates and Priorities:**

- Use the **due date feature** to establish deadlines.

- Assign **priority levels** (e.g., High, Medium, Low) for better task prioritization.

3. **Monitor Task Completion Status:**

- Completed tasks are checked off in real time.

- Task history provides insights into progress trends and bottlenecks.

3. Using Progress Indicators for Better Visualization

Tracking multiple tasks requires clear progress indicators. Loop provides several methods for visualizing task status:

- **Checklists and Completion Tracking:** A simple but effective way to mark tasks as done.

- **Progress Columns:** Divide tasks into sections such as "Not Started," "In Progress," and "Completed."

- **Color Coding and Labels:** Highlight critical tasks with different colors.

To implement a progress tracking system:

1. **Create a Table Component in Loop:**

- Type **"/Table"** to insert a table.

- Label columns as **Task Name, Assigned To, Due Date, Status, and Notes.**

2. **Use Drop-Downs for Task Status Updates:**

- Customize a column with drop-down options:

  - Not Started

  - In Progress

- Waiting for Review

- Completed

3. **Update Task Status Regularly:**

    o Encourage team members to update progress after completing each milestone.

Leveraging Microsoft 365 Integration for Advanced Task Tracking

Microsoft Loop seamlessly integrates with other Microsoft tools, allowing users to track progress across multiple platforms.

1. Syncing Loop Tasks with Microsoft To Do

Microsoft To Do helps individuals and teams manage tasks beyond Loop. Here's how you can connect them:

- Any task assigned in Loop appears automatically in Microsoft To Do.

- Users can receive reminders and organize their task lists within To Do.

- Completed tasks update in real time, ensuring Loop remains synchronized.

2. Using Microsoft Planner for Project Tracking

For team-based projects, **Microsoft Planner** offers advanced task tracking:

- Convert Loop task lists into **Planner boards** for a visual overview.

- Assign due dates, track progress, and receive automated notifications.

- Use the Kanban-style board to organize tasks by progress level.

To sync Loop tasks with Planner:

1. Assign tasks in a Loop workspace.

2. Open **Planner** and navigate to your project.

3. Use **Power Automate** to create a workflow that syncs Loop tasks to Planner.

3. Connecting Loop with Microsoft Teams for Progress Updates

Since many teams use **Microsoft Teams** for communication, integrating Loop task tracking with Teams enhances productivity:

- Embed Loop components in Teams chats.

- Get automatic progress updates in Teams channels.

- Use @mentions in Loop components to notify team members directly within Teams.

Best Practices for Effective Progress Tracking in Microsoft Loop

To maximize efficiency, consider these best practices:

1. Establish a Clear Workflow

- Define **who** is responsible for updating task progress.

- Set **regular review intervals** (e.g., daily stand-ups, weekly progress reports).

2. Maintain Transparency and Accountability

- Use **@mentions** to remind team members of pending tasks.

- Keep a **log of completed tasks** for future reference.

3. Automate Repetitive Tasks

- Use **Power Automate** to trigger task reminders.

- Set up **recurring task lists** for ongoing projects.

4. Keep Task Tracking Simple

- Avoid overcomplicating workflows—stick to essential tracking elements.

- Ensure that all team members are comfortable using Loop for task management.

Conclusion

Tracking progress effectively in Microsoft Loop ensures teams stay organized, accountable, and productive. By leveraging task components, real-time updates, integration with Microsoft 365 tools, and structured workflows, users can manage projects efficiently.

Whether working individually or in a team, mastering task tracking in Loop helps streamline workflows and enhance collaboration.

2.4 Collaborative Content in Loop

Collaboration is at the heart of **Microsoft Loop**, and one of the key ways to make your workspace dynamic and interactive is by incorporating various content types. **Loop components** allow users to insert images and links, making shared pages more visually engaging and resourceful. This section will guide you through the process of adding images and links to Loop pages, explain their importance in collaboration, and provide best practices to maximize their impact.

2.4.1 Inserting Images and Links

Why Use Images and Links in Microsoft Loop?

Images and links serve multiple purposes in collaborative workspaces. They help:

- **Enhance communication**: Visual elements make content easier to understand.

- **Provide context**: Adding links to external documents or resources ensures team members have all necessary information.

- **Increase engagement**: Well-organized and visually appealing pages improve user experience and productivity.

Adding Images to Loop Pages

Step 1: Selecting an Image to Insert

There are multiple ways to add images to your Loop pages:

1. Uploading from your device: Add personal or company-branded images from your computer.

2. Using cloud storage: Insert images from OneDrive, SharePoint, or other cloud platforms.

3. Copy-pasting an image: Drag and drop or copy images directly into a Loop page.

4. Using Microsoft 365 integration: Insert images from Word, PowerPoint, or OneNote.

Step 2: Inserting an Image into a Loop Page

To insert an image in Microsoft Loop, follow these steps:

1. Open your Loop Workspace and navigate to the page where you want to insert the image.

2. Click on the "+" (plus) button or press "/" (slash command) to open the content menu.

3. Select "Image" from the list of available components.

4. Choose the source:

   o Upload from device

   o Insert from OneDrive or SharePoint

   o Paste an image URL

5. Adjust the placement and size if needed.

Tip: Using high-resolution images with clear labels improves readability and makes the document more visually engaging.

Step 3: Formatting and Positioning Images

Once an image is inserted, Microsoft Loop allows some basic formatting:

• Resizing: Drag the corners to resize the image.

- Alignment: Choose left, center, or right alignment for better layout structure.

- Captioning: Add a description to explain the image's relevance.

- Hyperlinking: Convert an image into a clickable link by embedding a URL.

Best Practice: Use consistent image styles across your Loop pages for a professional appearance.

Inserting Links in Loop Pages

Step 1: Understanding Link Options

Microsoft Loop allows different types of links:

1. External URLs – Links to websites, articles, research materials.

2. Microsoft 365 Files – Links to Word, Excel, PowerPoint, OneNote, SharePoint files.

3. Loop Components – Links to other Loop pages or workspaces for better navigation.

Step 2: Adding a Hyperlink in Loop

To add a link, follow these simple steps:

1. **Highlight** the text or phrase you want to turn into a hyperlink.

2. Use the **Ctrl + K (Cmd + K on Mac)** shortcut or click the **link button**.

3. Enter the URL or **search for a file** within Microsoft 365.

4. Press **Enter** to confirm.

Tip: Use **descriptive link text** instead of raw URLs to improve readability (e.g., "View the project plan" instead of "www.example.com/plan.pdf").

Step 3: Embedding Microsoft 365 Files as Links

Since Microsoft Loop integrates deeply with the Microsoft 365 ecosystem, you can link to files stored in:

- OneDrive

- SharePoint

- Teams

To embed a document link:

1. Type **"@"** followed by the document name (e.g., **@Marketing Plan 2024**).

2. Select the correct file from the pop-up suggestions.

3. The document will now appear as a clickable link inside your Loop page.

Best Practices for Using Images and Links in Microsoft Loop

1. Organize Content Logically

- Place relevant images next to corresponding text for better clarity.

- Use a structured format for hyperlinks to avoid cluttered pages.

2. Maintain Accessibility

- Use Alt Text: Describe images for visually impaired users.

- Avoid long URLs: Shorten links or use hyperlink text.

3. Keep Images and Links Updated

- Ensure all links are working and not broken.

- Regularly review and refresh images to keep content relevant.

Conclusion

Inserting images and links in Microsoft Loop enhances collaboration, makes information more accessible, and improves overall team efficiency. By following the outlined steps, you can create well-structured, visually engaging pages that enhance teamwork and knowledge sharing.

Now that you've mastered adding images and links, the next section will explore how to embed files from Microsoft 365 into your Loop workspace!

2.4.2 Embedding Files from Microsoft 365

Collaboration in Microsoft Loop is more than just text-based discussions and task management. A powerful feature that enhances productivity is the ability to embed files from Microsoft 365 into Loop pages and components. This integration allows teams to work with documents, spreadsheets, and presentations without switching between apps, ensuring seamless collaboration.

In this section, we'll explore:

- The benefits of embedding Microsoft 365 files into Loop

- The types of files that can be embedded

- Step-by-step instructions on embedding files from Word, Excel, and PowerPoint

- Best practices for efficient collaboration

Why Embed Microsoft 365 Files in Loop?

Embedding Microsoft 365 files in Loop provides several key advantages:

1. Real-Time Collaboration

By embedding files such as Word documents, Excel spreadsheets, or PowerPoint presentations, team members can edit content in real-time without leaving the Loop workspace. Changes made in the embedded file sync instantly, allowing for a truly collaborative experience.

2. Centralized Information

Loop acts as a centralized hub where teams can view and edit essential documents without switching applications. This reduces distractions and enhances workflow efficiency.

3. Enhanced Context and Organization

Instead of attaching files in emails or referencing them separately, embedding files in Loop allows users to place them within relevant discussions, ensuring that all necessary resources are available in one place.

4. Always Up-to-Date Files

Unlike static file attachments, embedded Microsoft 365 documents are always the latest version. Team members avoid version conflicts and access the most updated content at all times.

Supported File Types for Embedding

Microsoft Loop supports embedding files from various Microsoft 365 apps. Here are the primary file types that can be embedded:

Microsoft 365 App	File Type	Common Uses in Loop
Word	.docx	Meeting notes, project documentation, collaborative writing
Excel	.xlsx	Financial reports, data analysis, team budgets
PowerPoint	.pptx	Team presentations, marketing materials, project updates
OneNote	.one	Shared notes, brainstorming sessions, research data
SharePoint Files	Various	Centralized storage for team files and resources

How to Embed Files from Microsoft 365 in Loop

Embedding files from Microsoft 365 into Loop is a straightforward process. Follow these steps to embed Word, Excel, or PowerPoint files into a Loop page:

Step 1: Open Your Loop Workspace

1. Navigate to Microsoft Loop at loop.microsoft.com and sign in with your Microsoft account.

2. Select the workspace where you want to embed the file or create a new Loop page.

Step 2: Insert an Embedded File

1. Click on the "+" (Insert) button within the Loop page.

2. Select "Embed" from the dropdown menu.

3. Choose "Insert a Microsoft 365 file" and browse your OneDrive or SharePoint files.

Step 3: Select a File to Embed

1. Use the **search bar** to find your file or browse folders.

2. Click on the file you want to embed (e.g., a Word document or Excel spreadsheet).

3. Select **"Insert"** to embed the file within your Loop page.

Step 4: Collaborate on the Embedded File

- Once the file is embedded, click on it to open an interactive preview.

- Edit the file directly within Loop (if permissions allow) or open it in its respective Microsoft 365 app for advanced editing.

- Team members can leave comments, suggest edits, and update content in real-time.

Best Practices for Embedding and Collaborating on Files

To maximize efficiency when embedding Microsoft 365 files in Loop, consider these best practices:

1. Maintain Clear File Naming Conventions

- Use descriptive file names (e.g., "Project_Budget_Q1_2025.xlsx" instead of "Budget.xlsx") to avoid confusion.

- Keep files organized within SharePoint or OneDrive for easier access.

2. Set the Right Permissions

- Ensure that embedded files have appropriate sharing settings.

- Use "Can Edit" for collaborative documents and "Can View" for reference files.

- Regularly review permissions to avoid unintended access issues.

3. Keep Loop Pages Organized

- Embed files within relevant sections of a Loop page instead of placing them randomly.

- Use headings and bullet points to provide context for embedded files.

4. Use @Mentions for Collaboration

- Tag team members using @Mentions to notify them about specific files.

- Provide clear instructions on what actions are required for each embedded file.

5. Leverage Version History

- Microsoft 365 automatically tracks changes, allowing teams to restore previous versions if needed.

- If critical changes are made, inform team members to review the latest version.

Troubleshooting Common Issues

Despite its ease of use, embedding Microsoft 365 files in Loop may sometimes present technical challenges. Here's how to troubleshoot common issues:

1. File Not Loading Properly

- Check your internet connection to ensure it's stable.

- Refresh the Loop page or try reloading the embedded file.

- Ensure that the file isn't moved or deleted from OneDrive or SharePoint.

2. Permission Errors

- If you or a teammate cannot access the embedded file, check the file's sharing settings in OneDrive/SharePoint.

- Make sure the user is added to the correct permissions group.

3. Embedded File Does Not Update in Real-Time

- Refresh the page and check for updates.

- Open the file in its respective Microsoft 365 app and confirm that auto-save is enabled.

4. Large Files Causing Slow Performance

- Large Excel files with heavy formulas and data may slow down Loop.

- Consider embedding only essential sheets or summarized reports.

Summary

Embedding files from Microsoft 365 into Loop enhances collaboration, improves organization, and ensures that teams work with the latest content. Here's a quick recap:

✅ Microsoft Loop allows seamless embedding of Word, Excel, and PowerPoint files.
✅ Team members can collaborate in real-time without leaving the Loop workspace.
✅ Setting appropriate permissions ensures secure and efficient collaboration.
✅ Best practices like file naming, organization, and version control optimize workflow.
✅ Troubleshooting common issues ensures a smooth collaboration experience.

By integrating embedded files effectively, teams can boost productivity, streamline workflows, and stay organized—all within Microsoft Loop!

2.4.3 Using @Mentions for Team Collaboration

Collaboration is at the core of Microsoft Loop, and one of the most powerful features that enable seamless teamwork is the **@mentions** functionality. By using @mentions, you can quickly bring team members into the conversation, assign tasks, request input, or ensure that specific individuals see important updates within Loop workspaces, pages, and components. This feature enhances productivity by making communication direct and efficient, reducing the need for separate emails or messages.

In this section, we will explore how to use @mentions effectively in Microsoft Loop, covering the following topics:

- Understanding @mentions and their role in collaboration

- Adding @mentions to different Loop components

- Managing notifications and responses

- Best practices for effective @mention usage

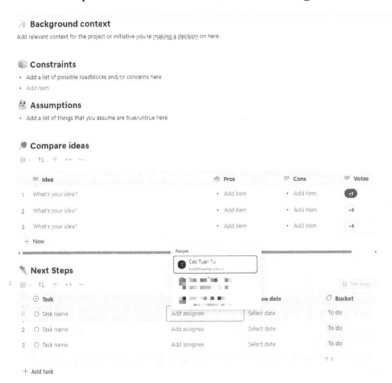

Understanding @Mentions and Their Role in Collaboration

What Are @Mentions?

@Mentions are a feature in Microsoft Loop that allows you to tag specific team members in a workspace, page, or component. When you mention someone by typing "@" followed by their name, they receive a notification, directing them to the relevant content. This ensures that the right people are involved in discussions, updates, or tasks without needing to search for information manually.

Why Use @Mentions?

- Improved visibility: Ensures that important updates and messages reach the right team members.

- Efficient task delegation: Helps in assigning responsibilities and tracking accountability.

- Faster responses: Encourages prompt feedback and action.

- Contextual communication: Keeps conversations organized within relevant Loop pages and components.

Where Can You Use @Mentions in Microsoft Loop?

- Inside text components (e.g., when leaving comments or discussing ideas).

- Within task lists (e.g., assigning tasks to specific people).

- In collaborative tables (e.g., requesting input on specific data points).

- Inside Loop workspaces and pages (e.g., highlighting key discussions).

Adding @Mentions to Different Loop Components

Microsoft Loop allows users to incorporate @mentions across various components to improve team collaboration. Here's how you can use them effectively:

Using @Mentions in Text Components

Text components are commonly used for notes, discussions, and documentation within Loop. You can tag a teammate inside a text block to bring their attention to a particular section.

How to Add an @Mention in Text Components:

1. Click inside the text component where you want to tag someone.

2. Type **"@"** followed by the person's name.

3. Select their name from the dropdown list.

4. The mentioned person will receive a notification with a direct link to the mention.

Example Use Case:

- You're drafting a project summary and need input from a marketing specialist. You can write:

"@JohnDoe Can you review this section and add details about the launch campaign?"

Using @Mentions in Task Lists

When managing tasks in Microsoft Loop, you can assign tasks to specific team members using @mentions. This ensures accountability and makes it easier to track responsibilities.

How to Assign Tasks Using @Mentions:

1. Create a new **task list component** within a Loop page.

2. Add a new task by typing a description.

3. Use **"@"** to mention the person responsible for the task.

4. The mentioned user will receive a notification and can mark the task as completed once finished.

Example Use Case:

- A project manager wants a team member to finalize a report:

"**Prepare final project report** – Assigned to @JaneSmith (Due Friday)"

Using @Mentions in Tables

Tables in Microsoft Loop are often used for organizing data, brainstorming ideas, or tracking progress. You can use @mentions to request input or assign ownership to a specific table entry.

How to Use @Mentions in Tables:

1. Insert a table component into your Loop page.

2. Select a cell where you need input or assign responsibility.

3. Type "@" followed by the team member's name in the cell.

4. The mentioned person will get a notification and can update the table accordingly.

Example Use Case:

- A content manager is tracking blog post assignments:

Topic	Writer	Status
AI in Marketing	@SarahLee	Drafting
Remote Work Trends	@MikeBrown	Under Review

Managing Notifications and Responses

When a team member is mentioned in Microsoft Loop, they receive a notification. Managing these notifications effectively ensures that collaboration remains productive without becoming overwhelming.

Where Do @Mention Notifications Appear?

- Microsoft Loop Notifications Panel – Inside the Loop interface.

- Microsoft Teams Notifications – If Loop is integrated with Teams.

- Outlook Email Notifications – Depending on individual notification settings.

Responding to @Mentions

- Click on the notification to jump directly to the mention.

- Read the context of the mention and take appropriate action.

- Reply within the Loop component or make the necessary updates.

- Mark the task as completed if it was assigned through @mentions.

Best Practices for Effective @Mention Usage

To maximize the benefits of @mentions in Microsoft Loop, consider the following best practices:

1. Be Clear and Concise

- When tagging someone, provide context for the mention to avoid confusion.
- Instead of just saying "@Mark," specify what you need:

"@Mark Please review the financial summary before the meeting tomorrow."

2. Use @Mentions Sparingly

- Avoid overusing @mentions for minor updates, as excessive notifications can be distracting.
- Instead, consolidate messages when possible.

3. Tag the Right Person

- Ensure you're mentioning the correct team member based on their role and expertise.
- If uncertain, consider mentioning a group instead of an individual.

4. Combine @Mentions with Due Dates for Tasks

- If you're assigning tasks, include deadlines to ensure timely completion.

"@Lisa Please finalize the client proposal by Monday."

5. Follow Up on Unanswered Mentions

- If you don't receive a response, send a follow-up message in the same Loop page or in Microsoft Teams.

Conclusion

Using @mentions in Microsoft Loop is a simple yet powerful way to enhance team collaboration. Whether you're assigning tasks, requesting feedback, or ensuring that critical information reaches the right people, @mentions make communication more efficient and organized. By mastering this feature, teams can improve workflow, reduce miscommunication, and ensure that work progresses smoothly.

In the next section, we'll explore **real-time collaboration features in Microsoft Loop**, including simultaneous editing, version history, and commenting features that further enhance teamwork. 🚀

CHAPTER III
Collaboration and Teamwork in Microsoft Loop

3.1 Real-Time Collaboration Features

3.1.1 Simultaneous Editing and Updates

Collaboration is at the core of Microsoft Loop, and one of its most powerful features is simultaneous editing and real-time updates. This functionality allows multiple users to work on the same Loop component, page, or workspace at the same time, ensuring a seamless and dynamic collaborative experience.

In this section, we will explore:

- How simultaneous editing works in Microsoft Loop

- The benefits of real-time updates for teams

- Best practices for efficient co-editing

- Potential challenges and how to overcome them

Understanding Simultaneous Editing in Microsoft Loop

Simultaneous editing in Microsoft Loop means that multiple users can edit, update, and contribute to a Loop component at the same time, without interference or version conflicts. Whenever a user makes a change—whether it's typing in a text component, updating a task list, or modifying a table—all other users can see the updates in real-time.

This real-time synchronization is powered by Microsoft's cloud infrastructure, which ensures that changes are reflected instantly across all connected devices. Unlike traditional document collaboration, where users may have to refresh or manually save changes, Microsoft Loop updates automatically and continuously, keeping all users on the same page.

How It Works Behind the Scenes

Microsoft Loop utilizes Microsoft's Fluid Framework, a real-time co-authoring technology that allows multiple users to interact with content simultaneously. Here's how it works:

1. Low Latency Synchronization – Changes made by any user are instantly propagated to others in milliseconds.

2. Conflict Resolution – If two users edit the same text at the same time, Loop intelligently merges changes or alerts users of potential conflicts.

3. Offline Mode Support – Even if a user is temporarily offline, they can continue making changes, which will sync as soon as they reconnect.

4. Cross-Application Integration – Loop components can be embedded in Microsoft Teams, Outlook, and other Microsoft 365 apps, ensuring real-time updates across platforms.

Benefits of Real-Time Collaboration in Microsoft Loop

The ability to work simultaneously on shared content offers numerous advantages, especially for teams and organizations.

1. Improved Team Efficiency

- With multiple users contributing at once, there's no need to wait for one person to finish before another can start.

- Teams can brainstorm ideas, refine project plans, or co-write documents without delays.

- The traditional "send-edit-wait" cycle of email attachments is eliminated, streamlining workflow.

2. Enhanced Transparency and Visibility

- Everyone on the team can see changes as they happen, ensuring **full visibility** into progress.

- There's no need to request updates or wonder if someone has completed their task—everything is visible in real time.

- Managers and team leads can **monitor changes live**, allowing for instant feedback.

3. Reduced Versioning Conflicts

- Unlike older document collaboration methods where multiple versions of a file could lead to confusion, Loop keeps everything **in sync and up-to-date**.

- No more "Version 1.2 - Final - Updated - Final2" file names!

- Every change is tracked, and previous versions can be restored if necessary.

4. Better Decision-Making and Faster Execution

- Teams can discuss, edit, and finalize content **on the spot**, reducing the back-and-forth of approvals.

- Real-time updates ensure that the latest information is always available, supporting **faster and more informed decisions**.

Best Practices for Effective Simultaneous Editing

While Microsoft Loop's real-time collaboration is powerful, it's important to follow **best practices** to ensure a smooth workflow.

1. Define Roles and Responsibilities

- Assign team members to specific tasks before they start editing.

- Example: One person formats text, another adds content, and a third reviews changes.

2. Use Comments and Mentions

- Instead of overwriting someone's input, use **@mentions** to ask for clarifications.

- Comments allow for **discussions within the document** without cluttering the content.

3. Avoid Overwriting Important Information

- When making major edits, inform teammates via chat or comments.

- If multiple people are editing, agree on a **color-coding system** or section ownership.

4. Take Advantage of Version History

- If a mistake is made, **Loop allows users to restore previous versions**.

- Regularly check the version history to track changes over time.

5. Organize Content for Readability

- Use **headings, bullet points, and tables** to keep information structured.

- Clearly label sections so multiple users know where to contribute.

Potential Challenges and How to Overcome Them

1. Content Overwrites and Conflicts

- **Challenge**: Two users may edit the same sentence at the same time, leading to conflicts.

- **Solution**: Loop's **automatic conflict resolution** helps, but best practice is to divide sections and communicate changes.

2. Too Many Edits at Once

- **Challenge**: If many people are making changes simultaneously, the content may become cluttered.

- **Solution**: Establish **editing guidelines**, and use **structured collaboration sessions**.

3. Distraction from Constant Updates

- **Challenge**: Real-time changes can be distracting if content moves too fast.

- **Solution**: Use the **"Follow" feature** in Microsoft Loop to focus only on relevant updates.

4. Connectivity Issues

- **Challenge**: A poor internet connection may cause delays in updates.
- **Solution**: Work in **offline mode**, and sync changes once reconnected.

Conclusion

Simultaneous editing in Microsoft Loop is a game-changer for team collaboration. With real-time synchronization, version control, and seamless integration with Microsoft 365 apps, teams can work together more efficiently than ever before. By following best practices and being mindful of common challenges, users can maximize their productivity and ensure smooth collaboration.

In the next section (3.1.2 Version History and Undo Options), we will explore how Microsoft Loop tracks changes and allows users to revert to previous versions when needed.

3.1.2 Version History and Undo Options

In a collaborative workspace like Microsoft Loop, keeping track of changes and being able to revert to previous versions is crucial. Whether you're working on a shared document, brainstorming with your team, or managing project notes, the ability to see past edits and restore earlier versions can help prevent mistakes and enhance productivity. In this section, we will explore the **Version History** and **Undo Options** available in Microsoft Loop, how they work, and best practices for using them effectively.

1. Understanding Version History in Microsoft Loop

Version History in Microsoft Loop is a feature that allows users to view past versions of a Loop component, page, or workspace. This is particularly useful when multiple team members are editing content simultaneously, as it provides a way to track changes, compare different versions, and restore previous content if needed.

How Version History Works

Every time a change is made to a Loop component or page, Microsoft Loop automatically saves a version in the background. This ensures that you can always revert to a previous state if necessary. The key features of Version History include:

- **Automatic Versioning:** Microsoft Loop periodically saves snapshots of your work, eliminating the need for manual saves.

- **Time-Stamped Versions:** Each version is labeled with the date and time of the edit, making it easy to track when changes occurred.

- **User Attribution:** If multiple people are collaborating, Loop records who made specific changes, ensuring transparency.

- **Version Comparison:** Users can compare different versions to identify modifications.

- **Restoration Options:** If a mistake is made, you can revert to an earlier version without affecting the rest of the content.

2. Accessing Version History in Microsoft Loop

To use the Version History feature, follow these steps:

Viewing Past Versions

1. **Open Your Loop Workspace:** Navigate to the Loop page or component you want to review.

2. **Access the Options Menu:** Click on the three-dot menu (⋮) in the top-right corner of the component or page.

3. **Select "Version History":** This will display a list of saved versions, including timestamps and the names of contributors.

4. **Browse Through Versions:** Click on any version to preview its contents and see the changes made.

Comparing Versions

Microsoft Loop highlights differences between versions, making it easier to track modifications. When comparing versions, consider the following:

- **What was added or removed?** Highlighted text or formatting changes help identify updates.

- **Who made the changes?** User names are displayed next to their modifications.

- **When were the changes made?** A chronological timeline provides context for edits.

Restoring a Previous Version

If you need to revert to an earlier version, follow these steps:

1. **Open the Version History Panel.**

2. **Find the Desired Version.** Browse through the list of saved versions.

3. **Click "Restore This Version."** Microsoft Loop will replace the current content with the selected version.

Restoring a version does not delete newer versions—it simply creates a new version based on the restored content.

---

3. Undo and Redo Options in Microsoft Loop

While Version History allows for recovering past versions, **Undo and Redo** functions are useful for quick fixes and minor mistakes made during real-time editing.

Using the Undo Function

Undo lets you revert recent changes without accessing the full version history. You can use it in two ways:

- Keyboard Shortcut: Press Ctrl + Z (Windows) or Cmd + Z (Mac) to undo the last action.

- Undo Button: Click the "Undo" icon (usually an arrow pointing left) in the Loop toolbar.

Undo works for:

- Text edits (typing, deleting, formatting)

- Table modifications (adding or removing rows/columns)

- Moving and restructuring components

Using the Redo Function

If you accidentally undo something you want to keep, the Redo function restores it.

- Keyboard Shortcut: Press Ctrl + Y (Windows) or Cmd + Shift + Z (Mac).

- Redo Button: Click the "Redo" icon (usually an arrow pointing right) in the toolbar.

4. Best Practices for Managing Version History and Undo Options

To maximize efficiency when working with Version History and Undo features, follow these best practices:

Regularly Check Version History

Even though Loop automatically saves versions, it's a good habit to periodically review changes, especially for long-term projects.

Use Descriptive Content Labels

When working with multiple versions, using clear labels and structuring Loop components effectively can make it easier to track changes.

Communicate with Your Team

If multiple team members are editing a page, coordinate with them before restoring a version to prevent overwriting important updates.

Combine Undo with Version History

Undo is best for quick fixes, while Version History is useful for major changes. Understanding when to use each feature will help improve productivity.

5. Common Issues and Troubleshooting

Version History Not Updating

If Version History doesn't show recent changes:

- Ensure you have a stable internet connection.

- Refresh the page to sync changes.

- Check if autosave is enabled in your Microsoft 365 settings.

Unable to Restore a Version

- Ensure you have **editing permissions** for the Loop page.

- Confirm that the version you want to restore is not locked by another user.

- If the issue persists, try signing out and signing back into Microsoft Loop.

Undo Not Working

- Some actions (like deleting entire components) may not be undone with **Ctrl + Z**. In such cases, check Version History instead.

6. Summary

Version History and Undo Options are essential tools for effective collaboration in Microsoft Loop. Understanding how to track, compare, and restore versions ensures that teams can work efficiently without fear of losing important updates. Additionally, using Undo and Redo for quick adjustments enhances real-time editing workflows.

By mastering these features, users can confidently collaborate in Loop while maintaining control over their content and ensuring accuracy in their shared workspaces.

3.1.3 Commenting and Feedback System

Collaboration is at the core of Microsoft Loop, and one of the most essential features that facilitate teamwork is the commenting and feedback system. This feature allows users to provide input, discuss ideas, suggest improvements, and resolve issues in a structured manner. Effective use of comments and feedback can significantly enhance communication and productivity within teams.

In this section, we will explore the commenting system in Microsoft Loop, including how to add, manage, and respond to comments. We will also discuss best practices for providing constructive feedback, managing discussions, and keeping track of changes in a collaborative workspace.

Understanding the Commenting System in Microsoft Loop

Microsoft Loop's commenting feature is designed to make collaboration smoother by enabling discussions directly within Loop components, pages, and workspaces. Unlike traditional document commenting systems, Loop offers a more interactive experience where comments are integrated into real-time collaborative content.

Key Benefits of the Commenting System

1. **Improved Team Communication** – Allows users to provide feedback without disrupting the content.

2. **Organized Discussions** – Keeps conversations structured and relevant to specific elements.

3. **Efficient Issue Resolution** – Enables quick decision-making by allowing team members to address feedback directly.

4. **Clear Accountability** – Assigns responsibility through mentions and action items in comments.

5. **Integrated Workflow** – Seamlessly works with other Microsoft 365 apps, making feedback management more efficient.

Adding Comments in Microsoft Loop

Adding comments in Microsoft Loop is a simple process that allows users to provide insights, suggestions, or ask questions within a collaborative document.

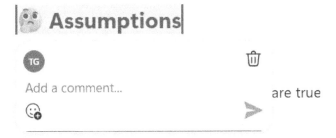

Steps to Add a Comment

1. **Select the content** – Highlight the specific text, table, or component where you want to add a comment.

2. **Right-click and choose "Add Comment"** – This will open a comment box next to the selected content.

3. **Type your comment** – Enter your feedback, question, or suggestion.

4. **Use @mentions** – Tag a team member using "@name" to notify them about the comment.

5. **Post the comment** – Click the submit button to save and share the comment with your team.

Where You Can Add Comments

- **Text components** – Comment on specific words, sentences, or paragraphs.

- **Tables and lists** – Provide feedback on data organization and structure.

- **Task lists** – Suggest changes or ask for clarifications on assignments.

- **Embedded files and links** – Give input on shared documents, images, or videos.

Managing and Resolving Comments

To keep collaboration productive, it's important to manage and resolve comments effectively. Microsoft Loop provides several tools to help teams track, reply, and resolve feedback efficiently.

Replying to a Comment

1. **Click on the comment bubble** – This opens the comment thread.

2. **Type your response** – You can acknowledge feedback, answer questions, or provide additional input.

3. **Use reactions** – Add quick reactions (👍, ❤️🗆, ✓) for simple acknowledgments.

4. **Resolve the comment when done** – Mark it as resolved once the issue is addressed.

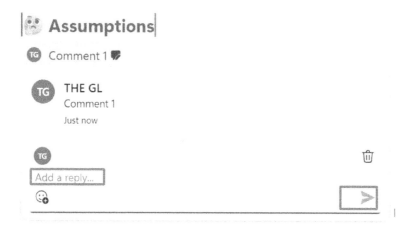

Editing or Deleting a Comment

*   **Editing** – Click on the comment and select "Edit" to modify your message.

*   **Deleting** – Click on the comment options (⋮) and choose "Delete" to remove a comment.

Tracking Unresolved Comments

Microsoft Loop provides options to filter and view unresolved comments, ensuring that all feedback is addressed before finalizing content.

Best Practices for Effective Feedback in Microsoft Loop

While the commenting system is a powerful tool, using it effectively requires a structured approach. Below are some best practices to enhance collaboration through comments.

1. Be Clear and Concise

- Use specific language when providing feedback to avoid misinterpretation.

- Instead of saying *"This needs improvement,"* say *"Consider adding more details in the second paragraph."*

2. Keep Discussions Focused

- Avoid off-topic comments; keep discussions relevant to the content.

- If a conversation becomes lengthy, consider moving it to a dedicated discussion area or a Microsoft Teams chat.

3. Use @Mentions to Assign Action Items

- Tagging specific team members ensures accountability.

- Example: *"@John, can you check the accuracy of this data?"*

4. Acknowledge and Close Resolved Comments

- Once feedback is implemented, mark the comment as resolved to keep the document clean.

5. Maintain a Professional and Positive Tone

- Constructive feedback should be polite and encouraging to foster a positive work environment.

Notifications and Comment Tracking

Microsoft Loop helps users stay updated on discussions by providing notifications and tracking features.

Receiving Notifications for Comments

Users receive notifications when:

- They are mentioned in a comment.

- Someone replies to a comment they created.

- A comment thread is resolved.

Checking Comments in the Activity Panel

- The Activity Panel in Loop shows all recent comments and discussions in a workspace.

- Users can filter comments to view only unresolved feedback.

Integrating Comments with Other Microsoft 365 Apps

Microsoft Loop's commenting system integrates seamlessly with other Microsoft 365 applications, enhancing the collaboration experience.

1. Microsoft Teams Integration

- Comments made in Loop components within Teams chats appear in both applications.

- Users can respond to comments directly from Teams.

2. Outlook and Email Notifications

- Comments tagged with @mentions can trigger email notifications.

- Users can reply via email, and their response will be recorded in Microsoft Loop.

3. SharePoint and OneDrive Synchronization

- Comments in Loop components embedded in SharePoint or OneDrive remain accessible across platforms.

Future Enhancements in Microsoft Loop's Commenting System

Microsoft continues to enhance Loop's collaborative features, and upcoming updates may include:

- AI-powered comment suggestions – Smart recommendations for resolving feedback.

- Threaded discussions – Improved organization of long comment threads.

- Advanced permission controls – More flexibility in managing comment visibility.

Conclusion

Microsoft Loop's commenting and feedback system plays a crucial role in fostering seamless collaboration. By allowing users to add, reply to, and resolve comments in real time, Loop ensures that teams stay aligned, feedback is efficiently addressed, and projects move forward smoothly.

Mastering these features will help you and your team communicate more effectively, reduce misunderstandings, and maintain well-organized discussions within Microsoft Loop.

3.2 Managing Permissions and Access Control

3.2.1 Sharing Loop Workspaces and Pages

One of the key strengths of Microsoft Loop is its seamless collaboration features, allowing users to work together in real-time while maintaining control over who can access and edit content. Understanding how to share Loop workspaces and pages effectively ensures that teams collaborate securely and efficiently. In this section, we will cover the fundamentals of sharing in Microsoft Loop, different access levels, how to manage sharing settings, and best practices for maintaining control over your work.

Understanding Sharing in Microsoft Loop

Before diving into the details of how to share workspaces and pages, it's essential to understand how sharing works in Microsoft Loop.

1. What Can Be Shared in Microsoft Loop?

Microsoft Loop is built around three primary components:

- Loop Workspaces – A shared space where users can collaborate on different pages and components.

- Loop Pages – A document-like interface within a workspace that contains different content blocks.

- Loop Components – Individual content elements (such as task lists, tables, or notes) that can be copied and shared independently across Microsoft 365 applications like Outlook and Teams.

Sharing can be done at different levels depending on whether you want to share an entire workspace, a single page, or a specific component within a page.

2. Types of Access in Microsoft Loop

When sharing a workspace or a page, Microsoft Loop provides different permission levels:

- Can Edit – Users with this permission can make changes to the workspace or page, including editing text, adding components, and modifying existing content.

- Can View – Users with this permission can see the content but cannot make any modifications.

- Can Comment (Future Feature) – While not available in all versions, Microsoft is expected to introduce a comment-only mode, allowing users to provide feedback without making direct changes.

Understanding these permission levels is crucial to prevent unauthorized changes while ensuring everyone has access to the content they need.

How to Share a Loop Workspace

Sharing a Loop workspace allows an entire team to collaborate on multiple pages and components within that space. Here's how you can do it:

Step 1: Open the Workspace Settings

1. Navigate to your Microsoft Loop dashboard.

2. Click on the workspace you want to share.

3. In the top-right corner, click on the Share button.

Step 2: Set Access Permissions

- A Share Workspace dialog box will appear.

- Enter the email addresses of the users you want to invite.

- Choose their access level (Can Edit or Can View).

- Click Send to invite them.

Alternative: Creating a Shareable Link

- Instead of adding individual emails, you can generate a link that allows multiple users to join.

- Click Copy Link and set the access level:

  o Anyone with the link (public access, recommended only for widely shared documents).

  o People in your organization (only users in your company can join).

o   Specific people (only invited users can access).

Security Tip: Always use "Specific people" or "People in your organization" for sensitive content to prevent unauthorized access.

Step 3: Managing Shared Workspaces

Once shared, you can manage access by:

- Removing users who no longer need access.

- Changing permissions (e.g., upgrading someone from Viewer to Editor).

- Revoking shared links if a workspace is no longer needed.

To manage permissions:

1. Open the workspace.

2. Click the Manage Access button.

3. Adjust settings for each user as needed.

How to Share a Loop Page

Sometimes, you may want to share only a single page instead of an entire workspace. This is useful when collaborating with external stakeholders or team members who only need access to a specific project section.

Step 1: Open the Page Settings

1. Navigate to the Loop workspace that contains the page.

2. Click on the page you want to share.

3. In the top-right corner, click the Share Page button.

Step 2: Choose Sharing Method

- Invite People Directly – Add their email addresses and select their access level.

- Generate a Shareable Link – Choose whether the link should be public, internal, or restricted.

Step 3: Adjust Advanced Sharing Settings

- Restrict Editing – Enable view-only mode to prevent changes.

- Set an Expiry Date – For temporary access, set an automatic expiration date for the shared link.

- Password Protect the Page – If the page contains sensitive information, set a password that users must enter to access it.

Pro Tip: Always review sharing settings before sending an invitation to prevent accidental data exposure.

Best Practices for Sharing in Microsoft Loop

1. Use Role-Based Access Control

Assign permissions based on team roles:

- Editors for content creators.

- Viewers for executives or external partners.

- Limited access for temporary collaborators.

2. Regularly Audit Shared Workspaces

Periodically check who has access to prevent unused or unauthorized users from retaining permissions.

3. Enable Microsoft 365 Security Features

For corporate environments, IT admins can:

- Enforce organization-wide sharing policies.

- Restrict external sharing based on compliance needs.

- Enable Microsoft Defender for additional security.

4. Use Comments Instead of Direct Edits (When Possible)

If a team member only needs to provide feedback, consider granting "comment-only" access instead of full editing rights.

Troubleshooting Sharing Issues in Microsoft Loop

Problem 1: Users Cannot Access the Shared Workspace

✅ **Solution:**

- Verify that the correct email address was used.

- Ensure the user is logged into the correct Microsoft account.

- Check if your organization's security policy restricts external sharing.

Problem 2: Users Cannot Edit a Shared Page

✅ **Solution:**

- Confirm that they have "Can Edit" permission.

- Ensure the page is not locked or restricted by an administrator.

Problem 3: The Shareable Link is Not Working

✅ **Solution:**

- Check if the link has expired.

- Verify that the correct permission settings were applied.

Final Thoughts

Effectively managing permissions and sharing settings in Microsoft Loop ensures that teams collaborate efficiently while maintaining security and control. By understanding the different sharing methods, setting appropriate permissions, and following best practices, you can maximize Microsoft Loop's collaboration potential while keeping your work safe and well-organized.

3.2.2 Setting Edit and View Permissions

Microsoft Loop is designed to facilitate seamless collaboration, allowing users to work on shared content in real time. However, managing permissions effectively is crucial to ensuring that information remains secure while still being accessible to the right people. In this section, we will explore how to set edit and view permissions in Microsoft Loop, including best practices for controlling access, managing roles, and maintaining security.

Understanding Permissions in Microsoft Loop

Before diving into how to set permissions, it is essential to understand the two primary permission levels available in Microsoft Loop:

1. **View Permission** – Users with view access can see the Loop components, pages, or workspaces but cannot make any changes.

2. **Edit Permission** – Users with edit access can modify, delete, or add content within the shared Loop component, page, or workspace.

Microsoft Loop's permission model ensures that users have the necessary level of access to collaborate effectively while protecting sensitive information from unwanted modifications.

How to Set Permissions for Loop Components

Loop components are small, portable pieces of content that can be shared across different Microsoft 365 applications such as Teams, Outlook, and OneNote. To control access to Loop components, follow these steps:

Step 1: Open the Loop Component

- Locate the Loop component you want to share within Microsoft Loop, Teams, or Outlook.

- If you have received a Loop component from someone else, ensure you have the necessary permissions to modify its sharing settings.

Step 2: Click on the Share Button

- In the top-right corner of the component, look for the **Share** button (represented by a link icon or "Share" text).

- Click on it to open the sharing options.

Step 3: Choose Who Can Access the Component

Microsoft Loop provides multiple options for sharing access:

- People in Your Organization – Grants access to anyone within your company or organization.

- People with the Link – Allows anyone with the link to access the component, with either view or edit permissions.

- Specific People – Restricts access to selected individuals who are explicitly invited.

Step 4: Set View or Edit Permissions

- Once you have selected the sharing method, choose whether users can **view** or **edit** the component.

- If necessary, disable **editing permissions** to ensure that shared users can only view the content.

Step 5: Share the Link or Invite Users

- Copy the generated link and send it via email, Teams chat, or any other communication channel.

- Alternatively, enter the email addresses of specific users and send them an invitation directly from Microsoft Loop.

Best Practices for Loop Component Permissions

- Avoid using the **"Anyone with the link"** setting unless necessary to maintain control over access.

- If granting edit permissions, ensure that only **trusted collaborators** receive access.

- Regularly review and update sharing settings to remove unnecessary users.

Managing Permissions for Loop Pages

Loop pages contain multiple components and serve as structured workspaces for collaboration. Permissions for Loop pages work similarly to components but apply to the entire page.

Step 1: Open the Loop Page

- Navigate to the page you want to share within your Loop workspace.

- Ensure that you have **owner** or **editor** permissions to modify sharing settings.

Step 2: Access the Share Settings

- Click the **Share** button located in the top-right corner.

- Select the **"Manage Access"** option to modify permissions for existing users.

Step 3: Define Access Levels

When sharing a Loop page, you can assign:

- **View Access** – Users can read but not edit the page.

- **Edit Access** – Users can add, modify, or remove content.

- **Owner Access** – Owners can change permissions and manage page settings.

Step 4: Set Expiry Dates and Restrictions (Optional)

- If necessary, apply **time-limited access** by setting an expiration date for external collaborators.

- Disable downloading or copying content if you want to prevent users from duplicating information.

Step 5: Share the Page with the Right People

- Send invitations via email or **copy the sharing link** and distribute it securely.

- Regularly audit permissions to **remove users who no longer need access**.

Controlling Access in Loop Workspaces

Loop **workspaces** are broader collaboration environments that contain multiple pages and components. Proper permission management at the workspace level ensures that only authorized team members can make modifications.

Step 1: Open the Loop Workspace

- Navigate to the **workspace settings** by selecting the workspace from the Microsoft Loop home screen.

Step 2: Access the Members and Permissions Settings

- Click on **"Manage Workspace Members"** to adjust access control.

- Identify users who currently have access and modify their roles.

Step 3: Assign Roles and Permissions

Microsoft Loop typically provides the following roles:

- **Owner** – Can manage workspace settings, permissions, and content.

- **Editor** – Can add, edit, and delete pages and components.

- **Viewer** – Can only view content but not modify it.

Step 4: Adjust Sharing Settings

- Restrict external sharing if necessary to **prevent unauthorized access**.

- Enable notifications to **track who joins or leaves the workspace**.

Step 5: Review Permissions Regularly

- Periodically check user roles and **remove inactive members**.

- Change permissions if a user's role within the team changes.

Advanced Permission Management

For organizations with stricter security policies, Microsoft Loop integrates with **Microsoft 365 compliance tools** to enforce advanced permissions.

Using Microsoft 365 Security Policies

- **Conditional Access** – Restrict Loop access based on user location or device.

- **Data Loss Prevention (DLP)** – Prevent sensitive information from being shared externally.

- **Audit Logs and Activity Monitoring** – Track changes and monitor access history.

Restricting External Sharing

If your organization requires high security, you can:

- Disable **external sharing** at the admin level.

- Require **multi-factor authentication (MFA)** for new collaborators.

- Set up **role-based access control (RBAC)** to limit permissions.

Best Practices for Managing Permissions in Microsoft Loop

1. **Use the Least Privilege Principle** – Grant only the **minimum access necessary** for each user.

2. **Monitor and Review Access** – Regularly check **who has access** and update permissions accordingly.

3. **Limit External Sharing** – Avoid unnecessary exposure of sensitive data by keeping access **internal**.

4. **Enable Microsoft 365 Security Features** – Utilize **DLP, audit logs, and compliance tools** for better control.

5. **Train Team Members** – Educate users on proper **sharing practices** to prevent accidental data leaks.

Conclusion

Setting edit and view permissions in Microsoft Loop is essential for secure and efficient collaboration. By properly configuring permissions for Loop components, pages, and workspaces, teams can ensure that only the right people have access while maintaining a streamlined workflow.

By following best practices and leveraging Microsoft 365 security features, organizations can maximize the benefits of Microsoft Loop while safeguarding sensitive information.

3.2.3 Managing External Collaborators

In today's interconnected work environment, teams often include not only internal employees but also external collaborators such as freelancers, contractors, clients, and business partners. Microsoft Loop enables seamless collaboration across organizations while maintaining security and access control.

This section will guide you through the process of managing external collaborators in Microsoft Loop, ensuring that they have the right level of access while keeping your workspace secure. We will cover:

- Understanding external collaboration in Microsoft Loop

- Adding external users to Loop workspaces and pages

- Managing permissions for external collaborators

- Best practices for working securely with external users

- Troubleshooting common issues with external collaboration

Understanding External Collaboration in Microsoft Loop

Who Are External Collaborators?

External collaborators refer to individuals who are not part of your organization's Microsoft 365 environment. These can include:

- **Freelancers and Consultants**: Professionals hired for specific projects

- **Clients and Business Partners**: External stakeholders who need access to project-related content

- **Vendors and Suppliers**: Third parties involved in logistics or operations

- **Temporary Employees and Interns**: Individuals working with your organization for a limited period

Since these users operate outside your company's domain, managing their access requires careful configuration to balance collaboration with security.

How External Collaboration Works in Microsoft Loop

Microsoft Loop operates within the Microsoft 365 ecosystem, meaning external users can only access Loop workspaces and components if they have been explicitly granted permission. Administrators and workspace owners can set access levels and restrictions to control how external users interact with content.

By default, external collaboration might be **restricted** depending on your organization's IT policies. Administrators can adjust settings to allow or block external users from accessing Loop workspaces and components.

Adding External Users to Loop Workspaces and Pages

Enabling External Collaboration in Microsoft 365

Before adding external users to Microsoft Loop, your organization's Microsoft 365 administrator must enable external sharing in **Microsoft Entra ID (formerly Azure AD) and SharePoint Online settings**. This ensures that external users can be invited and can access shared content securely.

To check if external sharing is enabled:

1. Go to the **Microsoft 365 Admin Center**.

2. Navigate to **Settings > Org settings > Security & Privacy**.

3. Look for **Sharing settings** under Microsoft Loop, SharePoint, and OneDrive.

4. Ensure that external sharing is **allowed** and set to an appropriate level.

Inviting External Users to Loop Workspaces

Once external sharing is enabled, you can invite users to your Microsoft Loop workspace by following these steps:

1. **Open Microsoft Loop** and go to the **workspace** you want to share.

2. Click on the **Share** button at the top-right corner of the workspace.

3. In the invite field, enter the email address of the external collaborator.

4. Choose their permission level:

    o **Can edit**: Allows them to modify content

    o **Can view**: Grants read-only access

5. Click **Send Invitation**.

The external user will receive an email with a link to access the Loop workspace. They may need to authenticate using a Microsoft account or a work email supported by Microsoft 365.

Sharing Individual Loop Pages with External Users

If you don't want to grant access to an entire workspace, you can share specific **Loop pages** instead:

1. Open the **Loop page** you want to share.

2. Click the **Share** button and select **Copy Link**.

3. Under **Link Settings**, choose one of the following options:

   o **Anyone with the link** (if allowed by IT policies)

   o **People in your organization**

   o **Specific people** (enter the external user's email)

4. Click **Apply**, then share the link via email or chat.

This allows you to collaborate on individual pages without exposing the entire workspace.

Managing Permissions for External Collaborators

Understanding Permission Levels

When adding external users to Microsoft Loop, you must carefully assign permissions to ensure proper security. Here are the three main permission levels:

Permission Level	Description	Recommended For
Can Edit	Full editing access to Loop workspaces, pages, and components	Trusted collaborators, project teams
Can View	Read-only access, can see updates but cannot make changes	Clients, stakeholders, auditors
No Access	Cannot open or view Loop content	Unauthorized users

Adjusting Permissions for External Users

To modify an external collaborator's access level:

1. Open the **Loop workspace** or **Loop page** where they are invited.

2. Click the **Share** button and navigate to **Manage access**.

3. Locate the external user's email under the access list.

4. Use the dropdown menu to change their permission (Edit, View, or Remove Access).

5. Click **Save Changes** to update their access.

Revoking Access for External Users

If an external collaborator no longer needs access, you can remove them:

1. Go to **Manage Access** in the Loop workspace.

2. Find the external user's email.

3. Click **Remove** to revoke their access.

4. Confirm the action.

Once removed, they will no longer be able to open the Loop workspace or view shared components.

Best Practices for Secure External Collaboration

To ensure a safe and productive collaboration experience, follow these best practices:

1. Use "Specific People" Sharing Instead of Open Links

Avoid using the "Anyone with the link" option unless necessary. Instead, restrict access to specific external collaborators.

2. Assign the Lowest Necessary Permission Level

Grant View access instead of Edit unless the external user needs to modify content.

3. Regularly Audit External Access

Periodically review and remove external users who no longer require access.

4. Use Expiration Dates for Shared Links

Set expiration dates for externally shared links to automatically revoke access after a project ends.

5. Enable Multi-Factor Authentication (MFA) for External Users

Ensure external users authenticate securely to prevent unauthorized access.

Troubleshooting External Collaboration Issues

Despite best efforts, external collaboration in Microsoft Loop may encounter some challenges. Here are solutions to common issues:

Issue	Possible Cause	Solution
External user cannot access Loop workspace	External sharing is disabled in Microsoft 365 settings	Check admin settings in Microsoft Entra ID and SharePoint
User gets a "You don't have permission" error	The user was invited but lacks permission	Verify and update their access level
Loop component doesn't update for an external user	Sync issues or outdated browser	Refresh the page, clear cache, or use Microsoft Edge/Chrome
External user cannot edit a Loop page	Page is shared as "View only"	Change their permission to "Can Edit" in Manage Access

If problems persist, contact your IT administrator for further troubleshooting.

Conclusion

Managing external collaborators in Microsoft Loop is essential for organizations working with clients, vendors, and freelancers. By carefully configuring permissions, regularly auditing access, and following security best practices, you can ensure smooth and secure collaboration.

Next, we'll explore how Microsoft Loop integrates with Microsoft Teams, enabling even greater productivity for teams working together in real-time.

3.3 Using Microsoft Loop with Microsoft Teams

Collaboration is at the heart of modern teamwork, and Microsoft Loop is designed to enhance real-time collaboration across different Microsoft 365 applications. One of the most powerful integrations of Loop is with **Microsoft Teams**, a widely used communication and collaboration platform. By embedding Loop components into Teams chats, users can work together more effectively, ensuring that information remains dynamic, up to date, and accessible to all team members.

In this section, we will explore:

- The benefits of using **Loop components within Microsoft Teams**

- Step-by-step instructions to **integrate Loop components into Teams chats**

- Best practices for **efficient collaboration using Loop and Teams**

3.3.1 Integrating Loop Components into Teams Chats

Microsoft Loop components can be embedded into Teams chats, allowing team members to edit content collaboratively in real time without leaving the conversation. These components ensure that important discussions, updates, and tasks remain fluid and accessible to all participants.

Benefits of Using Loop Components in Teams Chats

Before diving into the integration process, let's explore why you should use Loop components within Teams chats:

1. Real-Time Collaboration: Multiple users can edit, update, and view content simultaneously without switching between different apps.

2. Always Up-to-Date Information: Unlike static messages or attachments, Loop components stay live, meaning updates made anywhere (Teams, Outlook, Loop workspaces) are automatically reflected everywhere.

3. Enhanced Productivity: Teams members can contribute to shared tables, checklists, or brainstorming sessions directly within the chat, reducing context-switching.

4. Seamless Synchronization Across Microsoft 365 Apps: Loop components can also be accessed from Outlook, Word, and Loop Workspaces, ensuring continuity across different workflows.

How to Insert a Microsoft Loop Component in a Teams Chat

Step 1: Open Microsoft Teams Chat

- Navigate to Microsoft Teams and open an existing chat or start a new chat with your team members.

- This can be a one-on-one chat or a group chat in a specific channel.

Step 2: Select the Loop Icon

- In the chat's **message box**, locate the **Microsoft Loop icon** (▢).

- This icon allows you to insert a Loop component directly into the chat.

Step 3: Choose the Type of Loop Component

Microsoft provides several **Loop component options**, each designed for different use cases. You can select:

- **Paragraph** (for shared notes or discussions)

- **Table** (for structured information like task tracking)

- **Checklist** (for shared to-do lists and assignments)

- **Task list** (for project tracking and responsibility assignments)

- **Voting table** (for decision-making and feedback collection)

◆ **Example Use Case:** If you are planning a project, you might insert a **Task List** so that team members can see their assignments and update them in real time.

Step 4: Add and Edit Content

- Once you select a **Loop component**, it will appear inside the chat.

- You and your teammates can **start typing directly into the Loop component** within the chat window.

- Each edit is visible **in real time** to all participants, creating a **live, shared document** inside the conversation.

Step 5: Manage Access and Permissions

- By default, all members of the chat **can edit** the Loop component.

- You can adjust access settings by **clicking the "Share" button** on the Loop component.

- Options include:

  - **Can edit:** All chat members can make changes.

  - **Can view:** Only selected people can see the component without editing rights.

⬥ **Tip:** If you need **external collaboration**, ensure that sharing settings allow guests to access and edit Loop components.

How Loop Components Improve Teams Chats

Once you've added a Loop component, it enhances communication and collaboration in several ways:

1. **Reducing Message Overload**

   - Instead of sending multiple updates or long message threads, a single Loop component keeps everything in one place.

   - This prevents message clutter and ensures important information is not lost.

2. **Increasing Engagement and Participation**

   - Team members can actively contribute to shared ideas and tasks within the chat.

   - Since everyone can edit simultaneously, brainstorming and decision-making become faster.

3. **Improving Task Tracking and Accountability**

- o Task lists created in Loop components are visible to everyone, ensuring clarity in assignments.

- o Employees can mark tasks as completed in real time, reducing miscommunication.

◆ **Example Use Case:** A **marketing team** planning a campaign can use a **Loop checklist** to track deliverables, ensuring everyone knows what needs to be done.

Editing and Updating Loop Components in Teams

One of the best features of Microsoft Loop is that Loop components remain editable no matter where they are accessed. You can edit a component in Teams, and the changes will sync across all other locations, such as Outlook emails and Loop workspaces.

- Inline Editing: Click on a Loop component inside Teams chat and start typing.

- Access from Other Devices: If you access the same Teams chat on another device, the Loop component remains fully interactive.

- Version Control: You can track who edited what using version history, ensuring transparency in updates.

Best Practices for Using Loop in Teams Chats

To maximize productivity, here are some best practices when using Loop components in Microsoft Teams:

✅ Keep Loop Components Organized

- Name your Loop components **clearly** (e.g., "Q2 Project Deliverables") to avoid confusion in chats.

✅ Use Permissions Wisely

- Only grant **editing access** to relevant team members to prevent accidental changes.

✅ Encourage Real-Time Collaboration

- Assign specific responsibilities within **task lists** so team members are clear on their duties.

✅ **Avoid Too Many Loop Components in One Chat**

- If a conversation requires multiple Loop components, consider moving discussions to a Loop workspace for better organization.

✅ **Monitor Version History for Important Updates**

- If a project is evolving, periodically review version history to track key changes.

Final Thoughts

Integrating Microsoft Loop components into Microsoft Teams chats provides a powerful way to streamline collaboration, ensuring information is dynamic, editable, and always up to date. With the ability to edit in real time, track progress, and enhance teamwork, Loop components revolutionize the way teams communicate and manage projects.

As organizations move toward hybrid and remote work environments, tools like Loop inside Teams become indispensable for efficient collaboration. By mastering Loop's integration with Teams, you can ensure that your team stays connected, productive, and aligned on shared goals.

◆ Up Next: In Section 3.3.2, we will explore how Microsoft Loop enhances document editing within Teams, making it easier to collaborate on shared files and reports.

3.3.2 Collaborative Document Editing within Teams

Collaboration in the modern workplace demands flexibility, real-time communication, and seamless document editing. Microsoft Loop, when integrated with Microsoft Teams, provides an environment where team members can co-edit content dynamically, improving efficiency and reducing version conflicts.

In this section, we will explore how to collaboratively edit Loop components within Teams, including how to embed Loop content in Teams chats, co-edit documents, track changes, and leverage Loop's unique features to streamline team collaboration.

1. Embedding Loop Components in Microsoft Teams

Microsoft Loop components are designed to be dynamic and live, meaning any changes made to them reflect instantly across different Microsoft 365 applications. Teams is one of the most powerful platforms for communication and collaboration, and integrating Loop within Teams helps in real-time document editing without switching applications.

How to Add a Loop Component in a Teams Chat

To collaboratively edit a document using Loop in Microsoft Teams, follow these steps:

1. **Open Microsoft Teams** – Launch the Teams app and navigate to the chat or channel where you want to collaborate.

2. **Click on the Message Box** – At the bottom of the chat window, click on the message input field.

3. **Select the Loop Icon** – Click on the **Loop** button (usually represented by an infinity-like symbol).

4. **Choose a Loop Component** – You will see several options for Loop components, such as:

   o Paragraph (for text-based collaboration)

   o Table (for structured data)

   o Task list (for project tracking)

   o Voting table (for decision-making)

5. **Edit and Share** – After selecting a component, start editing the content. All team members in the chat can contribute in real-time.

Benefits of Embedding Loop Components in Teams

- **Real-Time Collaboration:** Changes made to the document are instantly visible to everyone.

- **Version-Free Editing:** Unlike traditional file-based collaboration, Loop components eliminate the need for multiple file versions.

- **Cross-App Integration:** The same Loop component can be accessed and edited in Teams, Outlook, and Loop Workspaces.

2. Co-Editing Loop Components in Microsoft Teams

Once a Loop component is embedded in a Teams chat, all participants in that chat can co-edit the content simultaneously. Microsoft Loop ensures smooth editing with features like live cursor tracking, auto-sync, and user presence indicators.

Understanding the Co-Editing Process

- Live Cursor Tracking: See exactly where other teammates are editing in the document.

- User Presence Indicators: Profile pictures or initials appear next to the content being modified.

- Instant Synchronization: Edits update in real time across all Microsoft 365 apps.

Editing Best Practices for Teams Collaboration

- Use Clear Formatting: To maintain readability, format text using bullet points, bold, and headings.

- Assign Responsibilities: Tag team members using @mentions to notify them about specific edits.

- Keep Updates Concise: Since everyone can edit, avoid overwriting important contributions.

- Review Before Finalizing: Use the version history feature (explained later) to ensure changes align with team objectives.

3. Tracking Changes and Version History

Unlike traditional file-based collaboration tools, Microsoft Loop components automatically save every change in real time. However, users might still need to track edits and restore previous versions.

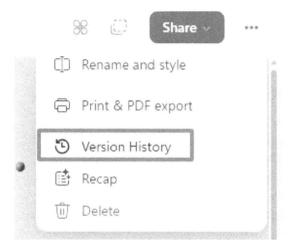

How to Access Version History

1. Click on the Loop component inside Microsoft Teams.

2. Look for the three-dot menu (:) at the top-right corner of the component.

3. Select Version History to view a timeline of changes.

4. Click on a previous version to review and restore it if necessary.

Benefits of Version History in Loop

-   Error Correction: Quickly revert to an earlier version if mistakes are made.

-   Accountability: Track who made specific changes and when.

-   Content Integrity: Prevent accidental deletion of important information.

4. Enhancing Collaboration with Additional Microsoft 365 Integrations

Microsoft Loop components don't just work in isolation—they integrate with other Microsoft 365 tools to improve document collaboration.

Using Loop with Microsoft OneDrive

-   Loop components automatically sync with OneDrive, ensuring accessibility even outside Teams.

-   Users can organize shared Loop documents into structured folders.

Using Loop with Microsoft Outlook

- Embed Loop components in Outlook emails to allow recipients to edit content directly from their inbox.

- Changes made in Outlook sync instantly with the Loop component inside Teams.

Using Loop with Microsoft Word and Excel

- Although Loop is designed for real-time collaboration, components can be converted into Word or Excel documents for long-form editing and advanced calculations.

5. Common Challenges and Solutions

Even with a seamless collaboration experience, users might encounter occasional challenges while editing Loop components in Teams. Here are some common issues and how to resolve them:

Sync Issues

Problem: Edits made in Teams don't appear in other applications.
Solution: Refresh the Teams chat or manually sync the Loop component by clicking on the refresh icon.

Permissions and Access Errors

Problem: Some team members cannot edit the Loop component.
Solution: Check the sharing settings in Teams and ensure users have edit permissions.

Formatting Limitations

Problem: Loop components do not support complex formatting like advanced tables or custom fonts.
Solution: Use Microsoft Word or Excel for detailed formatting and then link the file within Teams.

6. Best Practices for Collaborative Editing in Teams

To maximize productivity and ensure smooth collaboration, follow these best practices:

1. **Set Clear Editing Guidelines:** Establish a shared understanding of how team members should contribute to Loop documents.

2. **Use @Mentions Effectively:** Directly notify teammates about changes that require their attention.

3. **Regularly Review Version History:** Prevent accidental overwrites and ensure document accuracy.

4. **Limit Unnecessary Edits:** Avoid making changes that do not add value to the discussion.

5. **Organize Components in Workspaces:** Keep track of multiple Loop documents by structuring them in dedicated workspaces.

Conclusion

Collaborative document editing within Microsoft Teams using Loop components is a powerful way to enhance team productivity. With real-time synchronization, live editing features, and seamless integration with Microsoft 365 apps, Loop revolutionizes how teams work together.

By understanding how to embed, co-edit, and track changes in Loop components within Teams, users can streamline workflows and improve efficiency. As Microsoft continues to expand Loop's capabilities, mastering these collaboration techniques will be essential for modern teamwork.

3.3.3 Best Practices for Team Communication

Effective communication is the backbone of any successful team, and Microsoft Loop offers powerful tools to streamline collaboration and ensure seamless information flow. When used effectively within Microsoft Teams, Loop can enhance transparency, foster engagement, and boost productivity. In this section, we will explore the best practices for team communication using Microsoft Loop, covering strategies for organizing content, maintaining clarity, leveraging collaboration features, and integrating with Microsoft Teams.

1. Establish Clear Communication Guidelines

Before diving into the technical aspects of using Microsoft Loop, it's essential to establish clear communication guidelines for your team. Without a structured approach, even the most advanced collaboration tools can become chaotic.

Define the Purpose of Each Loop Component

- When creating a Loop page or component, clarify its purpose.

- Use consistent naming conventions to make it easy for team members to understand the context of shared components.

- Consider adding a brief introduction at the top of each Loop page outlining how it should be used.

Set Expectations for Collaboration

- Establish when and how team members should contribute to Loop components.

- Encourage real-time collaboration while also ensuring asynchronous work is structured.

- Assign specific responsibilities to team members within task lists to avoid confusion.

Maintain a Structured Organization

- Keep Loop components well-structured and categorized within Microsoft Teams channels.

- Use sections and headings within Loop pages for easy navigation.

- Archive outdated Loop components to reduce clutter.

2. Utilize Real-Time Collaboration Features

One of the biggest advantages of Microsoft Loop is its ability to enable real-time collaboration, allowing teams to work on the same content simultaneously. However, without clear best practices, real-time collaboration can quickly become overwhelming.

Enable Live Editing Without Overwriting Important Content

- Encourage team members to use comments and suggestions before making drastic changes to shared Loop components.

- Take advantage of version history to track changes and restore previous versions if needed.

- Assign a content owner for critical documents to manage updates efficiently.

Use @Mentions to Get Attention on Key Updates

- Tag relevant team members using @mentions to notify them about updates or requests.

- Avoid overusing @mentions to prevent notification fatigue.

- Use mentions strategically in task lists and discussion sections to keep the conversation focused.

Track Changes and Encourage Transparency

- Use the activity feed within Microsoft Teams to monitor updates on Loop components.

- Ask team members to provide brief status updates when making edits, either through comments or chat messages.

- Set up a weekly review session to discuss recent changes and improvements.

3. Leverage Microsoft Loop for Meeting Collaboration

Microsoft Loop integrates seamlessly with Microsoft Teams meetings, providing a central workspace where participants can contribute in real time.

Prepare a Collaborative Agenda with Loop

- Before a meeting, create a Loop page to outline the agenda.

- Allow team members to contribute discussion points in advance.

- Use tables and checklists to organize agenda items and action points.

Capture Meeting Notes in a Shared Loop Component

- During the meeting, designate a team member to take notes in a Loop component embedded within Teams.

- Use bullet points and formatting tools to improve readability.

- Tag action items with @mentions to assign follow-ups to specific team members.

Summarize Key Takeaways and Action Items

- After the meeting, refine the notes into a structured summary.

- Use a task list component to highlight assigned responsibilities and deadlines.

- Pin the Loop component in the Teams channel so everyone has easy access to meeting outcomes.

4. Optimize Loop Components for Asynchronous Work

Not all team members will be online at the same time, so Microsoft Loop must be optimized for **asynchronous collaboration** to ensure smooth workflows across different time zones.

Create Clear and Concise Content

- Avoid overly long and complex documents—keep Loop components short and structured.

- Use bullet points, numbered lists, and headings to improve readability.

- Include reference links to additional documents if needed.

Provide Context for Asynchronous Updates

- When making edits or suggestions, leave a brief comment explaining the reason for the change.

- Use timestamps and version history to keep track of major updates.

- Encourage team members to acknowledge updates through reactions or short responses.

Ensure Easy Access to Important Loop Components

- Pin essential Loop components in Teams channels for quick reference.

- Use search and tagging features to make finding documents easier.

- Organize Loop pages logically within Teams workspaces.

5. Integrate Loop Components with Other Microsoft 365 Apps

For enhanced efficiency, Microsoft Loop can be integrated with other Microsoft 365 tools like OneNote, Outlook, SharePoint, and Planner.

Use Loop Components in Outlook for Email Collaboration

- Embed Loop components in emails to allow recipients to update content directly from their inbox.

- Use this feature for collaborative decision-making or gathering team feedback asynchronously.

Sync Loop Components with Planner for Task Management

- Convert Loop task lists into Planner tasks for more detailed tracking.

- Assign due dates and monitor task progress in Planner while keeping Loop as the discussion hub.

Embed Loop Components in SharePoint for Centralized Knowledge Sharing

- Store important Loop pages in SharePoint for easy access.

- Create a knowledge base using Loop pages to document team processes.

6. Encourage a Culture of Continuous Improvement

Successful communication isn't just about using the right tools—it's also about fostering a collaborative culture within the team.

Provide Training and Onboarding for New Team Members

- Organize training sessions on how to effectively use Microsoft Loop.

- Create a Loop onboarding guide for new employees with best practices.

Gather Feedback on Collaboration Workflows

- Periodically ask team members for feedback on how Microsoft Loop is being used.

- Identify pain points and adjust workflows accordingly.

Keep Up with Microsoft Loop Updates

- Stay informed about new features and improvements from Microsoft.

- Encourage team members to explore advanced functionalities to enhance their productivity.

Conclusion

Using Microsoft Loop within Microsoft Teams offers a dynamic and flexible approach to team communication. By following these best practices—establishing clear guidelines, optimizing real-time and asynchronous collaboration, leveraging integration with other Microsoft 365 tools, and fostering a culture of continuous improvement—your team can maximize productivity and ensure seamless information flow.

Mastering these techniques will not only improve efficiency but also create a more engaged and connected team, making Microsoft Loop a powerful asset in your digital workspace.

CHAPTER IV
Advanced Features and Customization

4.1 Automating Workflows with Loop

As teams and organizations increasingly rely on digital tools for collaboration, automation has become an essential part of streamlining workflows. Microsoft Loop, while primarily a collaboration platform, can be significantly enhanced when integrated with **Power Automate**, a Microsoft service that allows users to create automated workflows between apps and services.

In this section, we will explore how **Microsoft Loop and Power Automate** work together, how to set up automation, and practical use cases where automation can boost productivity and efficiency.

4.1.1 Connecting Loop with Power Automate

Understanding Power Automate and Its Role in Microsoft Loop

Microsoft Power Automate (formerly known as **Microsoft Flow**) is a cloud-based service that enables users to create **automated workflows** between their favorite apps and services. These workflows, known as **"flows"**, can perform actions such as sending notifications, synchronizing files, collecting data, and automating repetitive tasks.

When integrated with **Microsoft Loop**, Power Automate can help teams:

- Automate routine tasks like sending reminders, tracking updates, or triggering actions based on specific events.

- Connect Loop components with other Microsoft 365 applications such as Teams, Outlook, SharePoint, and OneDrive.

- Improve collaboration efficiency by ensuring data flows smoothly across multiple platforms without manual intervention.

How Microsoft Loop Integrates with Power Automate

Microsoft Loop supports Power Automate connectors, which allow users to set up flows that interact with Loop workspaces, pages, and components. By using pre-built templates or custom workflows, users can automate processes like:

- Automatically creating Loop pages when a new project starts in Microsoft Planner.

- Sending notifications when a Loop component is updated.

- Syncing task lists from Loop with Microsoft To Do or Planner.

- Archiving completed Loop pages in OneDrive or SharePoint for future reference.

Setting Up Power Automate for Microsoft Loop

To get started with Power Automate and Microsoft Loop, follow these steps:

Step 1: Access Power Automate

1. Open Microsoft Power Automate by navigating to https://flow.microsoft.com.

2. Sign in with your Microsoft 365 account.

3. Click on Create to start building an automation flow.

Step 2: Choose a Trigger for Your Flow

A trigger is an event that starts the automation. Power Automate provides multiple triggers related to Microsoft 365 applications, such as:

- "When a Loop component is updated" – Triggers a flow when a Loop page or component is modified.

- "When a new Loop page is created" – Automates actions whenever a new workspace or page is added.

- "When a new task is added to a Loop task list" – Helps sync Loop with other task management tools.

Step 3: Define Actions to Perform

After selecting a trigger, you need to define the actions that will take place. Some common actions include:

- Sending notifications via Teams or Outlook when Loop content changes.

- Creating tasks in Planner based on Loop component updates.

- Saving completed Loop documents to SharePoint for archiving.

- Synchronizing data between Loop and other Microsoft apps like OneNote, Excel, or Lists.

Step 4: Test and Deploy the Flow

1. Click Save and Test your flow to ensure it works as expected.

2. If everything functions correctly, enable the automation.

3. Monitor the workflow in Power Automate to track activity and troubleshoot errors if needed.

Practical Use Cases for Automating Microsoft Loop with Power Automate

Now that we've covered the setup process, let's look at some real-world scenarios where automation with Loop and Power Automate can enhance productivity.

1. Automating Project Management Updates

Scenario: A team uses Microsoft Loop for project tracking and needs automatic updates whenever a task is completed.

Solution:

- Create a Power Automate flow that monitors a Loop task list.

- When a task is marked as "Complete," Power Automate updates Microsoft Planner or sends an email notification to the team.

2. Sending Automated Meeting Summaries

Scenario: After a meeting, a Loop page is created for notes and action items. Team members often forget to check the updates.

Solution:

- Configure Power Automate to detect when a Loop meeting notes page is updated.

- Automatically send an email summary to all meeting participants.

- Save meeting notes to a OneNote section for future reference.

3. Integrating Loop with Microsoft Teams for Instant Alerts

Scenario: A manager wants to stay updated whenever a Loop component related to a project is modified.

Solution:

- Set up a Teams notification flow in Power Automate.

- When a Loop component (e.g., budget tracker or task list) is updated, send a Teams alert to relevant stakeholders.

4. Archiving Completed Loop Workspaces in SharePoint

Scenario: Once a project is finished, teams want to archive their Loop workspace to SharePoint.

Solution:

- Use Power Automate to detect completed projects in Loop.

- Automatically move all related Loop pages to a designated SharePoint folder for future reference.

5. Syncing Loop with Microsoft Planner for Task Management

Scenario: A marketing team plans campaigns using Loop, but they also rely on Microsoft Planner to manage execution.

Solution:

- Set up a two-way sync between Loop task lists and Planner.

- When a new task is added in Loop, create a corresponding task in Planner.

- When a task is completed in Planner, update the Loop task list accordingly.

Best Practices for Automating Microsoft Loop with Power Automate

To get the most out of automation, keep these best practices in mind:

1. Start with Simple Automations

Begin with basic workflows (e.g., sending notifications) before implementing complex multi-step automations.

2. Monitor and Optimize Flows

Regularly review flow performance in Power Automate and refine them to ensure they run efficiently.

3. Use Pre-Built Templates

Microsoft provides ready-to-use Power Automate templates that simplify automation setup. Browse templates to find ones that match your needs.

4. Maintain Security and Access Controls

Ensure that only authorized users can trigger or modify automation flows, especially for sensitive data.

5. Keep Automations Aligned with Team Needs

Before deploying automation, discuss with your team to ensure that the workflow genuinely improves efficiency and doesn't create unnecessary complexity.

Conclusion

Integrating Microsoft Loop with Power Automate unlocks a new level of efficiency for teams and individuals. By automating repetitive tasks, syncing data across apps, and improving communication, Loop becomes a more powerful collaboration tool.

In the next section, we will explore how Microsoft Loop integrates with other Microsoft 365 applications, providing even more ways to enhance productivity and teamwork.

🚀 Key Takeaways from This Section:

✅ Microsoft Power Automate allows users to create workflows that automate tasks in Microsoft Loop.

✅ Common use cases include sending notifications, syncing tasks, and archiving data.

✅ Setting up an automation involves choosing a trigger, defining actions, and testing the workflow.

✅ Best practices include starting small, monitoring flows, and keeping automations aligned with team needs.

4.1.2 Setting Up Automated Notifications

Introduction

Automated notifications are an essential feature in modern collaboration tools, ensuring that users stay informed about updates, changes, and actions required in their workflows. Microsoft Loop allows users to set up automated notifications to streamline communication, improve efficiency, and reduce the risk of missing critical tasks or updates. By integrating Loop with Microsoft 365 and Power Automate, users can customize notifications based on their specific needs.

This section explores how to configure automated notifications in Microsoft Loop, covering different notification types, integration with other Microsoft 365 tools, best practices for managing alerts, and troubleshooting common notification issues.

4.1 Understanding Automated Notifications in Loop

Before setting up notifications, it's important to understand how notifications work in Microsoft Loop.

What Are Automated Notifications?

Automated notifications in Microsoft Loop are alerts triggered by specific events, such as:

- Changes in Loop components (e.g., edits, new content added).

- Task assignments and status updates.

- Mentions in comments or discussions.

- Deadlines and due dates approaching.

- External app integrations (e.g., Outlook, Teams, Planner).

These notifications can be sent through email, Microsoft Teams, push notifications, or directly within the Loop workspace.

Why Use Automated Notifications?

Setting up automated notifications in Microsoft Loop has several benefits:

- Improved Communication: Ensures that team members are always informed.

- Efficiency: Reduces manual follow-ups and reminders.

- Task Management: Helps users keep track of deadlines and assignments.

- Customization: Allows users to set up personalized alerts based on priorities.

4.2 Configuring Automated Notifications in Microsoft Loop

Enabling Basic Notifications in Loop

By default, Microsoft Loop provides basic notification settings. Here's how to access and configure them:

1. **Access Notification Settings:**

    o Open Microsoft Loop.

    o Click on your profile icon (top-right corner).

    o Select Settings → Notifications & Alerts.

2. **Adjust Notification Preferences:**

    o Enable or disable notifications for:

        ▪ Edits in shared Loop components.

        ▪ New comments or mentions.

        ▪ Task updates and deadline reminders.

    o Select preferred notification channels (email, Teams, push notifications).

3. **Save Changes:**

    o Click **Save** to apply the settings.

Setting Up Notifications for Task Management

Microsoft Loop integrates seamlessly with Microsoft To Do and Planner, allowing users to receive automated notifications when tasks are assigned or updated.

Steps to enable task-related notifications:

1. **Create a Task Component:**

    o   Open a Loop workspace and insert a Task List component.

    o   Add tasks and assign them to team members.

2. **Enable Task Alerts:**

    o   Click on the three-dot menu in the Task component.

    o   Select Notify me about task updates.

    o   Choose how you want to be notified (email, Teams, or Loop notifications).

3. **Sync with Microsoft Planner:**

    o   Open Microsoft Planner.

    o   Go to Settings → Notifications.

    o   Enable "Send email notifications when a task is assigned or completed".

This ensures that users receive alerts whenever a task status changes, keeping teams informed about project progress.

4.3 Advanced Notifications with Power Automate

For more advanced automation, Microsoft Loop can be integrated with Power Automate to create custom notification workflows.

What is Power Automate?

Power Automate (formerly Microsoft Flow) is a cloud-based tool that allows users to automate repetitive tasks by connecting Microsoft apps, including Loop, Outlook, Teams, and Planner.

Creating a Power Automate Flow for Loop Notifications

Follow these steps to set up a custom automated notification in Microsoft Loop using Power Automate:

1. **Open Power Automate:**

   o Go to Power Automate https://make.powerautomate.com/ and sign in with your Microsoft account.

2. **Create a New Flow:**

   o Click Create → Automated Cloud Flow.

   o Name the flow (e.g., "Loop Task Alerts").

   o Select When a new task is created in Loop as the trigger.

3. **Set Up Conditions for Notifications:**

   o Add a condition:

     ▪ If a task is assigned to me, send a Teams notification.

     ▪ If a task is due within 24 hours, send an email reminder.

4. **Choose a Notification Action:**

   o Select Send an email notification (Outlook) or Post a message in Teams.

   o Customize the message content (e.g., task name, due date, assigned user).

5. **Test and Activate the Flow:**

   o Click Test to ensure it works correctly.

   o Click Save and Turn on the flow.

Now, Loop will automatically send notifications based on the defined triggers, ensuring users never miss an update.

4.4 Best Practices for Managing Notifications

To avoid notification overload, follow these best practices:

Prioritize Important Notifications

- Enable only essential alerts to reduce distractions.

- Set priority levels for different notifications (e.g., urgent vs. non-urgent).

Optimize Notification Frequency

- Avoid excessive notifications by consolidating updates into daily summaries instead of real-time alerts.

- Use Power Automate to batch notifications for better management.

Utilize Multiple Notification Channels

- Use Teams notifications for team-wide updates.

- Use email alerts for important deadlines.

- Enable mobile push notifications for urgent tasks.

4.5 Troubleshooting Common Notification Issues

Not Receiving Notifications

- Ensure that notifications are enabled in Loop settings.

- Check email spam/junk folders.

- Verify Power Automate flows are running correctly.

Receiving Too Many Notifications

- Reduce notification settings for low-priority updates.

- Modify Power Automate flows to combine multiple alerts into one.

Notifications Delayed or Not Syncing

- Refresh Loop and Teams apps.

- Reconnect Loop with Microsoft 365 apps.

- Ensure internet connection is stable.

Conclusion

Automated notifications in Microsoft Loop are a powerful way to stay informed, improve team collaboration, and manage tasks efficiently. Whether using built-in settings or integrating with Power Automate, users can customize alerts to fit their workflow. By following best practices and troubleshooting common issues, users can ensure they receive only the most relevant and timely notifications for their work.

4.1.3 Using Loop for Project Management

Microsoft Loop is a powerful tool for project management, allowing teams to collaborate dynamically and efficiently. With its flexible structure, real-time updates, and integration with other Microsoft 365 tools, Loop provides a seamless environment for managing tasks, tracking progress, and ensuring that projects stay on schedule. In this section, we will explore how Microsoft Loop can be leveraged for project management, covering key use cases, best practices, and integration with essential tools.

1. Why Use Microsoft Loop for Project Management?

Traditional project management tools often rely on rigid structures, requiring teams to navigate multiple applications for communication, task tracking, and document collaboration. Microsoft Loop addresses these challenges by offering:

- **Real-Time Collaboration** – Teams can simultaneously update project components, ensuring that everyone is aligned.

- **Modular Components** – Tasks, notes, and data can be easily rearranged and embedded across Microsoft 365 apps.

- **Seamless Integration** – Loop works alongside Microsoft Teams, Outlook, Planner, and other essential productivity tools.

- **Flexibility** – Unlike static documents or spreadsheets, Loop provides a living workspace that evolves as the project progresses.

By leveraging Loop's capabilities, teams can reduce inefficiencies, enhance communication, and keep projects well-organized.

2. Setting Up a Project Workspace in Microsoft Loop

Creating a Dedicated Project Workspace

To begin managing a project in Microsoft Loop, follow these steps:

1. Open Microsoft Loop and navigate to the homepage.

2. Click on "New Workspace" to create a dedicated project space.

3. Name your workspace (e.g., "Marketing Campaign Q2 2025").

4. Invite team members by sharing the workspace link or adding them via email.

5. Customize the layout by adding pages and components relevant to the project.

A well-structured workspace ensures clarity, enabling team members to access information quickly and collaborate efficiently.

Organizing Project Pages and Components

Each project may have different areas of focus, which can be organized using Loop Pages. Here's an example of how you might structure a project workspace:

- Project Overview Page – Contains project objectives, key milestones, and a summary of deliverables.

- Task Management Page – Lists assigned tasks, deadlines, and progress updates.

- Meeting Notes Page – Stores discussions, decisions, and action points from team meetings.

- Resource Hub Page – Houses important files, links, and reference materials.

Each page can include Loop Components like task lists, progress trackers, and collaborative notes, ensuring that all aspects of the project remain accessible and up to date.

---

3. Key Microsoft Loop Features for Project Management

Task Lists and Assignments

One of the most powerful features of Loop is its ability to create and manage task lists collaboratively.

How to Create a Task List in Loop:

1. Navigate to the Task Management Page within your project workspace.

2. Insert a Task List Component by typing "/task list" and selecting the option.

3. Add tasks, assign owners, and set due dates directly within the list.

4. Use @mentions to notify team members of their assigned tasks.

5. Track completion status with real-time updates.

Progress Tracking and Milestone Management

Keeping a project on track requires continuous monitoring of progress. Microsoft Loop provides multiple ways to track and visualize progress:

- Checklists and Status Updates – Use task components to indicate completed and pending tasks.

- Milestone Tracking – Create a dedicated Milestone Table that outlines key dates and progress.

- Dynamic Updates – Loop Components update automatically across Microsoft Teams and Outlook, ensuring visibility.

Example Milestone Table in Loop:

Milestone	Owner	Due Date	Status
Project Kickoff	Alice	Feb 15	✓ Completed
Initial Draft Submission	Bob	Mar 5	☐ In Progress
Final Approval	Team	Apr 10	☐ Pending

These tools help project managers quickly assess project health and identify bottlenecks.

4. Integrating Loop with Other Microsoft 365 Tools

Microsoft Teams for Communication

- Loop Components can be embedded within Teams chats and channels, allowing discussions and updates to happen in real time.

- Project updates can be shared as dynamic Loop Components, reducing the need for static reports.

- Teams notifications can be automated using Power Automate (covered in Section 4.1.1).

Planner for Task Management

While Loop provides a flexible workspace, Microsoft Planner adds structured task tracking. Teams can:

- Sync Loop task lists with Planner for advanced tracking.

- Use Planner's Kanban-style board to visualize work in progress.

- Set reminders and due dates that integrate with Outlook.

SharePoint and OneDrive for File Management

Managing project documents efficiently is crucial. Teams can:

- Embed SharePoint documents within Loop Pages for easy reference.

- Use OneDrive links to ensure the latest versions of files are accessible.

- Automatically sync Loop Workspaces with project folders.

By integrating these tools, Loop serves as a central hub for all project-related resources.

5. Best Practices for Using Loop in Project Management

To maximize efficiency, teams should follow these best practices:

Establish Clear Naming Conventions

- Use standardized naming for pages and components (e.g., "Project Updates - March 2025").

- Tag Loop Components appropriately to improve searchability.

Keep Information Organized

- Regularly review and update project pages to remove outdated information.

- Assign a team member as a Loop Workspace Manager to oversee organization.

Promote Adoption and Training

- Encourage team members to use Loop by conducting training sessions.

- Provide guidelines on Loop best practices to ensure consistency.

6. Case Study: Using Microsoft Loop for a Marketing Campaign

To illustrate Loop's effectiveness, consider a marketing campaign project managed entirely within Loop.

Scenario:

A marketing team is launching a new product campaign and needs to coordinate efforts across different departments.

Implementation in Loop:

1. A Project Workspace is created with dedicated pages for strategy, content, and analytics.

2. Loop Components for task lists and brainstorming notes are embedded in Teams chats.

3. The team tracks milestones and KPIs using a progress dashboard.

4. Integration with Outlook ensures that updates and reminders are sent automatically.

Results:

- Increased team alignment through real-time collaboration.

- Improved project transparency with dynamic status updates.

- Faster decision-making with centralized access to information.

Conclusion

Microsoft Loop is revolutionizing project management by offering a flexible, real-time, and integrated workspace for teams. By leveraging Loop's features—task lists, milestone tracking, and seamless integration with Microsoft 365—teams can enhance productivity and streamline project execution.

For best results, combine Loop with Teams, Planner, and SharePoint, ensuring that all project components are well-connected. As Microsoft Loop continues to evolve, adopting best practices will help organizations maximize its potential and drive successful project outcomes.

🚀 Ready to optimize your projects? Start using Microsoft Loop today!

4.2 Integrating Loop with Other Microsoft 365 Apps

4.2.1 Embedding Loop Components in Outlook

Microsoft Loop is designed to enhance collaboration across different Microsoft 365 applications. One of the most powerful integrations is with Microsoft Outlook, allowing users to embed Loop components directly into emails, calendar events, and shared notes. This integration makes it easier for teams to collaborate in real time without switching between applications.

In this section, we will explore how to embed Loop components in Outlook, their benefits, and best practices to maximize efficiency.

Understanding Loop Components in Outlook

Loop components are dynamic, interactive content blocks that can be embedded in various Microsoft 365 apps, including Outlook. These components allow multiple users to edit and update information in real time, ensuring that everyone has the latest data. Some common Loop components that can be embedded in Outlook include:

- **Task Lists** – Assign and track tasks within an email thread.
- **Tables** – Share structured data that updates dynamically.
- **Checklists** – Collaborate on to-do lists with real-time updates.
- **Notes** – Share meeting notes that can be edited by multiple participants.
- **Progress Trackers** – Monitor project updates within an email.

Embedding these components into Outlook emails or calendar events enables seamless communication, reducing the need for endless email threads and document attachments.

How to Embed Loop Components in Outlook Emails

Step 1: Open a New Email in Outlook

To begin, open Outlook and click on **"New Email"** to compose a new message. You can also reply to an existing email thread where you want to include a Loop component.

Step 2: Insert a Loop Component

1. In the email composition window, click on the **Loop icon** in the toolbar.

2. Select the type of Loop component you want to embed, such as a task list, table, or checklist.

3. The selected component will appear in the body of the email. You can start adding content immediately.

Step 3: Collaborate in Real Time

- Once the Loop component is embedded, recipients of the email can **edit it directly within the email thread** without needing to switch to another app.

- Any changes made to the component will **sync across all Outlook clients**, ensuring that everyone is working with the latest version.

Step 4: Send the Email

After inserting and formatting the Loop component, click **"Send"** to share it with your recipients. The embedded component remains interactive, meaning updates will be visible to all participants even after the email is sent.

Embedding Loop Components in Outlook Calendar Events

Step 1: Open Outlook Calendar

Navigate to your Outlook calendar and create a new meeting or edit an existing event.

Step 2: Insert a Loop Component in the Meeting Notes

1. In the meeting details section, look for the **"Loop Components"** button.

2. Choose a Loop component such as a meeting agenda, action items, or brainstorming notes.

3. The component will be embedded in the meeting invitation.

Step 3: Collaborate Before, During, and After the Meeting

- Before the Meeting: Participants can add agenda items or topics before the meeting starts.

- During the Meeting: Attendees can take notes in real time within the Loop component.

- After the Meeting: The Loop component remains accessible in the calendar event, allowing for continuous updates and follow-ups.

Benefits of Using Loop Components in Outlook

Real-Time Collaboration

Loop components update instantly, allowing team members to contribute simultaneously without version control issues.

Reduced Email Clutter

Instead of long email threads with multiple replies, a single email with an embedded Loop component keeps all updates in one place.

Seamless Integration with Microsoft 365

Since Loop is part of Microsoft 365, it works naturally with other tools like Teams, OneNote, and SharePoint, making collaboration more efficient.

Improved Meeting Productivity

Embedding Loop components in calendar events ensures that meeting agendas, notes, and action items are always accessible and up-to-date.

Best Practices for Using Loop Components in Outlook

1. Use the Right Loop Component for Each Use Case

- Use task lists for action items.

- Use tables for structured data.

- Use notes for collaborative meeting minutes.

2. Keep Emails Concise and Focused

- Instead of writing lengthy emails, let the Loop component do the work by keeping all necessary information in one place.

3. Encourage Team Collaboration

- Educate your team on the benefits of Loop components and encourage them to engage directly within the component instead of sending additional emails.

4. Combine Loop with Other Microsoft 365 Apps

- Link your Loop components in Outlook to Teams conversations, OneNote pages, or Planner tasks for a more connected workflow.

Troubleshooting Common Issues

Issue 1: Loop Component Not Displaying in Outlook

- Ensure that Microsoft 365 is up to date.

- Check if Loop is enabled for your organization by contacting your IT admin.

Issue 2: Changes Not Syncing in Real-Time

- Refresh Outlook or close and reopen the email thread.

- Ensure that all participants have permission to edit the Loop component.

Issue 3: Unable to Insert Loop Components in Emails

- Verify that you are using Outlook on the web or the latest desktop version (older versions may not support Loop).

Conclusion

Embedding Loop components in Outlook is a game-changer for team collaboration, streamlining workflows, and reducing unnecessary email back-and-forth. Whether you're embedding a task list in an email or adding a meeting agenda to a calendar invite, Loop helps teams stay organized and efficient.

By leveraging this feature, users can enhance communication, improve productivity, and create a more connected workplace within Microsoft 365.

In the next section, we will explore how to use Loop with OneNote and Planner, expanding on its capabilities to further integrate with your daily workflows.

4.2.2 Using Loop with OneNote and Planner

Microsoft Loop is a powerful tool for collaboration, but its true potential is unlocked when integrated with other Microsoft 365 applications. Two key apps that complement Loop's functionality are **OneNote** and **Planner**. OneNote is a digital notebook designed for capturing and organizing ideas, while Planner is a project management tool that helps teams track tasks and deadlines. When used together with Loop, these apps enhance teamwork, improve information organization, and streamline project execution.

This section explores how you can integrate **Loop with OneNote and Planner**, including practical use cases, step-by-step instructions, and best practices for maximizing efficiency.

Why Integrate Microsoft Loop with OneNote and Planner?

1. Enhancing Note-Taking and Documentation (OneNote + Loop)

- OneNote is a robust tool for taking notes, documenting meeting minutes, and capturing brainstorming sessions.

- Loop's dynamic components allow for real-time collaboration and sharing inside OneNote.

- By integrating Loop with OneNote, users can embed live components such as task lists, tables, and ideas that update in real time, eliminating version control issues.

2. Streamlining Task and Project Management (Planner + Loop)

- Planner is designed to manage tasks, assign responsibilities, and track deadlines.

- Loop can be used to embed Planner task lists inside workspaces, ensuring all team members have instant visibility into project status.

- By integrating these two tools, teams can keep discussions, project planning, and execution all in one place, reducing the need for constant app switching.

Integrating Microsoft Loop with OneNote

Step 1: Embedding Loop Components in OneNote

1. **Open OneNote** and navigate to the section where you want to add a Loop component.

2. In Microsoft Loop, create a new **Loop component** (e.g., a task list, table, or checklist).

3. Click the **Copy Link** button on the Loop component.

4. Switch to OneNote and paste the link into your notebook.

5. The component will appear as an interactive **live link**, allowing users to edit it directly from OneNote.

⬧ **Use Case:** Imagine a marketing team taking notes during a brainstorming session in OneNote. They can insert a **Loop table** to collect campaign ideas and update it in real time, ensuring that everyone has access to the latest input.

Step 2: Using OneNote as a Reference Hub for Loop Workspaces

- Instead of creating scattered notes, teams can use OneNote as a **centralized hub** for storing meeting notes, project outlines, and research.

- A **Loop workspace link** can be embedded in OneNote for easy access to all related discussions, documents, and tasks.

⬧ **Use Case:** A product development team could keep a OneNote notebook with notes on different features and insert **Loop workspace links** so that team members can jump directly into discussions.

Step 3: Syncing Notes from OneNote into Loop Workspaces

- OneNote allows users to **copy and paste structured content** into Loop pages.

- This is useful for transferring well-organized information into a Loop component where it can be actively discussed and refined.

⬧ **Use Case:** A manager who takes meeting minutes in OneNote can quickly copy important action items into a **Loop task list** to track follow-ups.

Integrating Microsoft Loop with Planner

Step 1: Embedding Planner Task Lists in Loop

1. Open **Microsoft Planner** and navigate to your desired project board.

2. Select the **task list** you want to integrate with Loop.

3. Click on the **three-dot menu (⬚)** next to the task list and choose **Copy Link**.

4. Open **Microsoft Loop**, go to the appropriate workspace or page, and paste the Planner link.

5. The task list will appear as an interactive link, allowing users to track progress from within Loop.

◆ **Use Case:** A software development team working on a new feature can embed a **Planner task list** inside Loop to ensure engineers and designers can track their assignments and deadlines in one place.

Step 2: Creating a Dynamic Task List with Loop Components

- Instead of just linking to Planner, teams can use **Loop's task list component** for real-time task tracking.

- Tasks assigned in Loop can later be **manually added to Planner** for full project visibility.

◆ **Use Case:** A sales team can use a Loop task list to jot down action items after a strategy meeting. Later, the manager can move critical tasks into Planner for long-term tracking.

Step 3: Automating Task Sync Between Loop and Planner (Using Power Automate)

- **Microsoft Power Automate** allows users to create workflows that sync Loop tasks with Planner.

- A common automation is:

   o **Trigger:** When a task is created in a Loop component.

   o **Action:** The task is automatically added to a specific Planner project.

- This ensures that all tasks are tracked systematically without manual effort.

✦ **Use Case:** A marketing manager can set up a **workflow** so that any new promotional campaign tasks created in Loop are instantly logged into Planner for tracking.

Best Practices for Using Loop with OneNote and Planner

1. Establish Clear Workflow Guidelines

- Decide **where** different types of information should live:
    - Use **OneNote** for static information and documentation.
    - Use **Loop** for real-time collaboration.
    - Use **Planner** for structured project tracking.

2. Keep Workspaces and Notes Organized

- Tag and categorize OneNote pages to match **Loop workspaces**.
- Use **consistent naming conventions** for Loop pages and Planner tasks.

3. Use Automation to Minimize Manual Updates

- Leverage Power Automate to keep Loop and Planner in sync.
- Automate reminders so that tasks assigned in Loop are followed up in Planner.

4. Encourage Team Adoption

- Train your team on how to **embed, sync, and track** content across Loop, OneNote, and Planner.
- Provide templates for common workflows to **reduce setup time**.

Conclusion

Integrating Microsoft Loop with OneNote and Planner creates a powerful collaboration ecosystem that combines note-taking, real-time editing, and task management in one seamless workflow.

- **OneNote** ensures that ideas and meeting notes are structured and easily accessible.
- **Loop** enables real-time collaboration, keeping discussions and updates dynamic.

- **Planner** ensures that projects stay on track with assigned tasks and deadlines.

By strategically using these tools together, teams can enhance productivity, improve communication, and streamline project execution. Whether you are brainstorming, planning, or executing, the combination of Loop, OneNote, and Planner ensures that all information stays organized, up-to-date, and actionable.

4.2.3 Syncing Loop with SharePoint and OneDrive

Introduction

Microsoft Loop is designed to seamlessly integrate with the Microsoft 365 ecosystem, and one of its most powerful capabilities is its synchronization with SharePoint and OneDrive. These integrations enable users to store, manage, and share Loop components, pages, and workspaces efficiently across teams and organizations. By syncing Loop with SharePoint and OneDrive, users can ensure content accessibility, improve collaboration, and maintain a structured workflow while leveraging Microsoft's cloud storage capabilities.

This section will explore how Microsoft Loop interacts with SharePoint and OneDrive, how to set up syncing, best practices for managing Loop content within these platforms, and troubleshooting common issues.

Understanding the Integration Between Loop, SharePoint, and OneDrive

Before diving into the technical setup, it is essential to understand how Microsoft Loop integrates with SharePoint and OneDrive:

1. **Loop and SharePoint**

   o SharePoint serves as the backend storage system for Loop workspaces and pages.

   o Loop components that are shared within an organization are typically stored in a connected SharePoint document library.

   o Permissions in SharePoint control how users access and edit Loop content, ensuring security and data governance.

2. **Loop and OneDrive**

- o OneDrive acts as the personal storage location for Loop components that an individual user creates and does not share with others.

- o Loop content stored in OneDrive can be managed like any other file, benefiting from OneDrive's file versioning, syncing, and sharing capabilities.

- o Users can move Loop components from OneDrive to SharePoint when they need team collaboration.

Why Sync Loop with SharePoint and OneDrive?

- Centralized Document Management: Organize all Loop components and workspaces within a structured storage system.

- Seamless Collaboration: Share content across teams and departments with controlled access.

- Data Security and Compliance: Use SharePoint and OneDrive's security policies to protect sensitive information.

- Cross-Device Accessibility: Access Loop components on different devices with automatic synchronization.

Setting Up Microsoft Loop Sync with SharePoint

By default, Loop workspaces and components are stored within **Microsoft 365 cloud storage**, but users can configure them to sync with SharePoint for better organization and team collaboration.

Step 1: Identify the SharePoint Storage Location

- Each Microsoft 365 Group has an associated SharePoint document library.

- When a Loop component is shared with a team, it is automatically stored in the corresponding SharePoint site under the Documents folder.

- Users can manually move Loop content to a different SharePoint site if needed.

Step 2: Sync Loop Components with SharePoint

To sync a Loop component or workspace with SharePoint:

1. Open the Loop component in Microsoft Loop.

2. Click on the Share button.

3. Select "Save to SharePoint" and choose the appropriate document library or folder.

4. The component will now be stored in SharePoint and accessible via Microsoft Teams, SharePoint Online, and OneDrive.

Step 3: Managing SharePoint Permissions for Loop Components

To ensure proper access control:

- Navigate to the SharePoint document library where the Loop component is stored.

- Click on Manage Access and specify whether users have view, edit, or owner permissions.

- Use SharePoint security groups to assign permissions to entire teams rather than individual users.

Setting Up Microsoft Loop Sync with OneDrive

When working individually or in small teams, storing Loop components in OneDrive offers flexibility and ease of access.

Step 1: Check OneDrive Storage for Loop Components

By default, personal Loop components are stored in OneDrive under the "Loop Components" folder. To locate them:

- Open OneDrive in your browser or file explorer.

- Navigate to Documents > Loop Components.

- Find the Loop component you want to sync across devices.

Step 2: Sharing Loop Components from OneDrive

Unlike SharePoint, OneDrive provides personal storage but allows sharing with external users. To share a Loop component from OneDrive:

1. Open OneDrive and locate the Loop component.

2. Click "Share" and enter the recipient's email address.

3. Choose whether they can view or edit the document.

4. Click "Send", and the recipient will receive a link to the Loop component.

Step 3: Moving a Loop Component from OneDrive to SharePoint

If a Loop component initially created in OneDrive needs to be moved to SharePoint for broader collaboration:

1. Open OneDrive and find the component.

2. Click Move To > Select SharePoint Site > Choose the appropriate folder.

3. Confirm the move. The component is now available in SharePoint and follows its permission settings.

Best Practices for Syncing Loop with SharePoint and OneDrive

To optimize workflow efficiency and data security, consider these best practices:

1. Use SharePoint for Team Collaboration, OneDrive for Personal Work

- Store Loop components in SharePoint when multiple users need real-time access and collaboration.

- Use OneDrive for drafts, personal notes, or temporary storage.

2. Set Up Clear Naming Conventions

- Create structured folder names in SharePoint (e.g., "Marketing - Loop Components" or "HR Collaboration - Loop").

- Standardize Loop component names to prevent confusion (e.g., "Q1_Project_Updates_Loop").

3. Enable Version History for Important Loop Documents

- SharePoint and OneDrive both support versioning, which allows tracking changes over time.

- This feature ensures data recovery in case of accidental deletions or edits.

4. Use Microsoft Teams for Easy Access to Loop Components

- Since Teams and SharePoint are interconnected, storing Loop components in SharePoint makes them easily accessible in Teams.

- Pin important Loop components in Teams channels for quick reference.

5. Monitor Permissions Regularly

- Regularly audit permissions in SharePoint to avoid unauthorized access.

- Use OneDrive's expiration date feature for shared links to ensure temporary access.

Troubleshooting Common Issues

Issue 1: Loop Component Not Syncing with SharePoint

Solution:

- Ensure the user has edit permissions on the SharePoint library.

- Check if the SharePoint storage limit has been exceeded.

- Refresh the browser or restart the Microsoft Loop application.

Issue 2: OneDrive Does Not Show the Loop Components Folder

Solution:

- Confirm that Microsoft Loop is enabled in your Microsoft 365 admin settings.

- Manually create a "Loop Components" folder in OneDrive and move Loop content into it.

Issue 3: Shared Loop Components Show as Read-Only

Solution:

- Verify sharing permissions in OneDrive or SharePoint.

- If the recipient cannot edit, update their access level to "Can Edit" in the sharing settings.

Conclusion

Syncing Microsoft Loop with SharePoint and OneDrive allows for seamless collaboration, structured data management, and improved workflow efficiency. By understanding how Loop interacts with these cloud storage platforms, users can maximize productivity, maintain security, and optimize teamwork within Microsoft 365.

By following the step-by-step setup guide, best practices, and troubleshooting tips, users can leverage the full power of Microsoft Loop while ensuring their content is organized, accessible, and securely managed.

4.3 Personalizing Your Loop Workspaces

4.3.1 Customizing Layouts and Themes

Microsoft Loop is designed to be a highly flexible and dynamic collaboration tool. However, simply using its default setup may not provide the most efficient experience. Customizing layouts and themes in Loop can significantly enhance productivity, improve clarity, and make workspaces visually appealing. This section will guide you through the various ways to tailor your Loop workspaces to meet your needs, covering layout structuring, visual customization, and best practices for optimizing usability.

1. Understanding the Importance of Customization

1.1 Why Customize Your Loop Workspace?

Customization is not just about making a workspace look better—it's about creating an environment that supports efficiency, collaboration, and ease of use. A well-structured workspace:

- Improves navigation and accessibility.

- Enhances readability and content organization.

- Reduces clutter, making information easier to find.

- Helps teams stay aligned with branding and corporate aesthetics.

Whether you're managing a personal workspace or a team collaboration hub, optimizing the layout and appearance of Loop can significantly impact productivity and engagement.

1.2 Key Elements of Layout and Theme Customization

Before diving into the customization process, it's important to understand the core components that influence a Loop workspace's look and feel:

- Workspaces and Pages – The structural foundation of Loop.

- Sections and Content Blocks – How information is arranged within a page.

- Themes and Color Schemes – Visual elements that define the workspace's aesthetic.

- Fonts and Text Styles – Typography choices that enhance readability.

By effectively managing these elements, you can create an environment that is both functional and visually appealing.

2. Structuring Your Layout for Maximum Efficiency

2.1 Organizing Workspaces and Pages

The foundation of an efficient Loop workspace starts with its structure. Consider the following best practices when organizing workspaces and pages:

2.1.1 Defining Your Workspace Structure

- Use Workspaces for Broad Categories: If you manage multiple projects or departments, create separate workspaces for each. For example, a marketing team may have workspaces for "Campaign Management," "Content Creation," and "Analytics & Reporting."

- Keep It Simple: Avoid excessive nesting of pages. Too many sub-pages can make navigation overwhelming.

- Standardize Naming Conventions: Use clear, consistent names for workspaces and pages to avoid confusion.

2.1.2 Structuring Pages for Clarity

- Use Headers and Sections: Break content into meaningful sections using headers (H1, H2, H3) to improve readability.

- Incorporate Tables and Bullet Points: Instead of long paragraphs, use tables and lists to present information concisely.

- Utilize White Space: Avoid cluttered pages by ensuring ample spacing between elements.

2.2 Enhancing Navigation with Link Structures

A well-structured Loop workspace should make it easy to navigate between different pages and components.

2.2.1 Adding Internal Links for Quick Access

- Use hyperlinks within Loop to connect related pages.

- Create a table of contents for longer pages.

- Add back-to-top buttons for improved user experience.

2.2.2 Creating a Dashboard-Style Homepage

A dashboard page can serve as a control center for your workspace, providing quick access to essential pages and tools. Consider adding:

- Navigation menus with links to key pages.

- Quick action buttons for common tasks (e.g., "Create a New Page").

- Recent activity feeds to track updates.

3. Customizing Themes and Visual Styles

3.1 Choosing the Right Theme for Your Workspace

Microsoft Loop offers a variety of customization options to tailor the workspace's appearance.

3.1.1 Light vs. Dark Mode

- Light Mode: Best for bright environments, improving visibility.

- Dark Mode: Reduces eye strain in low-light settings and saves battery life on mobile devices.

3.1.2 Custom Color Schemes

Users can select from preset themes or customize colors to align with personal or company branding. Consider:

- Neutral tones for a professional look.

- Vibrant colors to enhance creativity and engagement.

- Brand-aligned colors for corporate consistency.

3.2 Adjusting Font Styles and Sizes

Typography plays a key role in readability and accessibility.

3.2.1 Selecting the Right Font

- Sans-serif fonts (e.g., Arial, Calibri) – Best for digital reading.

- Serif fonts (e.g., Times New Roman, Georgia) – Suitable for formal documents.

- Monospace fonts (e.g., Courier New) – Ideal for displaying code or technical content.

3.2.2 Font Size and Spacing Recommendations

- Headings: Use larger font sizes (18-24 pt) for section titles.

- Body text: Keep at a readable size (12-16 pt).

- Line spacing: Maintain at least 1.5x for easy reading.

---

4. Creating Reusable Templates for Consistency

4.1 Why Use Templates?

Templates save time and ensure consistency across Loop pages. Common use cases include:

- Meeting notes templates with pre-filled agenda sections.

- Project management templates for tracking progress.

- Task assignment templates for team collaboration.

4.2 Setting Up a Template in Microsoft Loop

1. Create a new page with the desired structure.

2. Format text and sections based on your needs.

3. Save as a template so it can be reused for future pages.

4.3 Managing and Updating Templates

- Periodically review and refine templates to keep them relevant.

- Share templates with team members to standardize workflows.

---

5. Best Practices for Workspace Customization

5.1 Keeping Workspaces Organized

- Use **consistent naming conventions** for pages and workspaces.

- Archive or delete outdated content regularly.

- Pin important pages for quick access.

5.2 Balancing Aesthetics with Functionality

- Avoid excessive decorations that clutter the interface.

- Use color and formatting strategically to highlight key information.

5.3 Ensuring Accessibility and Inclusivity

- Choose **high-contrast colors** for better readability.

- Enable **screen reader compatibility** for visually impaired users.

- Provide **alternative text** for images and embedded content.

Conclusion

Customizing Microsoft Loop workspaces goes beyond aesthetics—it enhances usability, collaboration, and efficiency. By thoughtfully structuring pages, optimizing navigation, applying consistent themes, and using templates, you can create an environment that aligns with your workflow and team objectives.

Whether you're a solo user optimizing personal projects or a team leader designing an efficient workspace, applying these best practices will ensure that Microsoft Loop becomes a powerful tool for smarter collaboration.

4.3.2 Using Templates for Repeated Workflows

Introduction to Loop Templates

One of the most powerful ways to maximize efficiency in Microsoft Loop is by using templates for repeated workflows. Whether you're managing a recurring project, organizing team meetings, or maintaining a structured note-taking system, templates help standardize processes and reduce redundant setup work.

In this section, we'll explore how to create, customize, and effectively utilize templates in Microsoft Loop. By the end of this chapter, you'll be able to design your own templates to streamline collaboration and ensure consistency across your workspaces.

Why Use Templates in Microsoft Loop?

Using templates in Microsoft Loop brings several advantages, including:

- **Time Efficiency:** No need to recreate the same structure for recurring tasks.

- **Consistency:** Ensures uniformity in workflow across teams and projects.

- **Ease of Use:** Reduces errors and helps new team members onboard quickly.

- **Scalability:** Easily replicable for larger projects or expanding teams.

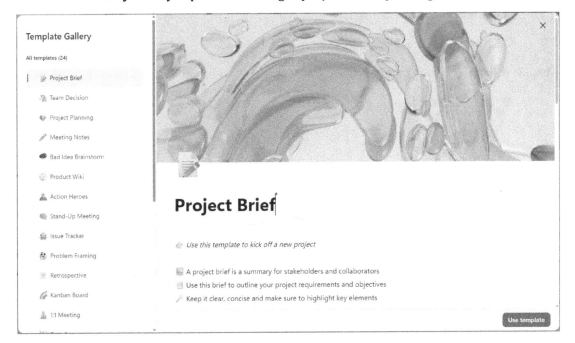

Templates are particularly useful for:

- Weekly and monthly reports

- Recurring meetings

- Task management workflows

- Standardized brainstorming sessions

- Project planning and tracking

Creating a Template in Microsoft Loop

To create a reusable template in Microsoft Loop, follow these steps:

Step 1: Identify the Workflow to Template

Before creating a template, determine what kind of process needs standardization. Some common examples include:

- A meeting agenda template

- A project status update template

- A content calendar template

- A task management template

Step 2: Build the Structure in a Loop Page

1. Open Microsoft Loop and navigate to your workspace.

2. Click **New Page** to create a blank template.

3. Structure your page using Loop components such as:

   o Text Components for descriptions and instructions.

   o Tables to organize data or assign tasks.

   o Task Lists for tracking actions.

   o Mentions (@) to designate responsibilities.

   o Embedded Links or Files for additional resources.

Example: If you are creating a **Meeting Notes Template**, you may structure it like this:

Weekly Team Meeting Notes

▦ Date: [Insert Date]

◎ Meeting Goal: [Define Objective]

☐ Attendees: @Mention Participants

📝 Agenda Items

1. [Topic 1]

2. [Topic 2]

3. [Topic 3]

📌 Key Discussion Points

- [Discussion Topic 1]

- [Discussion Topic 2]

Step 3: Save the Page as a Template

After structuring the page:

1. Click on the More Options (:) button at the top right.

2. Select Save as Template or Duplicate Page for Future Use (depending on availability in your Loop version).

3. Name the template and store it in a designated workspace for easy access.

Using and Managing Loop Templates

Applying a Template to a New Page

Once your template is saved, you can quickly reuse it:

1. Open a Loop workspace where you want to use the template.

2. Click **New Page → Choose from Templates** (if available).

3. Select your saved template from the list.

4. Modify the details as needed and start working immediately.

Modifying an Existing Template

Templates should be adaptable to fit evolving needs. To edit a saved template:

1. Locate the template in your workspace.

2. Open the page and make the necessary modifications.

3. Save the updated version as a **new template** or overwrite the existing one.

Best Practices for Using Templates in Microsoft Loop

1. Keep Templates Simple and Flexible

A good template should provide a structure without being too rigid. Allow space for customization based on project-specific needs.

2. Use Standard Naming Conventions

To keep templates organized, follow a clear naming pattern, such as:

- "▦ [Template] Monthly Report"

- "🚀 [Template] Project Kickoff"

- "✓ [Template] Task Management"

3. Incorporate Collaboration Elements

Use @mentions, dynamic checklists, and embedded files to encourage real-time updates and team participation.

4. Regularly Review and Update Templates

Templates should evolve based on feedback and new requirements. Schedule periodic reviews to refine them for better usability.

5. Store Templates in a Dedicated Section

Create a "Templates" workspace in Loop where team members can easily access and apply templates.

Real-World Use Cases of Microsoft Loop Templates

1. Project Kickoff Template

💡 **Purpose:** Standardizes the project initiation process.
📌 **Key Components:**

- Project goals and objectives

- Key stakeholders and responsibilities

- Initial timeline and milestones

- Resource links and reference materials

2. Weekly Team Standup Template

💡 **Purpose:** Organizes quick updates on ongoing tasks.
📌 **Key Components:**

- Tasks completed last week

- Current focus areas

- Blockers and challenges

- Actionable next steps

3. Content Planning Template

💡 **Purpose:** Streamlines content strategy and publishing schedules.
📌 **Key Components:**

- Content calendar

- Assigned writers and deadlines

- Draft review process

- Distribution strategy

Conclusion

Using templates in Microsoft Loop simplifies repeated workflows, enhances team productivity, and ensures consistency. Whether for personal use, team collaboration, or large-scale project management, well-structured templates allow you to work smarter, not harder.

Start creating and refining your Loop templates today to optimize efficiency and improve workflow management across your organization!

4.3.3 Organizing Content for Maximum Efficiency

Organizing content effectively in Microsoft Loop is crucial for maintaining productivity, ensuring seamless collaboration, and maximizing the platform's potential. Whether you're working on a personal project, collaborating with a team, or managing complex workflows, a well-structured Loop workspace can save time and improve efficiency. In this section, we will explore best practices for organizing content in Loop workspaces, Loop pages, and Loop components to create an intuitive and highly functional workspace.

Best Practices for Organizing Loop Workspaces

1. Define Clear Workspaces for Different Projects or Teams

- Avoid clutter by creating dedicated workspaces for **specific teams, projects, or functions**.

- For example, instead of keeping all marketing content in one workspace, create separate ones like **"Marketing Strategy"**, **"Social Media Campaigns"**, and **"Content Creation"**.

- Keep workspace names clear and concise for easy identification.

2. Establish a Standard Naming Convention

- Use a consistent naming format for workspaces and pages.

- Example: **"Q1_2025_Product_Development"** instead of **"New Product"** to ensure clarity on scope and timeframe.

- Include dates, departments, or objectives in titles to make them self-explanatory.

3. Manage Workspace Members and Permissions Wisely

- Assign appropriate permissions to prevent unauthorized changes.

- Regularly review access rights to keep security and collaboration efficient.

- Use guest access settings when collaborating with external partners.

Structuring Loop Pages for Easy Navigation

1. Use Sections and Subsections for Logical Flow

- Break down pages into **clear sections** to avoid overwhelming users with too much information.

- Example structure for a marketing campaign:

    o   Campaign Overview

    o   Target Audience & Strategy

    o   Content Calendar & Deliverables

    o   Performance Metrics & Reporting

2. Implement a Table of Contents for Long Pages

- If a Loop Page contains multiple sections, create a table of contents (ToC) at the top.

- ToC helps users jump to relevant sections quickly, especially in large documents.

3. Link Related Pages and Content

- Instead of duplicating content, use internal links to connect related Loop pages.

- Example: Link a "Budget Planning" page within a "Project Roadmap" to allow team members to access financial data without redundancy.

Optimizing Loop Components for Maximum Efficiency

Loop components are reusable blocks of content that can be shared across different applications like Microsoft Teams, Outlook, and Word. To keep them organized:

1. Categorize Loop Components in Dedicated Pages

- Instead of scattering components across multiple pages, create dedicated pages to store frequently used ones.

- Example: A "Task Management" page with reusable task lists for different teams.

2. Tagging and Labeling Components for Easy Retrieval

- Use clear labels and tags within your Loop pages to make components easy to find.

- Example: A "Meeting Notes" component can be tagged with #WeeklyCheck-in #ClientMeetings for better organization.

3. Managing Shared Components Across Multiple Workspaces

- If a Loop component is used frequently across multiple workspaces, ensure it remains updated.

- Example: A "Team Goals" table shared in multiple projects should be linked to a master document to avoid inconsistencies.

Automating Content Organization for Efficiency

1. Using Power Automate to Keep Content Structured

- Set up automation to organize content with Power Automate.

- Example: Automatically move outdated pages to an "Archived" section to reduce clutter.

2. Implementing Auto-Tagging and Categorization

- Automate tagging for new pages and Loop components based on content type.

- Example: Any new task list component added to a workspace gets tagged as #ActionItems for easy filtering.

3. Scheduling Regular Content Reviews

- Set up reminders to review and clean up Loop pages every month or quarter.

- Archive completed projects and remove redundant pages to keep the workspace clean.

Ensuring Long-Term Maintainability of Loop Workspaces

1. Periodically Review and Clean Up Content

- Remove obsolete pages and components to maintain clarity.

- Example: Archive old versions of documents but keep the latest iteration accessible.

2. Establish Governance Policies for Loop Usage

- Set workspace guidelines to standardize page creation, sharing, and component usage.

- Example: A best practices document pinned in every workspace.

3. Educate Team Members on Organizational Standards

- Provide training on best practices for organizing Loop content.

- Example: Host a monthly workshop to ensure all users understand workspace structures.

Conclusion

Efficiently organizing Microsoft Loop workspaces, pages, and components is essential for maximizing productivity and ensuring seamless collaboration. By implementing clear naming conventions, structured pages, categorized components, and automation, teams can reduce clutter, improve workflow efficiency, and make information retrieval easier.

By following the strategies outlined in this section, you will transform Microsoft Loop into a well-structured, intuitive, and highly productive tool that enhances team collaboration and personal efficiency.

CHAPTER V
Microsoft Loop for Different Use Cases

5.1 Using Loop for Personal Productivity

5.1.1 Organizing Daily Tasks and Notes

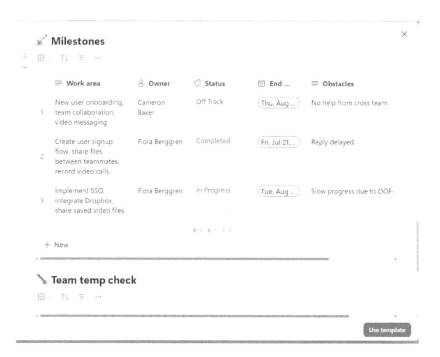

In today's fast-paced digital world, staying organized is essential for productivity. Microsoft Loop provides a dynamic and flexible way to manage daily tasks, notes, and to-do lists efficiently. Whether you are a student managing assignments, a freelancer handling multiple projects, or a professional keeping track of meetings and priorities, Loop offers a collaborative and interactive workspace to streamline your workflow.

This section will guide you through the process of organizing daily tasks and notes using Microsoft Loop. You will learn how to create structured to-do lists, categorize notes, and enhance productivity by integrating Loop with other Microsoft 365 applications.

1. Why Use Microsoft Loop for Daily Task Management?

Microsoft Loop is different from traditional note-taking apps and task managers because it provides:

- **Real-time collaboration:** Edit notes and to-do lists dynamically with updates syncing across all devices.

- **Flexible structure:** Unlike rigid task management tools, Loop allows users to create a fluid and adaptable workflow.

- **Integration with Microsoft 365:** Seamlessly connect with Outlook, Teams, OneNote, and other applications to centralize your tasks.

- **Interactive components:** Use tables, lists, and checkboxes to track progress efficiently.

With these features, Microsoft Loop becomes a powerful tool for managing tasks and notes without getting lost in endless lists or disorganized documents.

2. Creating a Daily Task List in Microsoft Loop

A well-structured task list is essential for productivity. Here's how you can create one in Microsoft Loop:

Step 1: Create a New Loop Page for Tasks

1. Open Microsoft Loop and navigate to your workspace.

2. Click on New Page and name it something like "Daily Tasks" or "Personal To-Do List."

3. Add an introductory section outlining your priorities for the day.

Step 2: Use a Task List Component

1. Click on the Insert (+) button and select Task List.

2. Start adding tasks to the list, such as:

    o   Morning Routine: Check emails, review schedule.

    o   Work Tasks: Complete report, attend meetings.

    o   Personal Tasks: Buy groceries, go to the gym.

3. Assign due dates, priorities, and task categories if needed.

Step 3: Organize Tasks with Sections and Categories

*   Group similar tasks together (e.g., work vs. personal tasks).

*   Use color coding or tags to identify high-priority items.

*   Break large tasks into subtasks for better clarity.

Step 4: Set Task Reminders and Notifications

*   Microsoft Loop allows task components to integrate with Outlook and Microsoft To Do, enabling reminders.

*   Assign deadlines and set up notifications to ensure completion.

By structuring tasks in this way, you create a streamlined workflow that keeps you focused throughout the day.

3. Taking Notes Efficiently with Microsoft Loop

Taking effective notes is crucial for managing information, brainstorming ideas, and tracking progress. Here's how Microsoft Loop can help:

Step 1: Create a Dedicated Note-Taking Page

1. Navigate to your Loop workspace and create a new page titled "Daily Notes" or "Meeting Notes."

2. Use Loop Text Components to write down key points.

3. Utilize @mentions to highlight important references or people involved.

Step 2: Structure Notes with Tables and Bullet Points

Instead of writing long paragraphs, structure notes using:

- Tables for comparisons and summaries.

- Bullet points for listing key takeaways.

- Checklists for action items resulting from discussions.

Step 3: Enhance Notes with Embedded Files and Links

- Embed Word documents, Excel sheets, and PowerPoint presentations directly into the page.

- Add hyperlinks to relevant resources for easy access.

Step 4: Convert Notes into Actionable Tasks

- Highlight important takeaways and convert them into task components.

- Assign deadlines and responsibilities to ensure follow-ups.

By implementing these steps, your notes remain organized and actionable, making it easier to track progress and recall key information.

4. Using Loop Components to Enhance Personal Productivity

Loop offers several interactive components that can boost personal efficiency:

Checklists for Task Tracking

- Instead of maintaining separate lists, use Loop Checklists to track progress dynamically.

- Tick off completed items, and they will automatically update for better visibility.

Tables for Data Organization

- Create tables to compare different projects, track expenses, or log activities.

- Customize columns for priority, deadline, and status tracking.

Embedded Calendars for Time Management

- Sync with Outlook Calendar to visualize deadlines and appointments.
- Use a Loop Calendar Component to track meetings, deadlines, and events.

Loop in Microsoft Teams for Better Collaboration

- Share your task list and notes in Teams for seamless integration with work discussions.
- Collaborate on shared projects while keeping personal notes private.

5. Best Practices for Organizing Daily Tasks and Notes in Loop

To maximize the benefits of Microsoft Loop, follow these best practices:

Keep Your Loop Workspaces Organized

- Create separate pages for work tasks, personal tasks, and general notes.
- Use consistent naming conventions to quickly find information.

Review and Update Tasks Daily

- Dedicate 5–10 minutes each morning to update your task list.
- Mark completed items and adjust priorities based on urgency.

Utilize Loop's Collaboration Features Wisely

- Keep personal notes private but share relevant content with teammates.
- Use @mentions to assign tasks to team members if needed.

Integrate Loop with Other Apps

- Sync Loop tasks with Microsoft To Do for better tracking.
- Use Power Automate to set up reminders and automate task updates.

Conclusion

Organizing daily tasks and notes in Microsoft Loop transforms your productivity by centralizing everything in a single, collaborative, and dynamic platform. Whether you're managing work projects, personal errands, or brainstorming ideas, Loop provides the flexibility and structure needed to stay on track.

By following the strategies outlined in this section, you can harness the full potential of Loop's task management and note-taking capabilities, ultimately leading to a more organized and efficient workflow.

Next Steps:

- Explore advanced task management techniques with Power Automate.

- Learn how to use Loop in team collaborations for better communication.

- Experiment with custom templates to optimize recurring workflows.

5.1.2 Managing Personal Projects with Loop

Introduction

Managing personal projects can be overwhelming, especially when juggling multiple tasks, deadlines, and resources. Microsoft Loop provides a flexible and intuitive workspace that helps individuals structure their projects, collaborate when needed, and track progress efficiently. Whether you're working on a side hustle, planning an event, or organizing personal goals, Loop offers powerful tools to streamline your workflow.

This section explores how to effectively use Microsoft Loop for personal project management, covering workspace setup, task organization, tracking progress, and leveraging integrations with Microsoft 365 apps.

1. Setting Up a Personal Project Workspace

Creating a Dedicated Loop Workspace

A Loop workspace serves as the foundation for organizing your personal projects. Instead of scattered notes, spreadsheets, or emails, you can centralize everything in one structured location.

To create a personal project workspace:

1. Open **Microsoft Loop** and click on **New Workspace**.

2. Name your workspace based on your project (e.g., "Freelance Design Portfolio" or "Wedding Planning").

3. Customize the workspace icon and color for easy recognition.

4. Invite collaborators if your project requires external input (optional).

Structuring Loop Pages for Better Organization

Within your workspace, Loop pages act as sections where you can break down different aspects of your project. Consider the following structure:

- Project Overview – Define objectives, key milestones, and a summary of what you aim to achieve.

- Task List – Keep track of to-dos, deadlines, and progress updates.

- Resources & Research – Store important links, documents, and reference materials.

- Budget & Expenses – Track spending if your project involves financial planning.

- Notes & Ideas – Jot down brainstorming notes or creative inspirations.

Each page can contain Loop components that make tracking, organizing, and updating information easy.

2. Organizing Tasks and Deadlines

Using the Task List Component for Action Items

Microsoft Loop's Task List component allows you to create interactive to-do lists directly within your project pages.

To set up a task list:

1. Open your Task List page.

2. Insert a Task List component by typing /task list and selecting it from the menu.

3. Add tasks with clear action items (e.g., "Create project outline" or "Contact suppliers").

4. Set due dates for each task to stay on schedule.

5. Assign tasks to yourself or collaborators if needed.

Prioritizing and Categorizing Tasks

To prevent feeling overwhelmed, categorize your tasks by priority and status:

- High Priority – Tasks that need immediate attention.

- Medium Priority – Important but flexible deadlines.

- Low Priority – Optional or long-term tasks.

You can also organize tasks by type:

- Research & Planning – Gathering information and brainstorming ideas.

- Execution – Actionable steps needed to complete the project.

- Review & Refinement – Quality checks and final touches.

Tracking Progress with Status Updates

Loop allows you to track task progress using status labels or updating task lists. A common approach includes:

- Not Started – Tasks yet to be worked on.

- In Progress – Tasks currently being worked on.

- Completed – Finished tasks.

Use checklists or insert a progress tracker component to visually monitor how far along you are in the project.

---

3. Enhancing Productivity with Loop Features

Using Loop's Collaboration Tools for External Input

Even for personal projects, you may need feedback or assistance from friends, mentors, or collaborators. Microsoft Loop allows you to:

- @Mention someone in a comment to ask for input.

- Share a specific Loop component (e.g., a budget table) without exposing the entire workspace.

- Use comment threads to discuss specific tasks or ideas.

Embedding External Content and Files

You can embed files from OneDrive, Google Drive, or websites directly into Loop pages. For example:

- If you're working on a writing project, embed a Word document with drafts.

- If you're organizing an event, embed a PowerPoint presentation with plans.

- If you need financial tracking, insert an Excel spreadsheet for budgeting.

To embed files, simply type /embed and paste the link to your document.

Automating Routine Tasks with Power Automate

If your project involves repetitive actions (e.g., setting reminders, syncing notes with Outlook), you can automate them using Power Automate:

1. Go to Power Automate and select "Create a Flow."

2. Choose triggers such as "When a new task is added in Loop".

3. Set automated actions, like sending email reminders or adding tasks to Microsoft To Do.

Automation helps reduce manual effort and ensures that no task is forgotten.

4. Monitoring Progress and Staying on Track

Visualizing Project Milestones

To track long-term progress, set milestones for your project. Example:

- Week 1: Research phase completed.

- Week 3: First draft ready.

- Week 5: Finalizing details.

Use a timeline component or an embedded calendar (via Microsoft Calendar or Planner) to visualize these milestones.

Reviewing and Refining Work

Regularly reviewing your project ensures continuous improvement. Loop's commenting and version history features help:

- Go back to previous versions if needed.

- Make incremental changes without losing previous work.

- Receive feedback from external reviewers.

Archiving Completed Projects

Once your project is complete, keep it accessible for future reference.

- Move finished projects to an "Archived" workspace in Loop.

- Export key documents to OneDrive for storage.

- Create a summary page for lessons learned and insights gained.

Conclusion

Microsoft Loop transforms personal project management by providing a centralized, flexible, and collaborative platform. With features like task tracking, embedded resources, collaboration tools, and automation, users can effectively manage projects of any scale.

By structuring workspaces effectively, leveraging Loop's task management tools, and integrating automation, you can stay organized, enhance productivity, and achieve personal project success with ease.

Now, let's move to the next section, where we explore Microsoft Loop for Team Collaboration and how it enhances remote work, brainstorming, and team meetings.

5.1.3 Creating a Digital Knowledge Hub

In today's fast-paced digital world, having a centralized space to store, organize, and retrieve information efficiently is crucial for productivity. A Digital Knowledge Hub serves as a repository of valuable insights, research, notes, and references that can be accessed anytime. Microsoft Loop provides the perfect platform to create a dynamic, easily searchable, and collaborative knowledge hub.

This section will guide you through the process of setting up a knowledge hub using Microsoft Loop, structuring information effectively, integrating external resources, and leveraging Loop's features to maintain an organized and accessible repository.

Understanding the Concept of a Digital Knowledge Hub

A Digital Knowledge Hub is more than just a collection of notes. It is a structured space where you can:

- Store important information in a way that is easy to retrieve.

- Link and interconnect ideas across different projects or topics.

- Collaborate with others on research, documentation, or learning materials.

- Update and refine content continuously as new insights emerge.

Traditionally, knowledge hubs have been created using tools like Notion, OneNote, and SharePoint, but Microsoft Loop introduces a new level of fluid collaboration and real-time content management, making it a powerful option for personal and professional knowledge management.

Setting Up Your Knowledge Hub in Microsoft Loop

Step 1: Creating a Dedicated Loop Workspace

To start building your Digital Knowledge Hub, create a separate Loop workspace dedicated to your personal or professional learning.

1. Open Microsoft Loop and navigate to the Workspaces section.

2. Click "+ New Workspace" and give it a meaningful name (e.g., "Personal Knowledge Hub" or "Research Repository").

3. Add a brief description to clarify the purpose of the workspace.

4. Choose who will have access (if it's just for you, keep it private; if you plan to share, add collaborators).

Step 2: Structuring Your Knowledge Hub with Pages

Loop Pages help you categorize information effectively. Some suggested sections include:

- General Knowledge – For random facts, insights, and key takeaways.

- Research Notes – A space to store articles, references, and citations.

- Books & Courses – Notes from books, podcasts, and online courses.

- Project Ideas & Brainstorming – A section for innovative thoughts.

- Personal Development – A space for skill-building, habits, and reflections.

To create these pages:

1. Inside your Loop Workspace, click "+ New Page" for each category.

2. Use headings, bullet points, and tables to structure content.

3. Pin frequently accessed pages to the **Favorites** section for easy retrieval.

Step 3: Using Loop Components for Dynamic Organization

Microsoft Loop allows you to create interactive components that can be reused across multiple workspaces or applications like Microsoft Teams, Outlook, and Word.

Some useful components for knowledge management:

- Task Lists – To track pending research or books to read.

- Tables – To compare different concepts or organize research findings.

- Checklists – To monitor progress on learning goals.

- Embedded Links & Media – To store videos, documents, or external resources.

By using these Loop Components, your knowledge hub remains interactive, structured, and easy to maintain.

Enhancing Your Knowledge Hub with External Integrations

Embedding Content from Microsoft 365 Apps

One of the strengths of Microsoft Loop is its deep integration with other Microsoft tools. Here's how you can enhance your Digital Knowledge Hub with external content:

1. Outlook Emails – Save important emails related to research or learning.

2. OneNote Integration – Sync your handwritten notes or sketches.

3. Microsoft Word & Excel – Embed documents and spreadsheets for detailed research data.

4. Microsoft SharePoint – Link corporate knowledge bases or organizational wikis.

Syncing Loop with Cloud Storage Services

Microsoft Loop also supports cloud storage like OneDrive and SharePoint, ensuring that your files are:

- Easily accessible across devices.

- Synced in real-time, so updates are immediately reflected.

- Securely stored with Microsoft's enterprise-grade security features.

Best Practices for Managing Your Knowledge Hub

Organizing Information for Easy Retrieval

A knowledge hub is only useful if you can quickly find what you need. Here are some best practices:

- Use a consistent naming system for Loop Pages and components.

- Tag your content with keywords or categories for quick search.

- Group related topics together to maintain logical structure.

- Review and clean up outdated content regularly.

Collaborating and Sharing Knowledge

Even if your knowledge hub is personal, you may want to share certain insights with colleagues or friends. To do this:

- Use Loop's real-time collaboration features to allow team members to edit or comment.

- Share specific components (instead of entire pages) when you only need to give access to certain information.

- Export pages or sections for external use in PowerPoint, Word, or Teams.

Maintaining an Evolving Knowledge Hub

A Digital Knowledge Hub is not static—it grows as you continue learning. To keep it updated:

- Schedule weekly or monthly reviews to refine and organize content.

- Add new insights as you acquire knowledge.

- Use Microsoft Loop's version history to track changes over time.

Real-World Use Cases of a Microsoft Loop Knowledge Hub

To illustrate the power of Microsoft Loop for knowledge management, here are some practical scenarios:

1. A Student's Learning Repository

A student can use Loop to:

- Collect lecture notes in a structured format.

- Organize study materials by subject.

- Create revision guides with embedded video links and diagrams.

2. A Researcher's Digital Archive

A researcher can:

- Store and categorize academic papers.

- Collaborate with peers by sharing Loop components.

- Maintain a list of citations and references.

3. A Professional's Knowledge Management System

A business professional can:

- Keep track of industry trends and insights.

- Create a personal learning journal.

- Collaborate with colleagues on best practices.

Conclusion

Creating a Digital Knowledge Hub in Microsoft Loop transforms the way you store, manage, and retrieve information. With Loop Workspaces, Pages, and Components, you can build a structured, dynamic, and collaborative knowledge system that grows with you.

By following the strategies outlined in this chapter, you will be able to:
✅ Organize knowledge efficiently with structured Loop Pages.
✅ Use Loop Components to create interactive and reusable content.
✅ Integrate with Microsoft 365 apps to centralize information.
✅ Maintain and update your hub regularly for maximum effectiveness.

Whether you're a student, researcher, or professional, Microsoft Loop offers a modern and seamless way to manage your knowledge, boost productivity, and enhance collaboration. Start building your Digital Knowledge Hub today, and experience smarter knowledge management with Microsoft Loop!

5.2 Microsoft Loop for Team Collaboration

5.2.1 Enhancing Remote Work with Loop

In today's digital age, remote work has become an essential mode of operation for many organizations. With teams distributed across different locations and time zones, effective collaboration tools are crucial to maintaining productivity, engagement, and efficiency. Microsoft Loop offers a dynamic and flexible platform for remote teams, enabling seamless communication, real-time collaboration, and structured project management.

This section explores how Microsoft Loop enhances remote work by improving teamwork, centralizing knowledge, facilitating asynchronous collaboration, and integrating with other Microsoft 365 applications.

1. The Challenges of Remote Work

Before delving into how Microsoft Loop addresses remote work challenges, it's important to understand the difficulties that remote teams often face:

- Lack of real-time collaboration – Many traditional collaboration tools are not optimized for simultaneous work, leading to version control issues and inefficiencies.

- Scattered communication – Teams often rely on multiple communication channels such as email, messaging apps, and video calls, making it hard to track conversations.

- Difficulty in knowledge sharing – Important information can get lost in long email threads or various file storage locations.

- Asynchronous work barriers – Different time zones can make it challenging to coordinate schedules for meetings and discussions.

- Task management inefficiencies – Keeping track of responsibilities and project updates can be difficult without a centralized system.

Microsoft Loop effectively addresses these issues by offering a collaborative, real-time, and structured workspace where remote teams can work together without friction.

2. Key Features of Microsoft Loop for Remote Teams

2.1 Real-Time Collaboration on Loop Components

One of the standout features of Microsoft Loop is its ability to facilitate real-time collaboration through Loop Components. These are dynamic, interactive elements that can be embedded in various Microsoft 365 apps like Microsoft Teams, Outlook, and OneNote, allowing remote teams to:

- Co-edit content simultaneously, ensuring everyone stays up to date.

- Eliminate version conflicts by having a single source of truth across platforms.

- Share task lists, voting tables, checklists, and notes within a conversation.

For example, if a marketing team is working on a campaign plan, they can create a Loop Component with a shared checklist in Microsoft Teams. Whether a team member updates the checklist in Loop or Teams, changes are instantly reflected everywhere.

2.2 Centralized Workspaces for Team Projects

In a remote work environment, having a centralized hub for all team-related content is crucial. Loop Workspaces act as a digital co-working space where teams can:

- Create and organize Loop Pages dedicated to different projects.

- Store meeting notes, brainstorming ideas, and project roadmaps in one place.

- Enable remote team members to contribute asynchronously.

For example, a software development team working across different time zones can maintain a shared workspace where developers log daily updates, designers upload UI prototypes, and project managers track milestones. This setup eliminates the need for excessive meetings while keeping everyone aligned.

2.3 Asynchronous Collaboration with Loop Pages

One of the biggest benefits of Microsoft Loop for remote work is support for asynchronous collaboration. Unlike traditional document-sharing tools, Loop Pages allow remote teams to:

- Contribute at different times without disrupting workflows.

- Provide inline comments and feedback on specific sections.

- Use @mentions to notify team members when input is needed.

For example, if a content team is drafting a blog post, writers can add their sections, editors can review and suggest changes asynchronously, and managers can approve the final draft—all without needing a live meeting.

2.4 Task and Project Management in Loop

For remote teams, keeping track of tasks and deadlines is essential. Microsoft Loop integrates with Microsoft Planner, To Do, and Teams, enabling teams to:

- Assign and track tasks within Loop components.

- Set due dates and priorities.

- Sync task updates across different Microsoft 365 apps.

For instance, if a sales team is working on an upcoming client proposal, they can create a task component within Loop to outline responsibilities. As team members complete their parts, updates automatically sync, providing transparency to the entire team.

2.5 Seamless Integration with Microsoft 365

Since Microsoft Loop is deeply integrated with Microsoft 365, remote teams can leverage other powerful tools without switching platforms:

- Microsoft Teams: Share Loop Components directly in Teams chats and channels for easy access.

- Outlook: Embed Loop notes in emails to collaborate on drafts or proposals.

- OneNote: Sync notes from Loop for structured documentation.

- SharePoint & OneDrive: Store and access Loop files securely.

For example, a HR team conducting remote hiring can embed an interview feedback Loop Component in a Teams chat, allowing recruiters to score candidates in real time without switching applications.

3. Best Practices for Using Microsoft Loop in Remote Work

To maximize the benefits of Microsoft Loop, remote teams should follow these best practices:

Define Clear Structures and Guidelines

- Establish clear naming conventions for Loop Workspaces and Pages.

- Organize information logically to avoid content sprawl.

- Assign responsibilities within shared documents.

Encourage Active Participation

- Use @mentions to request input from specific team members.

- Regularly review and update shared Loop Components.

- Host occasional check-ins via Microsoft Teams to reinforce collaboration.

Optimize for Asynchronous Workflows

- Encourage team members to log updates in Loop instead of long email chains.

- Utilize comments and suggestions to provide feedback without disrupting workflows.

- Set clear review and approval processes within Loop Workspaces.

Leverage Microsoft 365 Integrations

- Embed Loop Components in Teams, Outlook, and SharePoint for seamless access.

- Automate routine tasks using Power Automate workflows.

- Store critical documentation in OneDrive for backup and security.

4. Conclusion

Microsoft Loop is a game-changer for remote teams, offering a seamless, interactive, and real-time collaboration experience. By utilizing Loop Components, Workspaces, and integrations with Microsoft 365, remote workers can stay organized, communicate effectively, and enhance productivity.

Whether you're managing projects, brainstorming ideas, or tracking team progress, Microsoft Loop provides the tools needed to bridge the gap between remote team members. By implementing best practices and leveraging its full potential, remote teams can collaborate smarter and work more efficiently—no matter where they are in the world.

5.2.2 Brainstorming and Idea Generation

Collaboration and creativity go hand in hand in a modern workspace. Brainstorming sessions are essential for teams to generate ideas, solve problems, and innovate. Microsoft Loop offers a powerful, flexible, and real-time collaborative environment to make brainstorming more productive and engaging. In this section, we will explore how Microsoft Loop can enhance idea generation, discuss practical brainstorming techniques, and provide step-by-step guidance on how to maximize Loop's features for creative teamwork.

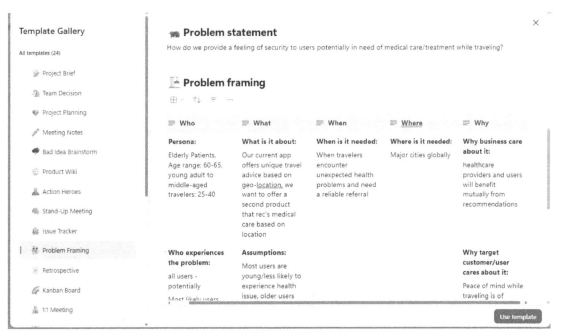

Why Use Microsoft Loop for Brainstorming?

Traditional brainstorming often involves whiteboards, sticky notes, or long email threads, which can lead to scattered ideas, lack of organization, and difficulty in tracking progress. Microsoft Loop overcomes these challenges by offering:

- Real-Time Collaboration: Team members can contribute ideas simultaneously, eliminating waiting times.

- Structured yet Flexible Format: Loop workspaces, pages, and components allow easy organization of thoughts while maintaining a free-flowing idea generation process.

- Integration with Microsoft 365 Apps: Users can pull in relevant documents, emails, and meeting notes to enrich brainstorming sessions.

- Persistent and Accessible Ideas: Unlike physical brainstorming boards, ideas remain available in Loop for future refinement and execution.

Setting Up a Brainstorming Workspace in Microsoft Loop

Before starting a brainstorming session, it's essential to set up a well-structured workspace to capture and refine ideas efficiently.

Step 1: Create a New Loop Workspace

1. Open **Microsoft Loop** and click on **"New Workspace"**.

2. Give the workspace a relevant name, such as *"Marketing Campaign Brainstorm"*.

3. Select a color and icon for easy identification.

4. Invite team members who will participate in the brainstorming session.

Step 2: Add a Brainstorming Page

1. Inside the workspace, create a new page and name it *"Brainstorming Ideas – Q2 Product Launch"*.

2. Add an introductory text component explaining the goal of the session.

3. Insert an **@mention** to key team members to notify them.

Step 3: Use Loop Components to Capture Ideas

1. Bullet Point Lists: Create a list where team members can quickly jot down initial ideas.

2. Tables: Use tables to categorize ideas based on feasibility, cost, or priority.

3. Task Lists: Assign follow-up tasks to refine and develop selected ideas further.

4. Voting Components: Allow team members to vote on their favorite ideas.

Best Brainstorming Techniques with Microsoft Loop

To maximize the effectiveness of a brainstorming session, teams can leverage different brainstorming techniques within Loop:

1. Mind Mapping in Loop

Mind mapping is a powerful technique to visually explore connections between ideas.

- How to do it in Loop:

    1. Create a Loop page titled *"Mind Map – New Product Features"*.

    2. Insert a Table component with two columns: *Main Idea* and *Supporting Ideas*.

    3. As team members generate ideas, they can add branches to the mind map by inserting new rows.

    4. Use @mentions to assign specific ideas to team members for further exploration.

2. SCAMPER Method in Loop

The SCAMPER technique (Substitute, Combine, Adapt, Modify, Put to another use, Eliminate, Reverse) is great for improving existing ideas.

- How to do it in Loop:

    1. Create a Loop table with seven columns (one for each SCAMPER category).

    2. Add the problem or idea to the first row.

    3. Ask team members to suggest changes based on SCAMPER questions.

    4. Use a Task List component to assign follow-up actions for promising ideas.

3. Rapid Ideation with Loop Components

Encourage fast idea generation without immediate filtering.

- How to do it in Loop:

    1. Set a 15-minute timer and ask participants to write as many ideas as possible.

    2. Use a Bullet List component where each participant adds ideas.

    3. Once the timer is up, review and refine the list together.

    4. Move top ideas to a new section for detailed discussion.

4. Dot Voting for Prioritization

Once ideas are generated, the team needs a way to prioritize them.

- How to do it in Loop:

    1. Create a Table component listing all generated ideas.

    2. Add a Voting component where each team member can vote for their favorite ideas.

    3. The top-voted ideas can be transferred to a Task List component for further development.

Enhancing Brainstorming Sessions with Microsoft 365 Integrations

1. Using Loop with Microsoft Teams for Live Brainstorming

- Create a Teams meeting and open the corresponding Loop page within the chat.

- Participants can add ideas in real time while discussing them over a video call.

- Ideas remain within the Loop page for follow-up discussions.

2. Embedding Loop Components in Outlook for Asynchronous Brainstorming

- Send a Loop component in an email to collect ideas from team members who can't join a live session.

- Responses sync automatically, ensuring no ideas are lost.

3. Linking OneNote for Idea Expansion

- Export brainstormed ideas from Loop to OneNote for further detailing.

- Use handwriting and annotation tools to sketch ideas visually.

Best Practices for Effective Brainstorming in Microsoft Loop

Encourage Open Participation

- Create a collaborative and judgment-free environment where all team members feel comfortable contributing.

- Use anonymous input options in Loop when discussing sensitive topics.

Keep Sessions Focused

- Define clear objectives before the brainstorming session begins.

- Use pre-made templates in Loop for structured discussions.

Document and Follow Up on Ideas

- Assign specific action items to ensure ideas don't get lost after the session.

- Use task lists to track the implementation of selected ideas.

Conclusion

Microsoft Loop revolutionizes the way teams brainstorm and generate ideas. By providing a flexible, interactive, and structured space, Loop enables teams to work efficiently, whether synchronously or asynchronously. The integration with other Microsoft 365 apps ensures that brainstorming sessions don't end when the meeting is over—ideas can be refined, expanded, and implemented seamlessly. By leveraging Loop's unique features and following best practices, teams can foster creativity and drive innovation more effectively than ever.

5.2.3 Running Effective Team Meetings

Effective team meetings are crucial for collaboration, decision-making, and keeping projects on track. However, many meetings suffer from inefficiency, lack of engagement, and poor follow-through. Microsoft Loop provides a modern, dynamic way to plan, conduct, and follow up on meetings, ensuring that discussions are productive and actionable.

In this section, we will explore how Microsoft Loop can enhance your team meetings by helping you:

- Plan meetings effectively with collaborative agendas and shared preparation materials.

- Conduct meetings efficiently with real-time collaboration, structured discussions, and note-taking.

- Follow up seamlessly with action items, shared summaries, and integration with other Microsoft 365 tools.

Preparing for a Productive Meeting with Microsoft Loop

Setting a Clear Agenda

A well-structured agenda is the foundation of an effective meeting. Microsoft Loop allows teams to collaboratively create and refine an agenda before the meeting starts. Here's how you can use Loop to streamline this process:

1. **Create a Loop Page for the Meeting**

   o Open Microsoft Loop and create a new Loop Page titled with the meeting name and date.

   o This will serve as the central hub for all meeting-related content.

2. **Use a Pre-Built Meeting Template**

   o Microsoft Loop provides ready-made templates for meeting notes, making it easy to set up an agenda quickly.

   o You can also create a custom template that includes sections such as:

     ▪ Meeting objectives

     ▪ Discussion topics

     ▪ Assigned presenters

     ▪ Time allocations

3. **Collaborate on the Agenda**

- o Invite team members to contribute agenda items in real time.

- o Use @mentions to assign topics to specific individuals.

- o Encourage team members to add supporting documents, links, or Loop components (such as tables or lists).

4. **Prioritize Discussion Points**

- o Ensure that key discussion points are arranged logically and timeboxed.

- o Microsoft Loop allows you to use checklists or voting components to determine the most important topics.

Gathering Pre-Meeting Inputs

Before the meeting starts, it's useful to gather input from participants to ensure everyone is prepared:

- Use Loop Poll Components to collect opinions on key topics before the meeting.

- Ask attendees to add their questions or comments directly to the Loop Page.

- Attach relevant reports, spreadsheets, or presentations from OneDrive or SharePoint for easy reference.

By structuring the agenda in Microsoft Loop, you create a single source of truth that keeps everyone aligned and engaged before the meeting even begins.

Conducting a Meeting Using Microsoft Loop

Collaborating in Real-Time

Microsoft Loop enables teams to work together on meeting notes and decisions as the discussion unfolds. Here's how to make the most of it:

1. **Live Note-Taking with Loop Components**

- o During the meeting, designate a notetaker (or multiple people) to document key points using a Loop Text Component.

- o Because Loop Components are live and shareable, even remote participants can contribute to the notes in real-time.

2. **Tracking Decisions and Action Items**

   o Create a Loop Task List Component to document key decisions and assign action items.

   o Assign tasks using @mentions so that team members receive notifications.

   o Set deadlines directly in the task list to ensure accountability.

3. **Enhancing Discussion with Embedded Content**

   o Embed files, tables, and charts from Excel, Word, and PowerPoint directly into the Loop Page for reference.

   o Use Loop Voting Components to quickly reach a consensus on key topics.

Encouraging Engagement and Participation

Microsoft Loop helps teams create a more interactive and engaging meeting experience:

- Use interactive brainstorming sessions: Create a Loop Page with an open-ended text component where team members can contribute ideas.

- Encourage asynchronous participation: Not all team members may be available at the same time. They can add comments or suggestions before or after the meeting.

- Keep discussions focused: Assign a moderator who ensures that discussions stay on track using the predefined agenda.

Following Up After the Meeting

Summarizing Meeting Outcomes

Once the meeting concludes, Microsoft Loop makes it easy to share a summary with all attendees:

1. **Compile Key Takeaways**

   o Use a Loop Summary Component to highlight major decisions, unresolved questions, and follow-up actions.

   o Summaries can be edited collaboratively so that everyone agrees on what was discussed.

2. **Distribute the Meeting Notes**

    o   Share the final meeting notes via Microsoft Teams, Outlook, or OneNote.

    o   Embed the Loop Page into a Teams Channel for easy reference.

Tracking Action Items and Next Steps

- Monitor progress on tasks: Since Loop integrates with Microsoft Planner and To Do, assigned action items can be tracked beyond the meeting.

- Schedule follow-up meetings: Use the summary document to determine if additional discussions are needed.

- Keep the conversation going: Add a Loop Page link to a Teams chat for ongoing discussions.

Best Practices for Running Effective Team Meetings with Microsoft Loop

To maximize the effectiveness of your meetings using Microsoft Loop, follow these best practices:

Before the Meeting

✓ Set a clear agenda and invite input from attendees.
✓ Share supporting materials ahead of time to allow for preparation.
✓ Use Loop's collaboration features to ensure everyone has a voice.

During the Meeting

✓ Take live notes using Loop Components to keep track of discussions.
✓ Assign action items immediately with clear owners and deadlines.
✓ Stay on track with the agenda and encourage participation.

After the Meeting

✓ Send a meeting summary with key takeaways and next steps.
✓ Use Loop to track action items and ensure accountability.
✓ Follow up with additional discussions asynchronously if needed.

Conclusion

Microsoft Loop revolutionizes the way teams conduct meetings by offering real-time collaboration, structured documentation, and seamless follow-up. By leveraging Loop's powerful features, teams can ensure that every meeting is productive, action-driven, and well-documented.

By integrating Microsoft Loop into your workflow, you can eliminate inefficient meetings, keep team members engaged, and ensure that decisions lead to concrete results. Whether your team is remote, hybrid, or in-office, Microsoft Loop provides the flexibility and structure needed to run effective meetings that drive progress.

5.3 Microsoft Loop for Project Management

5.3.1 Planning Projects with Loop Workspaces

Introduction

Project management is a complex process that requires careful planning, efficient communication, and seamless collaboration. Microsoft Loop, with its dynamic workspaces and real-time collaboration features, provides an innovative way to streamline project planning and execution. By leveraging Loop workspaces, project managers and teams can create a centralized hub where tasks, timelines, documents, and discussions are seamlessly integrated.

This section explores how to effectively plan projects using Microsoft Loop workspaces, covering key aspects such as workspace setup, content organization, and best practices for collaboration. Whether managing a small team project or coordinating a large-scale initiative, Loop can significantly enhance productivity and project visibility.

Why Use Loop Workspaces for Project Management?

Loop workspaces offer several advantages for project planning:

✅ Centralized Information – All project details are stored in one accessible location.

✅ Real-Time Collaboration – Team members can edit, comment, and update information simultaneously.

✅ Flexibility and Customization – Workspaces can be structured to fit different project needs.

✅ Integration with Microsoft 365 – Seamlessly connects with Teams, Outlook, Planner, and other productivity tools.

Setting Up a Loop Workspace for Your Project

Step 1: Creating a New Workspace

To begin planning a project in Microsoft Loop, follow these steps:

1.   Open Microsoft Loop and navigate to the Workspaces section.

2. Click Create a New Workspace and give it a relevant name (e.g., "Marketing Campaign 2025").

3. Choose a color and icon to visually differentiate the workspace.

4. Click Create to generate the workspace.

Once created, you can start adding pages and components to structure your project.

Step 2: Structuring the Workspace for Maximum Efficiency

A well-organized workspace ensures that project planning remains clear and manageable. Consider structuring your workspace as follows:

★ Project Overview Page – A high-level summary of the project, including objectives, stakeholders, and timelines.
★ Task Management Page – A breakdown of tasks, milestones, and responsibilities.
★ Meeting Notes Page – A dedicated space for tracking decisions and action items from meetings.
★ Resource Hub – A repository for important documents, reference materials, and external links.

Each page can contain Loop components like checklists, tables, and embedded documents to enhance interactivity.

Adding Key Components for Project Planning

Loop workspaces support various components that facilitate project management. Here are some essential ones:

Task Lists for Managing Workload

To create a task list in Loop:

1. Open a new Loop Page in your workspace.

2. Click Insert Component and select Task List.

3. Enter tasks, assign owners, and set due dates.

4. Enable progress tracking to monitor completion status.

◆ Pro Tip: Sync your task list with Microsoft Planner to get detailed tracking and notifications.

Tables for Budgeting and Scheduling

Tables are useful for tracking project budgets, deadlines, and deliverables. To insert a table:

1. Open a Loop Page and click Insert Component.

2. Choose Table and define columns such as Task Name, Owner, Due Date, Status, and Notes.

3. Use color coding to highlight priorities.

▥ Example:

Task	Assigned To	Due Date	Status	Notes
Develop Website Wireframe	Alice	Feb 15	In Progress	Review on Feb 10
Approve Budget	John	Feb 20	Pending	CFO approval required
Launch Social Media Ads	Team	Mar 1	Not Started	Awaiting content

Embedded Files and Documents

Project documentation is critical for smooth execution. Loop allows embedding files directly from OneDrive, SharePoint, and Teams.

*   Attach project briefs, contracts, or reference guides directly in Loop pages.

*   Use version history to track document changes.

*   Collaborate in real time without switching between apps.

Enhancing Team Collaboration in Loop

Using @Mentions for Communication

Project teams must stay connected throughout the planning phase. Using @mentions in Loop helps direct team members' attention to key updates.
✅ Tag individuals in discussions for immediate notifications.

✅ Use comments to clarify tasks and decisions.

✅ Leverage reactions (👍 🔥 ✅) for quick feedback.

Setting Up Notifications and Reminders

To ensure timely task completion, set up automated reminders using:

🔔 Loop's built-in notifications – Get alerts when tasks are assigned or updated.

🔔 Microsoft Teams integration – Receive project updates in Teams channels.

🔔 Power Automate workflows – Automate reminders for upcoming deadlines.

Best Practices for Effective Project Planning in Loop

✅ Keep Workspaces Organized

- Use clear naming conventions for pages and components.

- Archive completed projects to declutter the workspace.

✅ Encourage Team Collaboration

- Assign specific roles and responsibilities within the workspace.

- Regularly update pages with the latest information.

✅ Leverage Microsoft 365 Integration

- Sync with Planner, Teams, and OneDrive for enhanced functionality.

- Use Loop in Microsoft Outlook to keep stakeholders informed.

Conclusion

Microsoft Loop revolutionizes project planning by providing an interactive, real-time collaborative space where teams can stay organized and aligned. By leveraging workspaces, task lists, embedded files, and integrations with Microsoft 365, project managers can streamline workflows and improve efficiency.

5.3.2 Tracking Milestones and Deliverables

Introduction

Project management is all about keeping track of key milestones and deliverables to ensure a project is completed on time and within scope. Microsoft Loop provides a flexible, collaborative space where teams can define milestones, assign tasks, monitor progress, and adjust strategies in real-time. Whether managing a software development project, a marketing campaign, or a product launch, Loop helps teams maintain transparency and efficiency.

In this section, we'll explore how to use Microsoft Loop to track milestones and deliverables, set up progress tracking, and ensure accountability within teams.

Understanding Milestones and Deliverables

What Are Milestones?

Milestones are significant points in a project timeline that indicate progress toward completion. They serve as checkpoints that help teams stay aligned and measure success. Examples of milestones include:

- Completing the initial project plan
- Finalizing the first prototype
- Launching a marketing campaign
- Delivering a final product to the client

What Are Deliverables?

Deliverables are tangible or intangible outputs required to complete a project. They can be documents, software updates, reports, presentations, or even physical products. Examples include:

- A project proposal document
- A software version release
- A marketing report

- A design prototype

By effectively managing milestones and deliverables, teams can maintain clarity, ensure accountability, and prevent delays. Microsoft Loop provides a collaborative environment to facilitate this process.

Using Microsoft Loop to Track Milestones and Deliverables

1. Setting Up a Project Workspace in Microsoft Loop

Before tracking milestones and deliverables, it's important to set up a dedicated Loop workspace for your project. Here's how:

1. Create a new workspace in Microsoft Loop and name it after your project (e.g., "Website Redesign Project").

2. Add relevant pages within the workspace, such as:

   o Project Overview

   o Timeline & Milestones

   o Task Assignments

   o Progress Tracking

3. Invite team members and assign them different permissions (view, edit, or comment).

4. Link relevant documents and files from OneDrive or SharePoint for easy reference.

2. Creating a Milestone Tracking Page

Once the workspace is set up, the next step is to create a Milestone Tracking Page to document key project checkpoints.

How to Create a Milestone Table in Loop:

1. Open a new Loop page and name it "Project Milestones".

2. Insert a table component with columns such as:

   o Milestone Name (e.g., "Finalize Wireframe Design")

   o Deadline (e.g., "March 15, 2025")

      o   Responsible Team Member (e.g., "John Doe")

      o   Status (e.g., "In Progress", "Completed", "Delayed")

      o   Notes/Updates (for additional details)

3. Assign responsible team members using @mentions to notify them directly.

4. Regularly update the status column as milestones progress.

Example of a milestone tracking table:

Milestone	Deadline	Responsible	Status	Notes
Finalize Wireframe Design	Mar 15, 2025	John Doe	In Progress	Awaiting review
Develop Backend API	Apr 5, 2025	Sarah Lee	Not Started	Dependency on database setup
Launch Beta Version	Jun 20, 2025	Team	Pending	Final testing required

3. Managing Deliverables in Loop

Deliverables should be clearly defined and assigned to specific team members. Using Loop's task components, teams can manage these deliverables effectively.

Creating a Deliverables List:

1. Open a new Loop page and name it "Project Deliverables".

2. Insert a task list component and add key deliverables.

3. Assign deliverables to specific team members using @mentions.

4. Attach necessary files and documents directly to the deliverable items.

5. Set up due dates and enable progress tracking.

Example of a deliverables tracking list:

✅ Develop UI Mockups – Assigned to @Alex | Due: Mar 10, 2025
✅ Write Product Specification Document – Assigned to @Lisa | Due: Mar 20, 2025
✅ Conduct Beta Testing – Assigned to @Team | Due: June 15, 2025

4. Using Loop Components to Monitor Progress

Microsoft Loop's real-time collaborative features make progress tracking seamless. Here are a few powerful tools within Loop to monitor milestones and deliverables:

Progress Tracker Table

- Use a table component to visualize overall project progress.
- Include columns for task completion percentage, team comments, and roadblocks.
- Highlight urgent tasks or delayed milestones.

@Mentions and Notifications

- Keep everyone informed by using @mentions in updates.
- Notify team members when a milestone is reached.
- Set up automated reminders using Microsoft Power Automate.

Comments and Feedback Loops

- Add comments directly within deliverables for quick feedback.
- Use reaction emojis to acknowledge progress updates.
- Pin important notes for easy reference.

Integrating Microsoft Loop with Other Tools for Better Tracking

1. Loop and Microsoft Planner

- Sync your milestones and deliverables with Microsoft Planner.
- Create Planner tasks directly from Loop and track completion status.

2. Loop and Microsoft Teams

- Share milestone updates in Teams chat using Loop components.
- Use Teams meetings to review project progress.

3. Loop and Power Automate

- Automate notifications for upcoming deadlines.
- Set up triggers to move tasks forward when a milestone is completed.

Best Practices for Tracking Milestones and Deliverables in Loop

To ensure effective project tracking, follow these best practices:

✓ Define clear milestones and deliverables before starting.
✓ Regularly update the Loop workspace to keep information current.
✓ Use automation to reduce manual tracking efforts.
✓ Encourage team participation by making updates a shared responsibility.
✓ Leverage Loop integrations with Microsoft 365 for seamless collaboration.

Conclusion

Microsoft Loop provides a powerful and flexible environment to track milestones and deliverables in real-time. By setting up a structured workspace, using task-tracking components, and integrating with other Microsoft tools, teams can manage projects more efficiently and ensure successful outcomes.

By following the strategies outlined in this chapter, you'll be able to leverage Microsoft Loop to streamline project management, enhance team collaboration, and keep your deliverables on track.

5.3.3 Collaborating Across Departments

Introduction

Cross-departmental collaboration is crucial for organizations striving for efficiency, innovation, and seamless communication. Microsoft Loop offers a flexible and interactive platform that bridges gaps between teams, departments, and even external partners. By leveraging Loop's real-time collaboration features, organizations can streamline workflows, improve knowledge sharing, and ensure alignment across different functions.

In this section, we'll explore how Microsoft Loop enhances interdepartmental collaboration, the best practices for structuring workspaces, and real-world use cases that demonstrate its effectiveness in project management and cross-team coordination.

1. Challenges of Cross-Department Collaboration

Before diving into how Microsoft Loop helps, it's important to understand the common challenges organizations face when working across departments:

Communication Barriers

Different departments often use different tools and communication styles, leading to misunderstandings and information silos. Important updates may get lost in long email chains or scattered across multiple platforms.

Disconnected Workflows

Departments often have unique processes and workflows that don't always align. For example, the marketing team might use a different project tracking system than the product development team, making collaboration inefficient.

Lack of Centralized Information

With multiple departments working on a single project, key documents and data are often stored in separate locations, making it difficult to access up-to-date information.

Slow Decision-Making Processes

Cross-functional decision-making can be delayed due to a lack of visibility into project updates or difficulty in getting stakeholder approvals in a timely manner.

Microsoft Loop addresses these challenges by providing a centralized, interactive, and dynamic workspace where all teams can collaborate seamlessly.

2. Using Microsoft Loop for Cross-Department Collaboration

Microsoft Loop brings teams together in a shared, flexible environment where everyone can contribute in real time. Below are key ways Loop facilitates collaboration across departments.

Creating a Shared Workspace for Cross-Departmental Projects

A Loop workspace can serve as a central hub where all relevant teams—such as marketing, sales, product development, and customer support—can access project updates, share ideas, and contribute to ongoing discussions.

How to Set Up a Cross-Department Workspace:

- **Step 1:** Create a new Loop workspace and name it based on the project or initiative.

- **Step 2:** Invite key stakeholders from different departments, ensuring appropriate access permissions.

- **Step 3:** Organize Loop pages within the workspace to categorize project aspects (e.g., timelines, task lists, feedback sections).

- **Step 4:** Pin important resources such as meeting notes, guidelines, or shared files.

Breaking Down Information Silos with Loop Components

Loop components allow departments to share content in real time, whether inside Microsoft Teams, Outlook, or Word. This ensures that updates are instantly visible to all relevant stakeholders.

Examples of Using Loop Components Across Departments:

- **Marketing & Sales:** A Loop component containing customer insights can be shared between marketing and sales teams to align on campaign strategies.

- **Product & Support:** A Loop table tracking product issues can be updated by the customer support team and immediately reviewed by the product team.

- **Finance & Operations:** A budgeting Loop component can be embedded into financial planning meetings, allowing live edits from both departments.

Streamlining Approval Workflows with Loop

Many cross-functional projects require approvals at different stages. Microsoft Loop makes this process more efficient by enabling real-time feedback and sign-offs directly within the workspace.

Example of an Approval Workflow:

1. The product team drafts a new feature proposal in a Loop document.

2. The marketing team provides feedback and suggests changes directly within the document.

3. The finance team adds budget considerations in a separate Loop table.

4. The leadership team reviews and gives final approval within the same workspace.

This eliminates long email threads and scattered feedback, making decision-making faster and more transparent.

3. Best Practices for Successful Cross-Department Collaboration in Loop

Establish Clear Roles and Responsibilities

Clearly define who is responsible for what within the Loop workspace to avoid confusion and ensure accountability. Use checklists and task assignments to delegate responsibilities efficiently.

Encourage Real-Time Collaboration

Leverage Loop's real-time editing capabilities to hold collaborative meetings, brainstorm ideas, and make decisions faster. Encourage team members to use @mentions to tag colleagues for quick responses.

Keep Information Organized and Accessible

To avoid clutter, structure your Loop workspaces with clear sections for project updates, documents, and discussions. Regularly archive outdated content to keep the workspace relevant.

Integrate Loop with Other Microsoft 365 Tools

To maximize efficiency, connect Loop with other Microsoft 365 applications:

- Use **Teams** to embed Loop components in chat discussions.

- Link **OneDrive** or **SharePoint** for seamless file storage.

- Integrate **Power Automate** to automate repetitive tasks, such as notifying teams about project status changes.

Regularly Review and Optimize Collaboration Strategies

Periodically assess the effectiveness of your Loop workspaces. Collect feedback from team members on how the tool is being used and make adjustments accordingly.

4. Real-World Example: Microsoft Loop in Action

Scenario: Cross-Department Product Launch

A company is preparing for the launch of a new software product. The marketing, sales, product development, and customer support teams need to collaborate closely to ensure a successful release.

How They Use Microsoft Loop:

1. **Workspace Setup:** A "Product Launch 2025" Loop workspace is created, with separate pages for tasks, campaign planning, and product feedback.

2. **Live Content Updates:** The product team updates the development progress in a shared Loop component, ensuring real-time visibility for marketing and sales.

3. **Marketing & Sales Alignment:** A Loop table tracks target audiences, sales strategies, and content marketing materials, keeping both teams aligned.

4. **Customer Support Preparation:** Support teams add FAQs and anticipated customer concerns to a shared page, allowing proactive preparation before the launch.

5. **Approval & Sign-Offs:** The leadership team reviews final launch plans and provides approvals directly within the workspace.

Outcome:

By using Microsoft Loop, the teams eliminated communication delays, streamlined task management, and successfully launched the product with all departments fully aligned.

Conclusion

Microsoft Loop is a powerful tool for breaking down barriers between departments and enabling seamless collaboration. By providing a dynamic, real-time workspace, it ensures that projects progress smoothly, decisions are made faster, and teams remain aligned on shared goals.

Organizations that leverage Microsoft Loop for cross-departmental collaboration can significantly improve efficiency, reduce miscommunication, and enhance overall productivity. By following best practices and integrating Loop into existing workflows, teams can unlock its full potential for collaborative success.

CHAPTER VI
Troubleshooting and Best Practices

6.1 Common Microsoft Loop Issues and Fixes

6.1.1 Troubleshooting Sync and Access Issues

Microsoft Loop is designed to provide seamless collaboration across teams by syncing content in real time. However, like any cloud-based tool, users may sometimes encounter synchronization and access issues that disrupt workflow. This section covers common sync and access problems, their potential causes, and step-by-step solutions to help you get back on track quickly.

Understanding Sync and Access Issues in Microsoft Loop

Sync and access issues in Microsoft Loop typically occur due to three main factors:

1. **Network Connectivity Problems** – Slow or unstable internet connections can prevent Loop from syncing data properly.

2. **Permissions and Access Restrictions** – Users may lack the necessary permissions to access or edit certain Loop components.

3. **Microsoft 365 Service Interruptions** – Temporary downtime or maintenance in Microsoft 365 services can disrupt Loop's functionality.

Below, we'll explore these problems in detail and provide troubleshooting steps for each scenario.

Common Sync Issues and How to Fix Them

1. Loop Content is Not Updating in Real Time

Symptoms:

- Changes made by one user do not appear for others.

- Some users see outdated versions of Loop components.

- Components take a long time to update across different devices.

Possible Causes:

- Slow or unstable internet connection.

- Microsoft Loop servers experiencing delays.

- Browser cache interfering with real-time updates.

Solutions:
✅ **Check Your Internet Connection:**

- Run a speed test (e.g., Fast.com or Speedtest.net).

- If using Wi-Fi, switch to a wired connection for better stability.

- Restart your router or modem if the connection is weak.

✅ **Refresh Your Microsoft Loop Page:**

- Press **Ctrl + R (Windows)** or **Cmd + R (Mac)** to reload the page.

- Close and reopen your browser or Microsoft Loop app.

✅ **Try a Different Browser or Device:**

- If using Microsoft Loop in a browser, try switching to Microsoft Edge or Google Chrome.

- If using a mobile device, check if the issue persists on a desktop.

✅ **Clear Browser Cache and Cookies:**

- In **Google Chrome:**

    ○ Go to **Settings > Privacy and Security > Clear browsing data**

- Select **Cookies and other site data** and **Cached images and files**
- Click **Clear data**

- Restart your browser and log back into Microsoft Loop.

✓ **Check Microsoft Service Status:**

- Visit Microsoft 365 Service Health to check if there are any ongoing service disruptions.

2. Changes in Loop Components Are Overwritten or Disappear

Symptoms:

- Edits made by one user are replaced with an older version.
- Newly added components disappear after refreshing the page.

Possible Causes:

- Conflicts due to multiple users editing the same component simultaneously.
- Internet connection dropping while saving changes.
- Temporary data corruption in the Loop workspace.

Solutions:
✓ **Enable Version History to Restore Content:**

- Click on the **three-dot menu** (⋮) in the top right corner of the component.
- Select **Version history** and restore the correct version.

✓ **Avoid Simultaneous Editing of Critical Components:**

- Assign ownership to specific team members for key content.
- Communicate within the workspace before making major changes.

✓ **Manually Save Important Edits in Another Document:**

- Copy and paste critical content into **OneNote, Word, or Notepad** before making extensive edits.

✅ **Log Out and Log Back In:**

- Click on your **profile picture** in the top right corner and select **Sign Out**.

- Close the browser, reopen it, and log back in to refresh your session.

3. Loop Components Are Not Syncing Between Microsoft Teams and Loop App

Symptoms:

- A Loop component added in Teams is not updating in Loop.

- Edits made in Loop do not reflect in Teams.

- The Loop component disappears when reopening Teams.

Possible Causes:

- The component has not been shared correctly.

- Microsoft Teams cache interfering with updates.

- Loop is not fully integrated with the Teams account.

Solutions:

✅ **Ensure the Loop Component is Properly Shared:**

- Click on the **Share** button and verify that **Everyone in the organization** has access.

- Copy the link and paste it again in Microsoft Teams to refresh the connection.

✅ **Manually Refresh the Microsoft Teams App:**

- Click on your profile picture in Teams and select **Sign Out**.

- Restart Teams and sign back in.

✅ **Clear Microsoft Teams Cache:**

- Close Teams completely.

- On Windows:

    - Press **Win + R**, type %appdata%\Microsoft\Teams, and delete all files in the folder.

- On Mac:

  - Open Finder, press **Cmd + Shift + G**, type ~/Library/Application Support/Microsoft/Teams, and delete the cache files.

✓ **Try Accessing Loop from a Different Device:**

- If the component syncs correctly on another device, the issue may be local to the original device.

Common Access Issues and How to Fix Them

1. User Cannot Access a Loop Workspace or Page

Symptoms:

- "Access Denied" message appears when opening a workspace.

- User is unable to edit or view a shared page.

- The workspace does not appear in the list.

Possible Causes:

- The user does not have the correct permissions.

- The workspace is shared externally without proper authorization.

- The Microsoft 365 account used does not have Loop enabled.

Solutions:
✓ **Check and Adjust Sharing Permissions:**

- Click on the **Share** button and review permissions.

- Ensure the user has **Can Edit** access if they need to make changes.

✓ **Verify Microsoft 365 Licensing:**

- Loop is only available for Microsoft 365 business and enterprise plans.

- Check with your IT administrator if Loop is enabled for your account.

✓ **Try Opening Loop in Incognito Mode:**

- Open an incognito window in Chrome (Ctrl + Shift + N).

- Log into Microsoft 365 and access Loop.

- If it works, the issue may be related to cookies or stored login data.

Final Thoughts on Sync and Access Issues

Sync and access issues in Microsoft Loop can be frustrating, but with the right troubleshooting steps, most problems can be resolved quickly. By ensuring a stable internet connection, keeping browser settings optimized, and properly managing permissions, users can minimize disruptions and maintain smooth collaboration.

6.1.2 Resolving Formatting and Content Display Problems

Microsoft Loop is designed to provide a seamless and flexible collaboration experience, but users may occasionally encounter formatting and content display issues that disrupt their workflow. These issues can range from text misalignment and broken layouts to missing images and inconsistent component rendering. In this section, we will explore the most common formatting and display problems in Microsoft Loop and provide step-by-step solutions to resolve them.

1. Understanding Formatting and Display Issues in Microsoft Loop

Before diving into the solutions, it's important to understand why formatting and display issues occur. Some of the common causes include:

- **Browser Compatibility Problems:** Loop is a web-based tool, and different browsers may render content differently.

- **Sync Delays:** If content doesn't sync properly, formatting changes may not reflect instantly.

- **Corrupt Components:** Some Loop components may not load correctly due to network or cache issues.

- **Embedded Content Errors:** If external files, images, or links are embedded incorrectly, they might not display as expected.

- **Permissions Issues:** Sometimes, formatting problems arise because certain users lack editing rights to modify content properly.

Now, let's go through troubleshooting steps to resolve these problems.

2. Fixing Text and Formatting Issues

Misaligned or Overlapping Text

Problem: Text appears misaligned, overlapping with other elements, or not wrapping properly.

Solutions:

1. Use Proper Formatting Options: Select the text and use the formatting toolbar to adjust alignment, font size, and spacing.

2. Adjust Table or Component Width: If the text is inside a table or a narrow component, try expanding the width to allow better text flow.

3. Refresh the Page: Formatting issues can sometimes be a temporary glitch. Press F5 or manually refresh the page.

4. Check Browser Zoom Settings: Ensure your browser zoom is set to 100% to prevent unexpected rendering issues.

Inconsistent Font Styles or Sizes

Problem: Some text appears in a different font, size, or style than the rest of the content, even when formatting options seem uniform.

Solutions:

1. Use the Clear Formatting Option: Highlight the text and select the Clear Formatting option from the toolbar.

2. Apply Consistent Styles: If working with headings and paragraphs, ensure you are using the same style across different sections.

3. Manually Adjust the Font Size and Type: If necessary, manually set the font size and style to match the rest of the document.

4. Copy-Paste Without Formatting: When pasting external content, use Ctrl + Shift + V (Windows) or Cmd + Shift + V (Mac) to paste without retaining unwanted formatting.

Text Formatting Not Applying Properly

Problem: Bold, italics, or other text styles do not apply or disappear after saving.

Solutions:

1. Check for Sync Delays: If you are working in a shared environment, wait a few seconds and refresh the page.

2. Ensure You Have Editing Rights: If working on a shared document, check whether you have editing permissions.

3. Try Editing in Another Browser: Sometimes, browser-specific rendering issues can interfere with formatting.

3. Fixing Table and Layout Issues

Tables Not Displaying Correctly

Problem: Tables may appear broken, with incorrect column widths, missing rows, or misaligned text.

Solutions:

1. Manually Adjust Column Widths: Hover over the column dividers and drag to resize them.

2. Use the "Fit Content" Option: Microsoft Loop may allow resizing tables automatically to fit content.

3. Check for Copy-Paste Issues: If you pasted a table from an external source (like Excel), try recreating it manually to avoid format conflicts.

Embedded Components Not Displaying Properly

Problem: Microsoft Loop components (like task lists, notes, or tables) may not load or appear blank.

Solutions:

1. Refresh the Page: Sometimes, Loop components take time to load due to network delays.

2. Check Your Internet Connection: A slow or unstable connection can cause embedded components to fail.

3. Ensure the Component is Shared Properly: If you embedded a Loop component from another workspace, check if you have proper access permissions.

4. Fixing Image and Media Display Issues

Images Not Loading or Appearing as Broken Links

Problem: Inserted images may not appear, or they may show as broken links.

Solutions:

1. Check the Image Source: If the image was inserted via a URL, ensure the link is valid and accessible.

2. Reinsert the Image: Try deleting and re-uploading the image.

3. Use Supported File Formats: Microsoft Loop supports common image formats like JPEG, PNG, and GIF.

4. Clear Browser Cache: Sometimes, cached versions of the page cause images to fail to load.

Videos or External Links Not Displaying Properly

Problem: Embedded videos or external links appear as broken elements.

Solutions:

1. Verify the Source: Ensure the linked content is still available and accessible.

2. Use a Different Embed Method: If a direct embed fails, try inserting a hyperlink instead.

3. Check Browser Extensions: Some ad-blockers or security extensions may prevent embedded content from displaying.

5. Ensuring Proper Display on Different Devices

Content Appears Different on Mobile vs. Desktop

Problem: Formatting looks correct on one device but not another.

Solutions:

1. Use Responsive Layouts: Avoid excessive manual formatting and let Loop's default responsive settings handle layout adjustments.

2. Test on Multiple Devices: Check your content on both desktop and mobile to ensure compatibility.

3. Ensure You're Using an Updated Browser/App: Older versions of Microsoft Loop or web browsers may render content differently.

6. Preventing Formatting and Display Issues in the Future

Best Practices for Consistent Formatting

- Use predefined styles instead of manual formatting for text consistency.

- Avoid excessive copy-pasting from external sources to reduce format conflicts.

- Regularly refresh your page to ensure all content is updated properly.

- Use Microsoft Edge or Google Chrome for the best compatibility with Microsoft Loop.

Keeping Your Loop Content Organized

- Structure your workspaces properly to avoid clutter.

- Use clear section headings to keep information readable.

- Encourage team members to follow formatting guidelines for consistency.

Staying Updated with Microsoft Loop Enhancements

- Follow Microsoft 365 updates to stay informed about formatting improvements.

- Participate in the Microsoft Loop community to share best practices and troubleshooting tips.

Conclusion

Formatting and display issues can be frustrating, but with the right troubleshooting steps, they can be resolved quickly. By following best practices, ensuring proper component usage, and staying updated with Microsoft Loop improvements, you can create a seamless collaboration experience.

If issues persist, consider reaching out to Microsoft Support or checking online forums for additional solutions.

6.1.3 Dealing with Performance and Speed Issues

Microsoft Loop is a powerful collaboration tool, but like any cloud-based application, users may occasionally encounter performance and speed issues. Slow loading times, lag when editing, and delayed synchronization can be frustrating and hinder productivity. Understanding the common causes and solutions for these problems can help ensure a smooth experience while using Microsoft Loop.

This section will explore:

- The primary reasons why Microsoft Loop may experience performance issues

- How to optimize settings and configurations for better speed

- Best practices to prevent slowdowns in the future

Common Causes of Performance and Speed Issues

Before diving into solutions, it's essential to understand the root causes of performance problems in Microsoft Loop. Here are some of the most common factors:

1. Poor Internet Connection

Since Microsoft Loop is a cloud-based service, a stable and fast internet connection is crucial. A weak or unstable connection can result in slow loading times and delayed updates.

Symptoms:

- Loop pages take a long time to load
- Components sync inconsistently across devices
- Real-time collaboration feels sluggish

How to Fix:

- Check your internet speed using an online speed test tool
- Switch to a wired Ethernet connection instead of Wi-Fi for better stability
- Use a network with at least **10 Mbps download and 5 Mbps upload speed** for optimal performance
- Restart your router or modem to refresh the connection

2. High Browser or System Resource Usage

Running too many applications or browser tabs can consume excessive system resources, leading to slow performance in Microsoft Loop.

Symptoms:

- Loop pages freeze or become unresponsive
- Typing or clicking in Loop lags significantly
- High CPU or memory usage when checking the Task Manager (Windows) or Activity Monitor (Mac)

How to Fix:

- Close unnecessary browser tabs and applications
- Restart your computer to clear system memory

- Disable unused browser extensions that might interfere with Microsoft Loop

- Ensure your browser is updated to the latest version

3. Outdated Software or Browser

Microsoft Loop works best with modern web browsers and up-to-date system software. Using an outdated browser version can lead to compatibility issues and slow performance.

Symptoms:

- Loop pages fail to load or display incorrectly

- Features don't work as expected

- Frequent error messages when trying to access Loop

How to Fix:

- Update your browser (Google Chrome, Microsoft Edge, or Safari) to the latest version

- Ensure that your operating system (Windows or macOS) is up to date

- Try accessing Microsoft Loop in a different browser to check if the issue persists

4. Large Loop Workspaces with Too Many Components

Microsoft Loop allows users to create rich workspaces with multiple pages and components, but excessive content can slow things down.

Symptoms:

- Loop pages take a long time to open

- Scrolling or editing feels sluggish

- Search functionality is slow or unresponsive

How to Fix:

- Break large workspaces into smaller, focused workspaces

- Archive old or unused Loop pages to reduce workspace size

- Optimize content by limiting unnecessary large media files (images, videos, etc.)

5. Server-Side Delays and Microsoft Service Issues

Sometimes, Microsoft's servers may experience downtime or slowdowns due to high demand, maintenance, or unexpected issues.

Symptoms:

- Loop pages fail to load even with a strong internet connection

- Syncing takes longer than usual

- Microsoft Loop services show error messages

How to Fix:

- Check **Microsoft 365 Service Status** (https://status.office.com) for any reported outages

- If there's a known issue, wait for Microsoft to resolve it or try again later

- Restart your browser or log out and back into your Microsoft account to refresh the session

Optimizing Microsoft Loop for Better Performance

If you frequently experience slow performance in Microsoft Loop, consider optimizing your setup to improve speed and efficiency.

1. Adjust Your Browser Settings

Microsoft Loop performs best when the browser is optimized for speed.

Recommended Browser Settings:

- Enable **hardware acceleration** in Chrome or Edge for smoother performance

- Clear cache and cookies regularly to prevent data buildup

- Use **incognito mode** to see if extensions or settings are causing slowdowns

2. Manage Loop Workspaces Efficiently

A well-organized Loop workspace loads faster and is easier to navigate.

Best Practices:

- Use **folders and categories** to organize pages

- Delete **unused Loop components** to reduce clutter

- Regularly clean up old or inactive workspaces

3. Use Lightweight Content Formats

Avoid heavy media files that can slow down page loading times.

Tips:

- Upload images in **compressed formats (JPEG, PNG, WebP)**

- Use **links to large files** instead of embedding them directly

- Avoid inserting high-resolution videos; instead, link to them on OneDrive or SharePoint

---

Preventing Performance Issues in the Future

To ensure a consistently smooth experience with Microsoft Loop, adopt proactive measures:

1. Keep Your Software and System Updated

- Enable automatic updates for your **browser, operating system, and Microsoft 365 apps**

- Restart your computer regularly to clear temporary files and refresh system resources

2. Monitor and Optimize Your Network Connection

- Use **a wired connection** when possible for better stability

- Avoid using Loop on **public Wi-Fi** networks, which may be slow and unsecured

- If using Wi-Fi, ensure your **router firmware is up to date** and placed in an optimal location

3. Train Your Team on Best Practices

If you're using Microsoft Loop in a team setting, educate your colleagues on how to use it efficiently:

- Encourage team members to **avoid unnecessary large files**

- Teach them how to **properly structure workspaces**

- Share best practices for **collaborating without overloading the system**

Final Thoughts

Dealing with performance and speed issues in Microsoft Loop can be frustrating, but most problems can be resolved with simple adjustments. By understanding common causes, optimizing settings, and adopting best practices, you can ensure a smooth and efficient experience.

If issues persist, consider reaching out to **Microsoft Support** or checking Microsoft's official forums for updates. Staying informed and proactive will help you make the most of Microsoft Loop's powerful collaboration features.

6.2 Best Practices for Effective Collaboration

6.2.1 Structuring Workspaces for Clarity

Microsoft Loop is designed to facilitate seamless collaboration, but without a well-structured workspace, information can quickly become disorganized and difficult to navigate. A properly structured workspace ensures that team members can easily find relevant content, understand the flow of collaboration, and contribute efficiently. In this section, we will explore best practices for organizing workspaces in Microsoft Loop to maximize productivity and clarity.

Understanding the Role of Workspaces in Microsoft Loop

Before diving into structuring techniques, it's important to understand what a Loop workspace is and how it functions within Microsoft Loop.

- Workspaces serve as containers for related projects, topics, or teams, allowing users to group all relevant content in one place.

- Pages within workspaces hold structured information, such as meeting notes, project plans, or brainstorming sessions.

- Loop components (such as task lists, tables, and text blocks) allow for dynamic collaboration and can be shared across different Microsoft 365 applications.

Given this flexibility, structuring your workspaces effectively is crucial for keeping your team aligned and your projects organized.

Key Principles for Structuring a Microsoft Loop Workspace

To create a workspace that is intuitive and easy to navigate, consider the following principles:

1. **Define a Clear Purpose for Each Workspace**

- o Each workspace should have a specific function or goal. Avoid creating generic workspaces that mix unrelated projects.

- o Example: Instead of one workspace for an entire department, consider creating separate workspaces for specific projects, teams, or initiatives.

- o Naming convention: Use descriptive and consistent names like *"Marketing Campaign Q2 2025"* instead of just *"Marketing."*

2. **Create Logical Page Hierarchies**

- o Break down workspaces into structured pages with clear relationships.

- o Example: A project-based workspace could have:

    - A main overview page summarizing key goals and deadlines.

    - Subpages for meeting notes, task lists, research, and discussions.

- o Ensure each page has a clear title and relevant content to avoid redundancy.

3. **Utilize Templates for Consistency**

- o Microsoft Loop allows you to create custom templates for frequently used structures.

- o Example: A Meeting Notes template could include sections for agenda items, action items, and key takeaways.

- o Templates help maintain uniformity across different projects and teams.

4. **Keep Pages and Components Minimalistic**

- o Avoid cluttering pages with too many embedded elements, which can become overwhelming.

- o Example: Instead of adding multiple tables and lists on the same page, consider linking related components on separate pages.

- o Use collapsible sections to group information logically and improve readability.

Best Practices for Organizing Loop Pages

1. Structuring Pages for Quick Navigation

A well-organized page should allow users to find key information within seconds. Use the following techniques to improve navigation:

- **Use Clear Headers and Subheadings**
  - Example: Instead of a long block of text, break content into sections like:
    - Project Overview
    - Current Status
    - Action Items
  - This makes it easier for team members to scan for relevant details.

- **Leverage Tables and Bullet Points**
  - Use tables for structured data (e.g., task tracking, deadlines).
  - Use bullet points to highlight key takeaways and to-do items.

- **Create a Table of Contents for Long Pages**
  - If a page contains multiple sections, consider adding a table of contents at the top.
  - Example: A large project management page could include links to key sections such as *Milestones, Assigned Tasks, Budget Overview, and Risks.*

2. Categorizing Pages and Content

Instead of having one long, disorganized page, **categorize content into sections**:

Category	Example Content
Project Management	Goals, Roadmap, Task List
Meetings & Notes	Agendas, Key Discussions, Decisions
Research & Ideas	Brainstorming, Competitor Analysis
Resources	Reference Materials, Guidelines

This categorization helps users find what they need quickly without searching through unrelated content.

3. Using Workspaces for Cross-Team Collaboration

For large teams working on multiple projects, workspaces can be structured by function or collaboration type:

- Team-Based Workspaces: One workspace per department/team (e.g., *Marketing, Sales, Product Development*).

- Project-Based Workspaces: One workspace per project, with different teams contributing to relevant pages.

- Client/Partner Workspaces: Shared workspaces where external stakeholders can access relevant documents and updates.

Optimizing Workspaces for Efficiency

1. Establish Naming Conventions

Consistent naming conventions help users quickly understand the purpose of a workspace, page, or Loop component.

Best Practices for Naming

- Use clear, structured names: *"Project Alpha - Meeting Notes"* instead of *"Meeting Notes"*.

- Avoid vague or duplicate names: *"To-Do List"* could exist in multiple projects, so use *"Marketing Campaign - To-Do List"*.

2. Managing Permissions and Access

- Limit access to specific team members when necessary to prevent unnecessary edits.

- Assign view-only or edit permissions based on roles to ensure information security.

3. Archiving Old Content

- Regularly review and archive outdated pages to prevent clutter.

- Example: Move completed projects to an *Archived Workspaces* section.

Real-World Example of an Effective Microsoft Loop Workspace

Imagine a company managing a new product launch using Microsoft Loop.

- Workspace Name: *"Product Launch 2025"*

- Main Pages:

    o Overview & Objectives

    o Market Research & Competitive Analysis

    o Task Assignments & Deadlines

    o Marketing Strategy

    o Sales & Distribution Plan

Each page contains embedded Loop components (task lists, shared notes, and reports) to keep all stakeholders aligned.

Conclusion

A well-structured Microsoft Loop workspace enhances productivity, reduces confusion, and improves team collaboration. By defining clear workspace purposes, maintaining organized pages, using templates, and ensuring efficient navigation, you can maximize the benefits of Microsoft Loop.

By implementing these best practices, your team will work more effectively, reduce information overload, and enhance collaboration across projects. Start organizing your Microsoft Loop workspaces today for a smoother and more productive experience!

6.2.2 Keeping Content Organized and Up-to-Date

One of the key aspects of effective collaboration in Microsoft Loop is ensuring that content remains well-organized and up-to-date. As teams work together on projects, brainstorm ideas, and track tasks, the ability to maintain clarity and accessibility in shared workspaces can significantly impact efficiency and productivity.

In this section, we'll explore why content organization matters, best practices for structuring your Microsoft Loop pages and workspaces, strategies for keeping information current, and tools to help you manage content efficiently.

Why Content Organization and Updates Matter

Collaboration tools like Microsoft Loop thrive on real-time updates and shared access, but without a clear structure, content can quickly become chaotic. Here are some key reasons why organizing and updating your Loop content is essential:

1. Enhanced Productivity – A well-structured Loop workspace allows team members to locate information quickly without wasting time searching through cluttered pages.

2. Improved Collaboration – When content is systematically arranged, team members can seamlessly collaborate without confusion or duplication of work.

3. Better Decision-Making – Up-to-date data ensures that stakeholders make informed decisions based on the latest information.

4. Reduced Errors and Miscommunication – Keeping documents, notes, and task lists updated minimizes the chances of using outdated or incorrect information.

5. Increased Accountability – A structured system with clear ownership makes it easier to track progress and responsibilities within a team.

Now, let's break down the best practices to achieve an organized and up-to-date Microsoft Loop workspace.

Best Practices for Keeping Microsoft Loop Content Organized

1. Establish a Clear Folder and Page Hierarchy

Microsoft Loop offers Workspaces, Pages, and Components, and understanding how to structure them is critical for maintaining an orderly system.

✅ Define Workspaces Clearly – Assign one workspace per major project or team initiative to keep related information grouped together.

✅ Use Consistent Page Naming Conventions – Keep page names concise and descriptive (e.g., "Marketing Campaign Plan - Q3" instead of "Plan1").

✅ Organize with Sections and Headers – Use headings, bullet points, and dividers to structure long pages for easier readability.

✅ Leverage Templates – Create reusable templates for frequently used page layouts to maintain consistency.

💡 **Example:** Instead of dumping all notes into one long page, organize content into sections like: Workspace: Product Development

- Page: Meeting Notes (Weekly Syncs)

- Page: Feature Backlog & Prioritization

- Page: User Feedback & Surveys

- Page: Launch Timeline & Tasks

This structured approach ensures that content remains easy to navigate and intuitively accessible.

2. Use Tags, Labels, and Mentions for Quick Navigation

Microsoft Loop allows you to use @mentions, tags, and links to help categorize and cross-reference information.

✅ @Mention Team Members – Tagging a person ensures they are notified and can respond to content updates quickly.

✅ Use Status Labels – Assign status tags like "Draft," "In Review," "Approved" to indicate content status.

✅ Link to Related Pages and Components – Instead of duplicating content, insert links to relevant Loop components or pages.

💡 Example: A project status update page can include:

- @John to assign specific deliverables

- "#Urgent" for high-priority items

- Link to "Q2 Sales Report" to avoid unnecessary reuploads

This tagging system helps keep everyone aligned and aware of critical updates.

3. Maintain a Routine for Content Reviews and Updates

Content can quickly become outdated if left unchecked. To prevent outdated information from accumulating, teams should adopt a routine review process.

✓ Assign Content Owners – Designate responsible team members for updating key documents (e.g., project timelines, team charters).
✓ Set Recurring Review Reminders – Use Microsoft To-Do or Planner to set check-in reminders for updating key documents.
✓ Archive or Remove Old Content – Periodically clean up obsolete or redundant pages to declutter the workspace.

💡 Example: For a marketing campaign workspace, a monthly review can ensure that:

- The latest customer feedback and analytics are reflected.

- Old or completed campaigns are moved to an archive folder.

- The next quarter's plans are linked for easy transition.

By implementing a structured review routine, team members always work with current and accurate data.

4. Enable Version Control and Change Tracking

One of Microsoft Loop's powerful features is its ability to track changes and restore previous versions.

✓ Use Version History – Access previous document versions to revert mistakes or retrieve deleted content.
✓ Track Updates with Comments – Use inline comments for suggested edits rather than overwriting existing content.

✅ Create Change Logs – Maintain a simple table tracking who updated what and when to improve accountability.

💡 **Example:** A **product requirements page** may have a **"Change Log"** section at the bottom:

Date	Change Description	Updated By
Feb 1, 2025	Added new feature spec	@Alice
Feb 5, 2025	Updated launch timeline	@Bob

This prevents confusion and allows teams to revert changes when needed.

5. Keep Your Team Aligned with Notifications and Communication

Microsoft Loop integrates with Microsoft Teams and Outlook, allowing teams to stay updated without constantly checking Loop manually.

✅ Enable Notifications for Important Updates – Ensure team members receive alerts when content is updated.
✅ Discuss Changes in Microsoft Teams – Use Loop components inside Teams conversations to keep discussions centralized.
✅ Summarize Key Changes in a Weekly Update – Send a recap of important document updates to keep everyone aligned.

💡 **Example:** If a project timeline is adjusted, the project lead can post a summary in Teams:
🚀 Project Update:

- Deadline moved to March 15

- New milestone: User testing on Feb 20

- See Loop Page: "Project Plan" for details

This approach ensures critical updates are seen and acknowledged without cluttering emails.

Final Thoughts on Keeping Content Organized and Up-to-Date

To maximize productivity in Microsoft Loop, teams should proactively manage their content by:

✓ Creating a structured page hierarchy

✓ Using tags and links for easy navigation

✓ Regularly reviewing and updating documents

✓ Leveraging version control and notifications

By following these best practices, teams can eliminate chaos, reduce confusion, and enhance collaboration within Microsoft Loop. Keeping content organized and up-to-date isn't just a best practice—it's the foundation for efficient teamwork and seamless project execution.

6.2.3 Ensuring Secure and Efficient File Sharing

Microsoft Loop is designed to facilitate seamless collaboration, allowing users to share files and content dynamically across different teams and projects. However, ensuring that file sharing remains both secure and efficient is crucial to maintaining data integrity, protecting sensitive information, and maximizing productivity.

This section will guide you through best practices for secure and efficient file sharing in Microsoft Loop, covering access control, permission management, integration with Microsoft 365 security features, and collaboration workflows.

1. Understanding File Sharing in Microsoft Loop

Microsoft Loop enables users to share files, documents, and Loop components with colleagues in a flexible, interactive manner. Whether you're working within a Loop workspace, a Microsoft Teams chat, or Outlook, Loop ensures that information stays synchronized and accessible in real time.

However, improper file sharing practices can lead to security risks, including unauthorized access, data leaks, and compliance issues. Therefore, implementing best practices in file sharing is critical for organizations using Microsoft Loop.

2. Secure File Sharing Best Practices

Managing Permissions and Access Control

One of the most important aspects of secure file sharing in Microsoft Loop is defining access levels appropriately. Microsoft Loop allows you to manage permissions at different levels, ensuring that only authorized individuals can view or edit content.

Best Practices for Permission Management

- Use Least Privilege Access – Only grant users the minimum level of access required for their role. Avoid giving edit permissions to users who only need to view content.

- Set Expiration Dates on Shared Links – When sharing files externally, use expiration dates to automatically revoke access after a specific period.

- Restrict Anonymous Access – Always require authentication when sharing sensitive documents, even within your organization.

- Monitor and Review Permissions Regularly – Periodically audit user permissions to ensure they align with team roles and responsibilities.

How to Adjust Permissions in Microsoft Loop

1. Select the **Loop component or file** you want to share.

2. Click the **Share** button.

3. Choose **Who can access this file** (e.g., specific people, organization-wide, or public).

4. Set permissions:

   o **Can edit** – Allows full editing access.

   o **Can comment** – Allows users to leave feedback but not make direct changes.

   o **Can view** – Read-only access.

5. (Optional) Set an **expiration date** for temporary access.

6. Click **Apply** and then **Send** or **Copy link** to share.

Preventing Unauthorized Access

Unauthorized access is a major concern when sharing files across teams and external collaborators. Implement the following security measures to mitigate risks:

- Enable Multi-Factor Authentication (MFA) – Require users to authenticate using an additional security step before accessing shared files.

- Use Conditional Access Policies – Restrict file access based on device type, location, or security status.

- Encrypt Sensitive Documents – Store and share sensitive files using Microsoft's built-in encryption features.

- Disable Forwarding on Confidential Files – Prevent shared links from being re-shared without permission.

Using Microsoft Defender for Cloud Apps to Monitor File Sharing

Microsoft Defender for Cloud Apps provides real-time monitoring of file-sharing activities. You can:

- Detect unusual sharing behaviors (e.g., mass file downloads).

- Set alerts for sensitive document access.

- Block risky file-sharing actions automatically.

3. Efficient File Sharing Strategies

Optimizing File Structure and Organization

A well-organized file structure ensures that team members can easily find and access shared content without unnecessary delays. Follow these guidelines:

- Use Clear Naming Conventions – Name files and Loop components in a way that clearly describes their purpose. Example:

  - ✓ "Marketing_Strategy_2025_LoopComponent.docx"

  - ✗ "Document1.docx"

- Create Dedicated Workspaces for Projects – Instead of sharing individual files across multiple platforms, create a Loop workspace where related documents are stored together.

- Utilize Tags and Labels – Categorize Loop pages and components with relevant tags for easy retrieval.

Reducing File Duplication and Version Conflicts

Loop automatically syncs content, but users can still create conflicting versions when files are manually duplicated. To avoid this:

- Use Live Components Instead of Attachments – Instead of emailing separate versions of a document, embed a live Loop component in Microsoft Teams, Outlook, or OneNote.

- Leverage Version History – Microsoft Loop allows users to view previous versions of shared documents. If conflicts arise, you can restore an earlier version.

- Coordinate Real-Time Edits – Encourage team members to collaborate directly within Loop instead of downloading files, making edits, and re-uploading them.

Speeding Up Collaboration Without Sacrificing Security

Sometimes, strict security measures can slow down workflows. To balance security with efficiency:

- Predefine User Roles – Assign default access levels for departments or project teams.

- Use Shared Workspaces Instead of Individual File Shares – Reduce the number of separate file-sharing requests by maintaining a central collaboration hub.

- Automate Sharing Workflows with Power Automate – Set up rules to automatically share reports or updates with relevant team members based on predefined conditions.

4. Integrating Microsoft Loop with Other Microsoft 365 Security Features

Microsoft Loop seamlessly integrates with Microsoft 365's security and compliance ecosystem, enhancing both file security and accessibility.

Microsoft Purview for Compliance and Data Loss Prevention (DLP)

Microsoft Purview helps prevent accidental or intentional data leaks by enforcing policies such as:

- Blocking sharing of confidential files outside the organization.

- Detecting personally identifiable information (PII) in shared documents.

- Applying automated encryption based on content sensitivity.

Using OneDrive and SharePoint for Secure File Storage

Microsoft Loop components are stored in OneDrive and SharePoint, ensuring:

- Automatic backups and file recovery options.

- Enterprise-grade security with granular permissions.

- Seamless synchronization across devices.

Setting Up Alerts for Suspicious File Activity

Admins can configure Microsoft 365 Security Alerts to notify them of unusual file-sharing behaviors, such as:

- Multiple failed access attempts.

- Large-scale file transfers.

- Unusual geographic locations accessing corporate files.

5. Summary of Key Takeaways

Ensuring secure and efficient file sharing in Microsoft Loop requires a combination of:
✓☐ Managing permissions wisely – Use the least privilege model and review access regularly.
✓☐ Preventing unauthorized access – Enable MFA, restrict external sharing, and encrypt sensitive documents.

✓☐ Organizing content properly – Use clear naming conventions, workspaces, and tags.

✓☐ Reducing duplication and versioning issues – Rely on live Loop components and version history.

✓☐ Leveraging Microsoft 365 security tools – Use Purview, Defender, and SharePoint for advanced protection.

By following these best practices, teams can collaborate effectively while ensuring data security and compliance within Microsoft Loop.

6.3 Staying Up to Date with Microsoft Loop

6.3.1 Following Product Updates and New Features

Microsoft Loop is a dynamic tool designed to enhance collaboration and productivity. Like other Microsoft 365 applications, it undergoes continuous improvements, with new features, security updates, and integrations being introduced regularly. Staying informed about these updates ensures that users can maximize the tool's potential and adapt to changes smoothly.

This section will guide you through the best ways to keep track of Microsoft Loop's updates, understand their impact, and implement them effectively in your workflow.

Why Staying Updated is Important

Keeping up with product updates is crucial for several reasons:

- **Enhanced Productivity** – New features often introduce automation, efficiency improvements, or better collaboration tools. Staying updated ensures you benefit from these enhancements.

- **Security and Stability** – Updates often include security patches and performance improvements that keep your data safe and prevent disruptions.

- **Compatibility with Other Microsoft 365 Apps** – Since Microsoft Loop integrates with Teams, Outlook, OneNote, and other Microsoft 365 applications, staying updated ensures seamless integration.

- **Competitive Advantage** – Organizations and individuals who leverage the latest technology effectively often gain an edge in efficiency and collaboration.

How to Track Microsoft Loop Updates

1. Microsoft 365 Roadmap

The **Microsoft 365 Roadmap** is the best place to track upcoming features and improvements for Microsoft Loop. It provides:

- A **list of planned, rolling out, and launched features** for Microsoft 365 products, including Microsoft Loop.

- Expected release dates and descriptions of new capabilities.

- Status updates on feature development, categorized as **In Development, Rolling Out, or Launched**.

To use the Microsoft 365 Roadmap:

1. Visit the Microsoft 365 Roadmap.

2. In the **Search** bar, type "Microsoft Loop" to filter results.

3. Click on any feature to view details, expected rollout dates, and availability status.

4. Bookmark the page and check regularly for updates.

2. Microsoft Loop Official Blog and Announcements

Microsoft maintains a dedicated **Loop Blog** and announcement page within the Microsoft 365 ecosystem. These platforms provide:

- **Detailed articles** on major updates, explaining new features and how to use them.

- **Insights from Microsoft developers** on the future direction of Loop.

- **Case studies and real-world examples** of Loop being used effectively.

To stay informed:

- Follow the Microsoft Tech Community for official announcements.

- Check the Microsoft Loop blog for feature deep dives.

- Subscribe to **email updates** from Microsoft to receive news directly.

3. Microsoft Release Notes and Documentation

Every major Microsoft product has a **release notes page** where updates are documented in detail. These pages explain:

- What changes were made.

- How the new features work.

- Any known issues or important notes about the update.

You can find Microsoft Loop release notes on the **Microsoft Learn** platform or through the official Microsoft 365 documentation pages.

4. Following Microsoft Ignite and Build Events

Microsoft hosts **Ignite** and **Build** conferences yearly, where they announce major product updates, including new features in Microsoft 365 and Loop. These events:

- Provide early insights into **upcoming features** before they are released.

- Offer **live demonstrations** of new capabilities.

- Allow users to **ask questions** and provide feedback directly to Microsoft engineers.

To leverage these events:

- Register for Microsoft Ignite and Microsoft Build.

- Watch the keynote speeches and Loop-related breakout sessions.

- Review the event recordings and session summaries after the event.

Best Practices for Implementing Updates

1. Testing Updates in a Controlled Environment

If you are part of a business or enterprise using Microsoft Loop, consider testing new updates before rolling them out to all users. Microsoft often releases **preview versions** of features that can be tested before full deployment.

To manage this effectively:

- Assign a **test group** within your organization to experiment with new features.

- Use a **dedicated workspace** to evaluate how updates impact workflows.

- Provide **feedback to Microsoft** if you encounter issues or need additional features.

2. Educating Users About Updates

When a new update is released, ensure that your team or organization understands how to use it. You can:

- Conduct **short training sessions** to demonstrate new features.

- Share **internal guides or documentation** summarizing the most important changes.

- Encourage employees to join Microsoft's **Loop Community Forums** to stay engaged.

3. Subscribing to Insider Programs

Microsoft offers **Insider Programs** that allow users to access new features before the general public. By joining the **Microsoft 365 Insider Program**, you can:

- Test features before they are fully rolled out.

- Provide feedback to Microsoft to influence future developments.

- Prepare for changes before they reach the broader user base.

To join:

1. Open **Settings** in Microsoft Loop.

2. Navigate to **Insider Program** options.

3. Select **Beta or Preview Builds** to receive early access to updates.

Frequently Asked Questions About Microsoft Loop Updates

Q1: How often does Microsoft update Loop?

Microsoft releases updates on a **rolling basis**, with major updates typically announced every few months. Minor fixes and performance improvements may be introduced more frequently.

Q2: Will I be notified when a new feature is available?

Yes, Microsoft sends in-app notifications when a significant update is rolled out. You can also enable **email notifications** in your Microsoft 365 settings to receive update alerts.

Q3: What should I do if a new feature is not available to me yet?

If an update is rolling out gradually, it may take time before it reaches all users. Ensure that:

- Your Microsoft 365 subscription is **up to date**.

- You have the latest **Loop version** installed.

- You are in a region where the feature has been released.

If you still do not see the update, check the **Microsoft 365 Roadmap** or Loop's official documentation for rollout timelines.

Final Thoughts

Keeping track of Microsoft Loop updates ensures that you remain at the forefront of collaboration technology. By actively following the Microsoft 365 Roadmap, engaging with the Loop Community, and testing new features, you can optimize your workflow and make the most of this powerful tool.

As Microsoft Loop evolves, its capabilities will continue to expand, making collaboration even more seamless and dynamic. Stay proactive, embrace new features as they arrive, and keep exploring ways to enhance your productivity with Microsoft Loop! 🚀

6.3.2 Exploring Microsoft's Loop Community

Introduction

Microsoft Loop is a dynamic and evolving tool designed to enhance collaboration and productivity. To make the most of it, users should not only familiarize themselves with its features but also stay engaged with the wider **Microsoft Loop community**. This community provides a wealth of resources, discussions, and support channels where users can learn, share insights, and troubleshoot issues.

In this section, we will explore the different aspects of the **Microsoft Loop community**, including official Microsoft forums, user groups, social media discussions, and online learning platforms. By actively engaging with these communities, users can stay informed about new features, best practices, and innovative use cases.

Understanding the Microsoft Loop Community

The Microsoft Loop community consists of various groups, forums, and online spaces where users, developers, and Microsoft experts come together to discuss, support, and enhance their experience with Loop. This community serves multiple purposes:

- **Learning from others** – Users share their experiences, tips, and best practices.

- **Getting technical support** – Microsoft engineers and experienced users often provide answers to common problems.

- **Staying updated** – Microsoft frequently shares announcements, updates, and previews of upcoming features.

- **Networking and collaboration** – Users can connect with like-minded professionals to exchange ideas and solutions.

Microsoft supports its user communities through official platforms, while independent groups and forums also play a significant role in fostering discussion and collaboration.

Official Microsoft Loop Community Resources

Microsoft Learn and Documentation

Microsoft provides official **documentation and learning resources** through Microsoft Learn. These resources include:

- Step-by-step tutorials on using Loop.

- Guides on integrating Loop with Microsoft 365 applications.

- FAQs and troubleshooting guides.

This is an excellent starting point for both beginners and advanced users who want to deepen their understanding of Microsoft Loop.

Microsoft Tech Community

The **Microsoft Tech Community** is a hub where users discuss Microsoft products, including Loop. Here, you can:

- Join **Loop-specific forums** where users ask questions and share tips.

- Read about **new feature announcements** and Microsoft's development roadmap.

- Participate in **feedback discussions** where Microsoft gathers user suggestions for improving Loop.

To engage, visit Microsoft Tech Community and search for "Microsoft Loop" to find relevant threads.

Microsoft Insider Program

For users who want **early access to new features**, the **Microsoft Insider Program** is a valuable resource. By joining, you can:

- Test beta features before they are officially released.

- Provide direct feedback to Microsoft developers.

- Report bugs and contribute to improving the software.

This is ideal for businesses and power users who want to stay ahead of changes in the Microsoft ecosystem.

Microsoft 365 Roadmap

To keep track of **upcoming updates** to Microsoft Loop, users should frequently check the **Microsoft 365 Roadmap** (https://www.microsoft.com/en-us/microsoft-365/roadmap). This site provides details on:

- Features currently **in development**.

- Features that have been **released** recently.

- **Expected timelines** for future updates.

This ensures that users are always aware of the latest improvements and can plan their workflows accordingly.

Engaging with Independent Microsoft Loop User Groups

While Microsoft's official channels provide excellent resources, independent user groups and communities often offer **real-world insights and practical applications** that are not always covered in official documentation.

Reddit Communities

Reddit hosts several technology-focused groups where Microsoft Loop is discussed, including:

- r/Microsoft365 – A general Microsoft 365 community that includes discussions on Loop.

- r/sysadmin – Ideal for IT professionals managing Loop in workplace settings.

- r/productivity – A space where users share how they use Loop to boost efficiency.

Engaging in these discussions can help users learn practical use cases, discover workarounds for limitations, and exchange productivity **tips** with other users.

LinkedIn Groups

LinkedIn hosts professional groups focused on Microsoft tools and workplace productivity. Examples include:

- Microsoft 365 User Group

- Modern Workplace Community

- Collaboration Tools & Best Practices

These groups are great for networking, learning about corporate use cases, and staying informed about how businesses are implementing Microsoft Loop in their operations.

Facebook and Discord Groups

Facebook and Discord have many communities where users actively discuss Microsoft Loop. Some of the most popular groups include:

- Microsoft 365 & SharePoint Community (Facebook) – Focuses on integrating Loop with other Microsoft apps.

- Microsoft Loop Power Users (Discord) – A dedicated server where tech enthusiasts discuss advanced Loop features.

These platforms allow users to ask questions in real-time, share screenshots, and engage in deeper discussions.

Microsoft Loop on Social Media

Social media platforms provide **instant access to news, tutorials, and discussions** about Microsoft Loop. Following key accounts and hashtags can help users stay informed.

Twitter (X)

On Twitter, Microsoft experts and tech influencers frequently share:

- Feature updates and Loop release notes.

- Tips and tricks for maximizing efficiency.

- Short video guides on how to use new Loop features.

Suggested accounts to follow:

- @Microsoft365 – Official Microsoft 365 news.

- @MSFTEnable – Accessibility and collaboration updates.

- @LoopCommunity – User-led discussions on best practices.

Popular hashtags: #MicrosoftLoop, #MSLoop, #Microsoft365.

YouTube Channels

YouTube is a valuable platform for visual learners who prefer step-by-step guides. Some top channels for Loop tutorials include:

- Microsoft Mechanics – Official Microsoft tutorials.

- Kevin Stratvert – Easy-to-follow Loop tutorials for beginners.

- Modern Work Mentor – Productivity tips using Loop in workplace settings.

Watching these videos can provide a deeper understanding of practical use cases for Loop.

Contributing to the Microsoft Loop Community

Users can actively participate in the Microsoft Loop community by:

- Providing feedback – Microsoft values user input for feature improvements. Users can submit feedback directly within Loop using the "Help" section.

- Sharing experiences – Posting on forums or writing blog articles helps others understand new ways to use Loop.

- Creating tutorials – If a user finds a unique way to utilize Loop, sharing it via YouTube, LinkedIn, or Medium can help others learn.

- Answering questions – Engaging in Q&A discussions on Microsoft Tech Community or Reddit fosters knowledge sharing.

By contributing, users not only help others but also establish themselves as experts in Microsoft Loop, which can be beneficial for professional growth.

Conclusion

The Microsoft Loop community is an essential resource for staying informed, troubleshooting issues, and discovering innovative ways to enhance collaboration. By actively engaging with Microsoft's official resources, independent user groups, and social media discussions, users can maximize their productivity with Loop and stay ahead of new developments.

Whether through reading forums, watching tutorials, or participating in discussions, the Microsoft Loop community ensures that users are always equipped with the latest insights, solutions, and best practices.

By being an active member of this community, users can leverage Microsoft Loop to its fullest potential, optimize their workflows, and contribute to the growing knowledge base surrounding this powerful collaboration tool.

Conclusion

Final Thoughts on Microsoft Loop

In today's fast-paced digital world, where collaboration and efficiency are at the heart of success, Microsoft Loop emerges as a revolutionary tool that redefines how teams work together. Throughout this book, we have explored the fundamentals of Microsoft Loop, its core features, best practices, and troubleshooting methods. As we conclude, let's reflect on the key takeaways and what Microsoft Loop means for the future of teamwork and productivity.

The Power of Microsoft Loop in Modern Workflows

The way we work has evolved dramatically over the past few decades. The traditional workspace, once confined to office buildings and desktop computers, has expanded into a dynamic and decentralized digital ecosystem. Businesses and professionals across the globe are embracing remote work, hybrid models, and cross-functional collaboration. In this context, Microsoft Loop stands out as a tool designed for the modern workforce.

At its core, Microsoft Loop is not just another collaboration platform; it is an **ecosystem of dynamic components** that enable real-time teamwork. Unlike static documents and emails, Loop provides a fluid and flexible environment where information is always **up-to-date, interactive, and context-aware**. Whether it's brainstorming ideas, managing projects, or keeping track of important updates, Microsoft Loop ensures that teams stay **aligned, informed, and productive**.

One of the key advantages of Microsoft Loop is its ability to **integrate seamlessly** with other Microsoft 365 applications. This means that users don't have to switch between multiple tools to get work done—Loop brings everything into one interconnected space. From Outlook emails to Teams chats and SharePoint files, Loop components remain **accessible and editable across different applications**, ensuring continuity in workflows.

Key Takeaways from This Guide

As we conclude, it's important to highlight the major lessons and insights covered in this book. If you've followed along, you should now have a solid understanding of:

- Getting Started with Microsoft Loop: Understanding the fundamental concepts, such as Loop Workspaces, Pages, and Components, and setting up your first workspace.

- Working with Loop Components: Learning how to create, edit, and collaborate on different types of Loop components, such as text, tables, and tasks.

- Collaboration and Teamwork: Exploring how real-time co-authoring, commenting, and sharing enhance productivity within teams.

- Advanced Features and Customization: Discovering how to integrate Loop with Microsoft Teams, OneNote, Outlook, and SharePoint for a seamless experience.

- Practical Use Cases: Using Loop for personal productivity, project management, and remote collaboration.

- Troubleshooting and Best Practices: Learning how to solve common issues, structure workspaces efficiently, and adopt best practices for optimal collaboration.

This knowledge empowers you to unlock the full potential of Microsoft Loop, making it a powerful asset for both individuals and organizations.

The Future of Microsoft Loop

Microsoft Loop is still evolving. As Microsoft continues to refine and expand its capabilities, we can expect new features, integrations, and improvements that will further enhance collaboration. Some potential future developments include:

- AI-powered automation: Loop could integrate AI assistants to automate routine tasks, summarize discussions, and provide smart suggestions.

- Enhanced integrations with third-party tools: Microsoft is likely to expand Loop's compatibility with non-Microsoft applications, allowing users to connect with tools like Trello, Slack, or Notion.

- More customization options: Future updates may introduce more ways to personalize workspaces, making them more adaptable to different industries and workflows.

- Advanced security and compliance features: As organizations adopt Loop for enterprise-level collaboration, Microsoft may introduce more granular control over permissions, compliance tracking, and data security.

Staying informed about these updates will ensure that you continue to leverage Microsoft Loop to its fullest potential.

Embracing a Collaborative Mindset

While having the right tools is essential, the true success of any collaboration platform lies in how people adopt and integrate it into their daily workflows. Microsoft Loop is designed to enhance teamwork, transparency, and efficiency, but its impact depends on how teams embrace a collaborative mindset.

To make the most of Microsoft Loop, consider the following principles:

- Encourage openness and shared responsibility: Foster an environment where team members feel comfortable contributing, sharing ideas, and taking ownership of tasks.

- Stay organized and intentional: Use Loop's structure to prioritize tasks, set clear objectives, and avoid information overload.

- Balance flexibility with structure: While Loop offers dynamic and flexible components, it's important to establish guidelines on how to use workspaces effectively.

- Commit to continuous learning: As Microsoft Loop evolves, staying up to date with new features and best practices will help you maximize productivity.

By integrating these principles, you can ensure that Microsoft Loop becomes a valuable and sustainable part of your workflow.

Final Words

As we wrap up this guide, remember that Microsoft Loop is more than just a collaboration tool—it's a new way of working that fosters fluid teamwork, transparency, and efficiency. Whether you are using it for individual projects, team collaboration, or enterprise-level management, Loop offers unmatched flexibility to support your workflow.

The key to success lies not only in mastering its features but also in adapting a mindset that values seamless communication, organization, and teamwork. If you take the time to explore and experiment with Microsoft Loop, you will discover endless possibilities for enhancing your productivity.

With this knowledge, you are now well-equipped to harness the power of Microsoft Loop and drive meaningful collaboration in your personal and professional life.

That brings us to the end of our journey through **Microsoft Loop for Everyone: A Simple Guide to Smarter Collaboration**. If you found this book helpful, I encourage you to **continue exploring** and applying what you've learned. The world of digital collaboration is ever-changing, and Microsoft Loop is at the forefront of this evolution.

Thank you for taking the time to learn about Microsoft Loop. Now, go forth and collaborate smarter! 🚀

Next Steps for Mastering Loop

As we wrap up this guide on Microsoft Loop, you should now have a solid understanding of how to use this powerful tool for seamless collaboration. From setting up workspaces and using Loop components to integrating it with Microsoft Teams and troubleshooting common issues, you've gained valuable knowledge to enhance your productivity. However, mastering Microsoft Loop doesn't stop here. To truly leverage its capabilities, continuous learning, exploration, and adaptation to new features are essential.

This chapter will guide you through the next steps in your journey with Microsoft Loop, helping you move from basic proficiency to expert-level efficiency. Whether you are an individual user looking to improve personal productivity, a team leader aiming to optimize collaboration, or an organization wanting to integrate Loop into workflows, these steps will help you get the most out of the platform.

1. Explore Advanced Features and Integrations

Now that you have grasped the fundamentals, it's time to explore Microsoft Loop's advanced features and integrations with other Microsoft 365 applications.

Experiment with Power Automate for Workflow Automation

- Microsoft Loop can be even more powerful when integrated with Power Automate.

- Automate repetitive tasks such as sending notifications when a task is updated, logging meeting notes into a structured document, or syncing Loop components with Microsoft Planner for better task management.

- Explore the Power Automate library to find templates that fit your workflow.

Connect Loop with OneNote, Outlook, and SharePoint

- If you frequently take notes, integrating Loop with OneNote allows you to structure information efficiently.

- Use Loop components within Outlook to enhance email collaboration, allowing recipients to edit documents in real-time directly from their inbox.

- Store and organize Loop workspaces in SharePoint to improve document management and version control.

Leverage Loop with Microsoft Teams for Maximum Productivity

- Use Loop components in Teams channels and meetings to enable real-time brainstorming and decision-making.

- Assign tasks, track progress, and ensure smooth communication using a combination of Loop and Planner.

- Encourage your team to use Loop as a centralized hub for ongoing discussions and project updates.

2. Develop Best Practices for Efficient Use

To maximize the benefits of Microsoft Loop, it's crucial to establish best practices that promote clarity, organization, and security.

Standardize Workspace Structures in Your Organization

- Create workspace templates tailored to different project types (e.g., product development, marketing campaigns, client collaboration).

- Establish guidelines for naming conventions, content structuring, and archiving old workspaces to maintain an organized environment.

Encourage Collaboration Through Training and Knowledge Sharing

- Schedule periodic training sessions within your team or organization to ensure everyone understands how to use Loop effectively.

- Share best practices and tips through internal documentation or knowledge bases.

- Encourage employees to contribute insights on how they use Loop for various tasks.

Maintain Security and Compliance

- Educate users on access controls and permissions to prevent unauthorized edits or data breaches.

- Regularly audit who has access to critical workspaces and remove inactive users.

- Ensure your organization follows data retention policies to comply with regulations and avoid data loss.

3. Stay Updated with Microsoft Loop's Latest Features

Microsoft Loop is continuously evolving, with Microsoft regularly introducing new features and enhancements. Staying informed about these updates will ensure you remain ahead of the curve.

Follow Official Microsoft Channels

- Subscribe to Microsoft's official blogs, newsletters, and announcements to receive updates on Loop's new capabilities.

- Participate in Microsoft Loop webinars and training sessions hosted by Microsoft experts.

Join the Microsoft Loop Community

- Engage with other Loop users in Microsoft's official community forums and discussion groups.

- Share your experiences, ask questions, and learn from real-world use cases.

Experiment with New Features in the Insider Program

- Join the Microsoft 365 Insider Program to gain early access to upcoming Loop features.

- Test beta functionalities and provide feedback to Microsoft to help shape the future of the platform.

4. Expand Your Knowledge with Additional Resources

While this book has covered the essential aspects of Microsoft Loop, there are always more learning opportunities available.

Read Microsoft's Official Documentation

- Microsoft provides detailed documentation on Loop, including best practices, troubleshooting guides, and feature walkthroughs.

- Visit Microsoft Learn for interactive tutorials.

Take Online Courses and Certifications

- Platforms like LinkedIn Learning, Udemy, and Coursera offer courses on Microsoft 365 collaboration tools, including Microsoft Loop.

- Consider obtaining Microsoft certifications related to collaboration and productivity tools.

Follow Tech Blogs and Influencers

- Many tech experts and bloggers share valuable insights on using Microsoft Loop efficiently.

- Follow YouTube channels, LinkedIn influencers, and technology blogs that focus on Microsoft 365.

Final Thoughts

Microsoft Loop represents the future of modern collaboration, enabling individuals and teams to work more efficiently in a connected digital environment. By mastering its features, adopting best practices, and staying updated with new developments, you can maximize its potential and transform the way you work.

The journey of learning doesn't stop here. As you continue exploring Microsoft Loop, remember to experiment, engage with the community, and seek out new ways to enhance your workflows. Whether you're using Loop for personal productivity, team collaboration, or enterprise-level project management, there's always room to improve and innovate.

Thank you for taking the time to learn about Microsoft Loop through this book. We hope it serves as a valuable resource in your journey toward smarter collaboration. Now, go ahead and start applying what you've learned—your next level of productivity awaits! 🚀

Additional Resources and References

- Microsoft Loop Official Website: https://www.microsoft.com/

- Microsoft Learn: https://learn.microsoft.com/

- Microsoft Community Forums: https://techcommunity.microsoft.com/

- LinkedIn Learning – Microsoft 365 Courses: https://www.linkedin.com/learning/

- Power Automate Templates: https://powerautomate.microsoft.com/

Acknowledgments

First and foremost, I want to extend my deepest gratitude to you, the reader. Thank you for choosing *Microsoft Loop for Everyone: A Simple Guide to Smarter Collaboration*. Whether you are a beginner exploring Microsoft Loop for the first time or an experienced user looking to refine your skills, I appreciate the time and effort you've invested in reading this book.

Your decision to embark on this journey of learning and improving collaboration through Microsoft Loop is truly commendable. In today's fast-paced digital world, mastering the right tools can make all the difference in enhancing productivity, teamwork, and efficiency. My goal with this book was to provide a clear, practical, and easy-to-follow guide that empowers you to make the most of Microsoft Loop—and I sincerely hope it has been helpful to you.

I would also like to express my appreciation to the Microsoft 365 community, whose insights, discussions, and shared experiences continue to inspire and shape the way we use collaboration tools. The ever-evolving nature of technology means there is always something new to learn, and being part of a community of learners and innovators is what makes this journey exciting.

Finally, I encourage you to keep exploring, experimenting, and growing. The best way to master Microsoft Loop—or any tool—is to use it in real-world situations, adapt it to your needs, and continuously seek new ways to enhance your workflow. If this book has helped you in any way, I would love to hear your thoughts. Your feedback, stories, and experiences are invaluable, and they help shape future resources for other learners like yourself.

Once again, thank you for your support. I wish you success in all your collaborative endeavors—may Microsoft Loop be a powerful ally in your journey toward smarter and more efficient teamwork!

www.ingramcontent.com/pod-product-compliance
Lightning Source LLC
LaVergne TN
LVHW081333050326
832903LV00024B/1139